great songs...

of 2000-2009

edited by milton okun

ISBN 978-1-57560-895-2

INTRODUCTION

If any proof is needed, in this first decade of the 21st century, of the timeless, if not indestructible, nature of the love song, look no further than the winsome piano ballad "Love Song," a 2008 hit for Sara Bareilles. Peaking at Number 4, it's not only the sixth different song with this title to appear on the charts since Tommy James hit the Bottom 40 in 1972, it's by far the biggest, easily besting Tesla's Top 10 showing in 1990. (Fittingly, the seventh different version of "Heaven" was done in 2005 by Los Lonely Boys, coming in third to songs with that title by Bryan Adams and Warrant.)

In similar fashion, the songs from the last ten years collected in this book can hold their own with the best of any decade. From the hardiest of rockers, like "Seven Nation Army," by the White Stripes, through the power punk of Avril Lavigne ("Complicated") and Jimmy Eats World ("The Middle"), to the sophisticated hip-hop of the Black Eyed Peas ("Where Is the Love"), to the breeziest of singer/songwriter ditties ("Suddenly I See," by KT Tunstall), this is a diverse and tuneful play list, destined to keep musicians young and old, amateur and professional, happily at their instruments for hours on end.

With much of the decade defined by the iPod and *American Idol*, it's no surprise that the songs here have been selected by the judges with care, including the keynote epic by the very first American Idol, Kelly Clarkson ("A Moment Like This") and the second hit by the winner of *The X Factor* (the British *Idol*), Leona Lewis ("Better in Time"). As that monolithic international TV franchise has proven, the right song, done with the perfect, creative interpretation, can be a very satisfying experience, sometimes enough to launch a career, or at least to win some kudos down the street at Karaoke.

Whether your iPod is stacked with R&B or country music, rock or pop, or even jazz, this book is filled with peak moments, starting ten years back, with one of 2000's biggest songs, the Latin-tinged "Smooth," by Carlos Santana and Rob Thomas, and rolling right into the charts of '09, with singer/songwriter Jason Mraz's "I'm Yours."

The recent country music renaissance is captured here with some of the biggest performances of the decade, among them Keith Urban's heartfelt "You'll Think of Me," Lonestar's romantic gem "Amazed," and Faith Hill's explosive "This Kiss."

After going head to head early in the decade for the "bad girl of rock" title with Britney Spears ("Oops!...I Did It Again"), Christina Aguilera turned back to her best asset, her voice, in 2003's "Beautiful." By decade's end, Black Eyed Peas member Fergie was battling Christina for the "queen of blue-eyed soul" crown. On the other end of the spectrum, Norah Jones reinvented the jazz ballad ("Come Away with Me"), Beyoncé ("If I Were a Boy") reinvented the feminist R&B anthem, and Shakira reinvented concert choreography ("Underneath Your Clothes").

From Connecticut by way of Georgia, John Mayer led a dapper brigade of swanky gentlemen to the charts with his unique performing style and unabashed take on love with "Your Body Is a Wonderland" and the new wedding classic, "Daughters." But other wordy crooners, like Jack Johnson ("Bubble Toes"), were mining the same fertile turf. England's James Blunt had an international bestseller with the lovelorn "You're Beautiful." The emerging "king of blue-eyed soul" was California's Robin Thicke ("Lost Without U"). R&B newcomer John Legend ("Ordinary People") accepted the challenge and the chalice from the genre's previous mainstay, Alicia Keys ("If I Ain't Got You").

In the devastating wake of 9/11, rockers from Foo Fighters ("Times Like These"), Hoobastank ("The Reason"), Coldplay ("The Scientist"), and Dave Matthews Band ("The Space Between") were not afraid to cry or change or play the piano. And yet, as fear and uncertainty raged in the world outside throughout the decade, music's ability to remain largely unaffected served a soothing purpose. With Maroon 5 ("This Love") and the Killers ("Mr. Brightside") stepping into the shoes of Counting Crows ("Accidentally in Love"), everything could remain safe and secure underneath your headphones. As the economy crashed, the music business reeled, and Presidential politics reached historic heights of hope and change, it was somehow comforting to know that Adam Schlesinger was still as agonized as ever in outsider anthems like "Stacy's Mom," by his group Fountains of Wayne.

With a faltering economy and a new Internet-based "everyone's a radio programmer" philosophy now in place, musicians and labels were forced to turn to alternate means of delivering the message. Propelled by *American Idol*, TV and movies played a bigger role than ever in creating the perfect environment for a song to gain popular attention. Canadian Feist's "1,2,3,4" and Parisian Yael Naim's "New Soul" gained prominence in commercials for iTunes. Anna Nalick's moody confessional "Breathe (2AM)" found favor with the *Grey's Anatomy* set. The 2007 Oscar-winning "Falling Slowly," from the movie *Once*, started out in life on an obscure album called *The Swell Season*, released by its singers, Glen Hansard and Marketa Irglova. But the song that got the biggest benefit from movie exposure was probably "Paper Planes," by M.I.A., which was used in the trailer for *Pineapple Express* and featured in the multi-Oscar-winning *Slumdog Millionaire*.

With (legal) downloading on the rise and the Presidential mandate for change in the process of being created, the next ten years should be amazing ones, in music as well as in politics. What kind of songs will be found in the 2010–2019 edition of this series is anybody's guess. The only thing for certain is that no matter how the tunes are discovered and stored, and who the artists are, most of them will be love songs.

—Bruce Pollock

Bruce Pollock is the author of *By the Time We Got to Woodstock: The Great Rock Revolution of 1969* (Backbeat Books) and ten other books on popular music.

CONTENTS

1,2,3,4

Words and Music by
Feist and Sally Seltmann

Oh, _____ you're chang - in' your heart. Oh, _____ you

know who you __ are. Sweet - heart, bit - ter - heart, now I can't tell you a - part.

Co - zy and cold, __ put the horse be - fore the cart. Those teen - age __ hopes __ who have

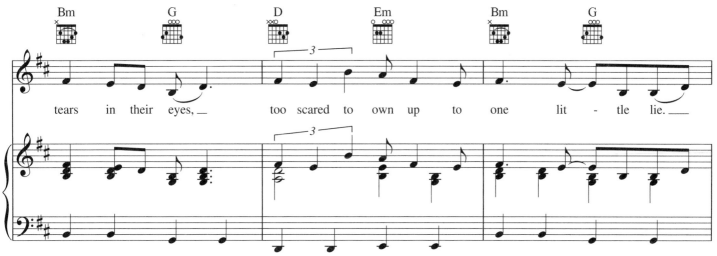

tears in their eyes, __ too scared to own up to one lit - tle lie. __

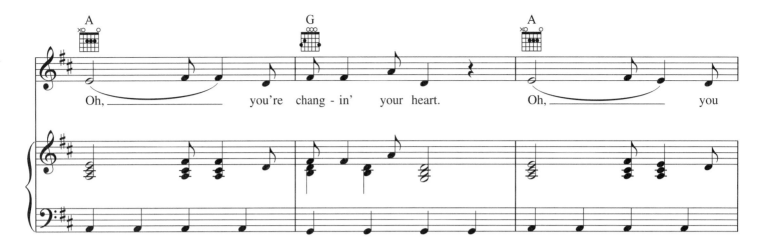

Oh, _____ you're chang - in' your heart. Oh, _____ you

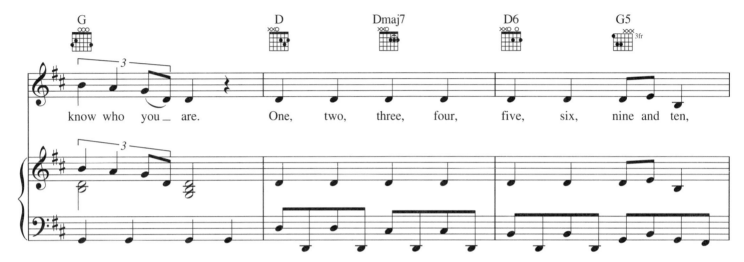

know who you _ are. One, two, three, four, five, six, nine and ten,

mon - ey can't buy you back the love that you had _ then. _____

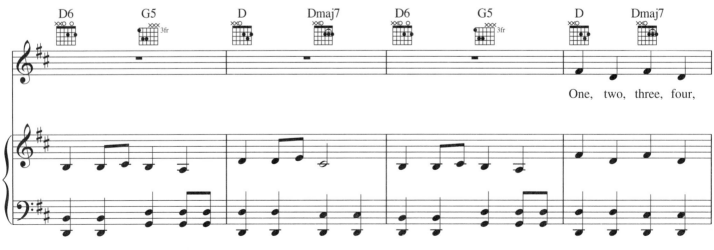

One, two, three, four,

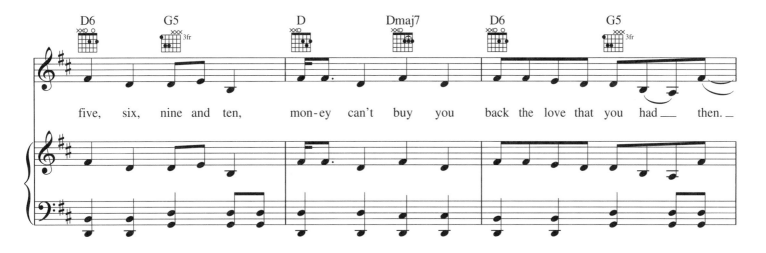

five, six, nine and ten, mon-ey can't buy you back the love that you had ___ then. ___

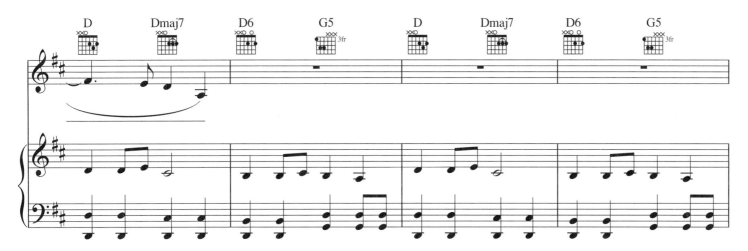

Oh, ___ you're chang-in' your heart. Oh, ___ you know who you are. ___

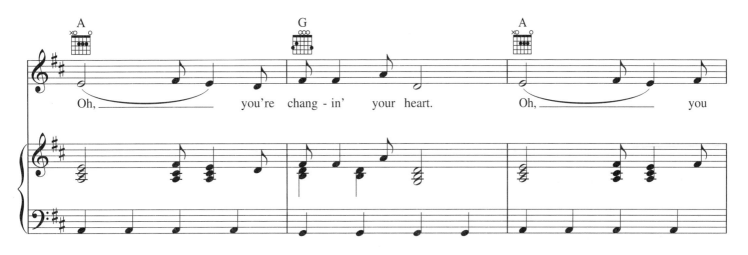

Oh, ___ you're chang-in' your heart. Oh, ___ you

know who you are. _____

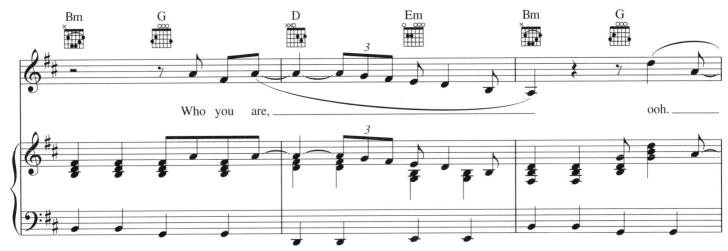

Who you are, _____ ooh. _____

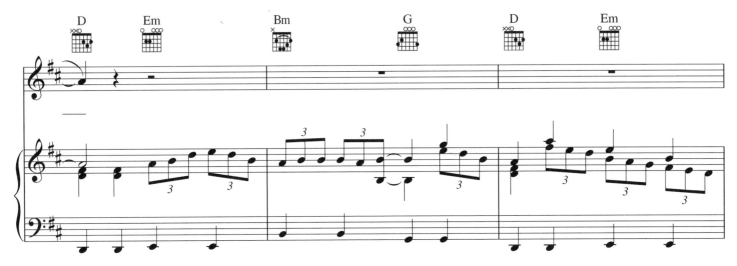

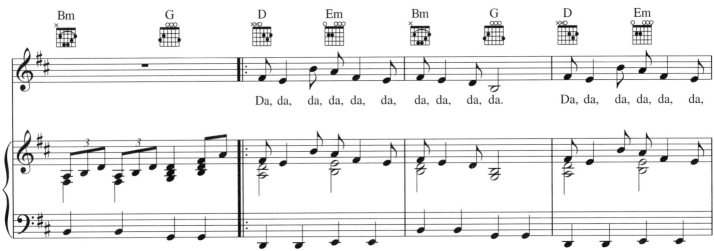

Da, da, da da, da, da, da, da, da, da. Da, da, da da, da, da,

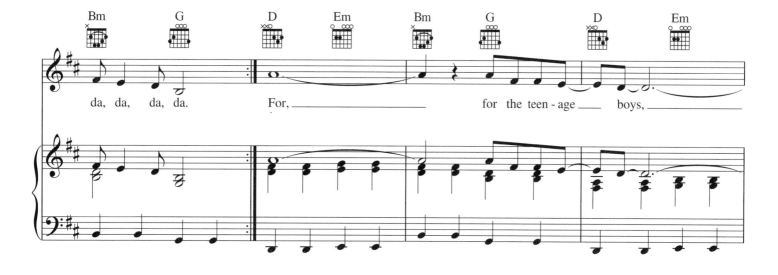

da, da, da, da. For,_____ for the teen - age ___ boys, ____

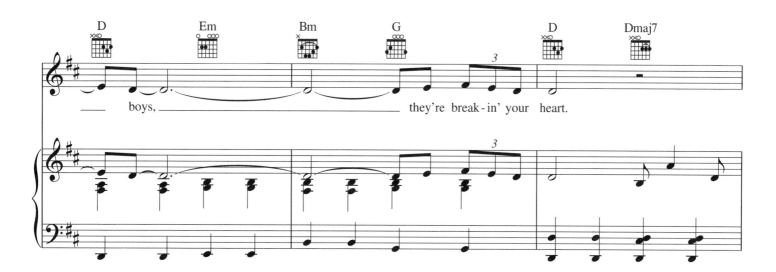

_____ they're break - in' your heart. For the teen - age __

_ boys, _____ they're break - in' your heart.

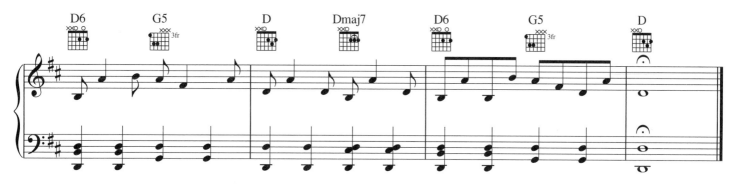

from the Motion Picture SHREK 2

Accidentally In Love

Words and Music by Adam F. Duritz,
Dan Vickrey, David Immergluck,
Matthew Malley and David Bryson

Moderately fast

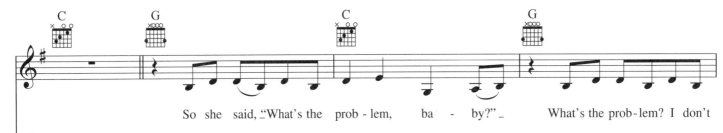

So she said, "What's the prob-lem, ba - by?" _ What's the prob-lem? I don't

know. Well, may-be I'm in love (love). Think a-bout it, ev-'ry time I think a-bout it,

can't   stop   think-ing 'bout it.   How much long-er will it take to cure this? __

Just to cure it 'cause I can't ig - nore it if it's love (love). Makes me wan-na

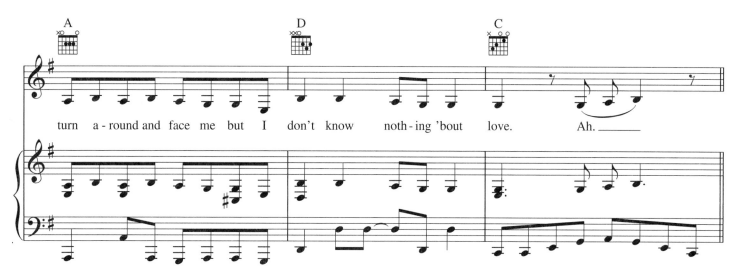

turn a - round and face me but I don't know noth-ing 'bout love.   Ah. _____

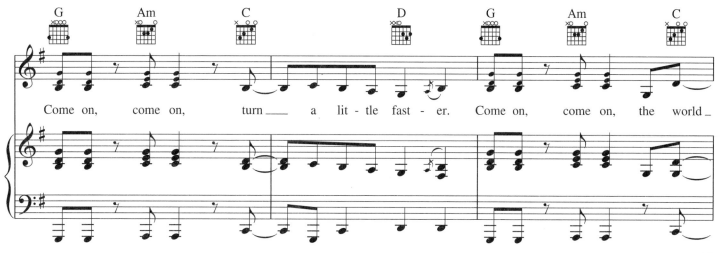

Come on,   come on,   turn ___ a lit-tle fast-er.   Come on,   come on,   the world __

will fol-low af - ter. Come on, come on, 'cause ev-'ry-bod-y's af - ter love. ___

___ So I said ___ I'm a

snow - ball run - ning, ___ run - ning down in - to the spring that's com - ing. All this ___

___ love melt - ing un - der blue skies, belt - ing out sun - light, shim - mer - ing

love.　　Well, ba - by, I　sur - ren - der to the straw - ber - ry ice　cream,

nev - er ev - er end of all this ___ love.　　Well, I　did - n't mean to　do it, but there's

no es - cap - ing ___ your　love.　　Ah. ____　These　lines　of

light - ning　mean　we're　nev - er a - lone, ___　nev - er a - lone,　no, no.

Again

Words and Music by Lenny Kravitz

with - out her king,   my love, for - ev - er. ____
lone - ly queen   I've longed for you,)

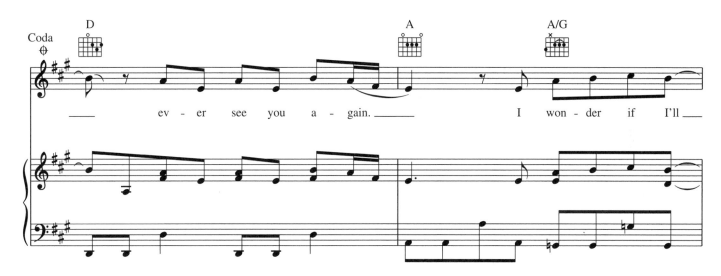

____   ev - er see you a - gain. ____   I won - der if I'll ____

____   ev - er see you a - gain. ____   I won - der if I'll ____   ev - er see you a - gain. ____

Amazed

Words and Music by Marv Green,
Chris Lindsey and Aimee Mayo

Moderately slow Country Ballad

Ev-'ry time our eyes meet, this feel-in' in-side me
The smell of your skin, the taste of your kiss,

is al-most more than I can take.
the way you whis-per in the dark.

*Recorded a half step lower.

With pedal

ba-by, I'm a-mazed __ by you. __

ba-by, I'm a-mazed __ by you. __

Ev-'ry lit-tle thing that you do. __

I'm so in love __ with you. __ It just keeps get-tin' bet - ter. __

24

Beautiful

Words and Music by Linda Perry

Moderately slow

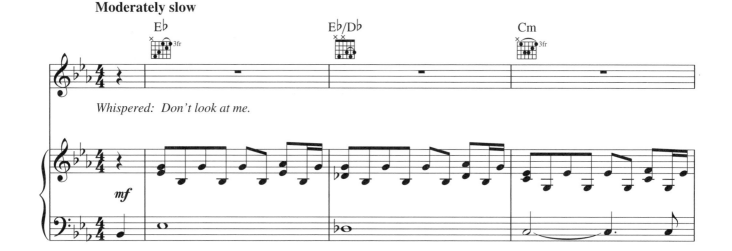

Whispered: *Don't look at me.*

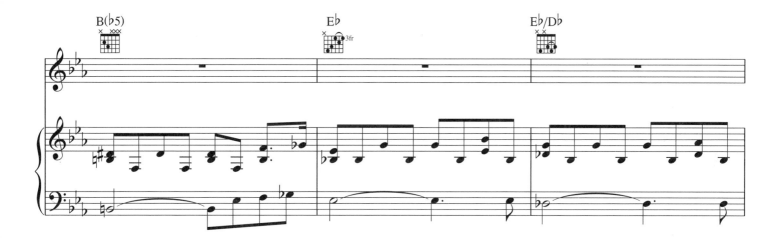

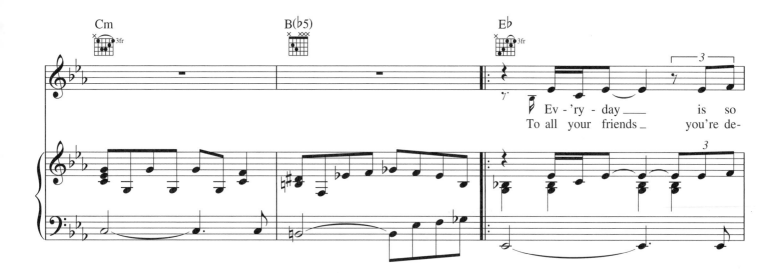

Ev-'ry-day ___ is so
To all your friends ___ you're de-

won-der-ful, then sud-den-ly, _____ it's hard to breathe. _

lir - i - ous. So con - sumed _ in all your doom. _

Now and then _____ I get in - se-cure _____ from all the pain, _

Try - ing hard _____ to fill the emp - ti - ness. _____ The piec - es gone, _____

feel so a - shamed. _____

left the puz - zle un - done. _____ Ain't that the way it is? _____

I am beau - ti - ful _____ no mat - ter what _ they say. _____

You are beau - ti - ful _____ no mat - ter what _ they say. _____

'Cause we are beau - ti - ful _____ no mat - ter what _ they say. _____

Words can't bring me ___ down. ___
Words can't bring you ___ down. ___
Words won't bring us ___ down. ___

I am beau - ti - ful ___ in
You are beau - ti - ful ___ in
We are beau - ti - ful ___ in

ev - 'ry sin - gle way. ___
ev - 'ry sin - gle way. ___
ev - 'ry sin - gle way. ___

Yes, words can't bring me ___ down, ___
Yes, words can't bring you ___ down, ___
Yes, words won't bring us ___ down, ___

___ oh ___ no.
___ oh ___ no.
___ oh ___ no.

So don't you bring me down ___ to - day. ___
So don't you bring me down ___

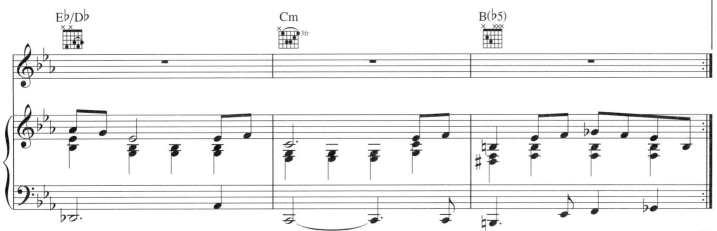

27

Fm7   Eb

So don't you bring me down to-day. _____ No mat-ter what we do. _

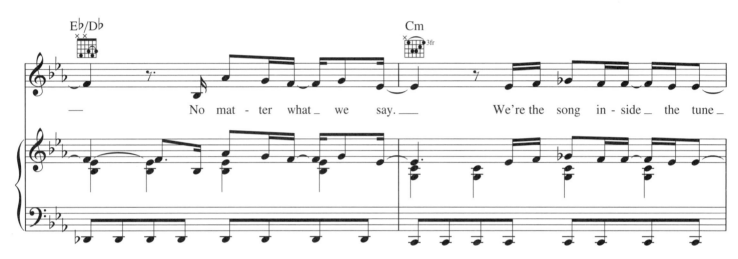

Eb/Db   Cm

_ No mat-ter what _ we say. _ We're the song in-side _ the tune _

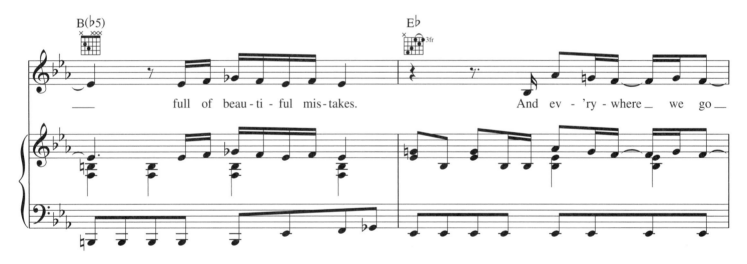

B(b5)   Eb

_ full of beau-ti-ful mis-takes. And ev-'ry-where _ we go _

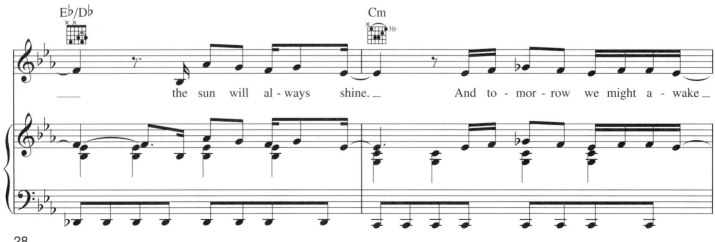

Eb/Db   Cm

_ the sun will al-ways shine. _ And to-mor-row we might a-wake _

28

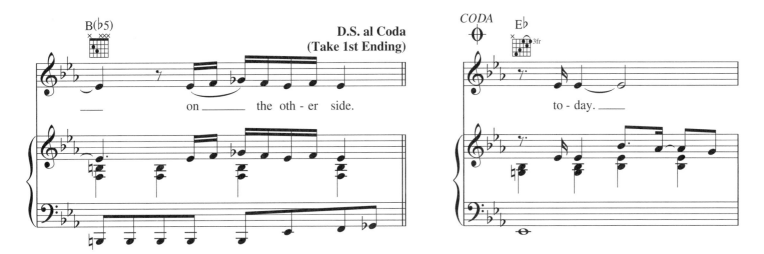

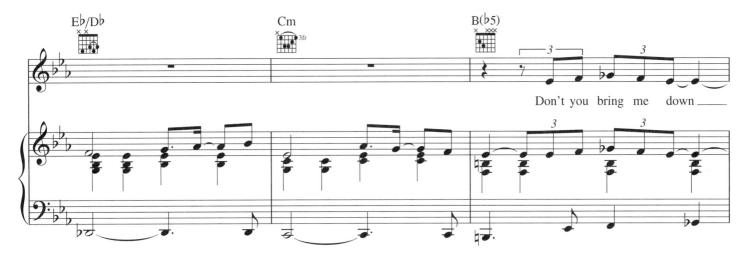

Better In Time

Words and Music by
Andrea Martin and Jonathan Rotem

It's been the long-est win-ter with-out ___ you; ___
I could-n't turn on the T - V ___

I did-n't know where to turn ___ to. ___ (Ah.) ___
with-out some-thing there to re-mind ___ me. ___ (Ah.) ___

* Recorded a half step higher.

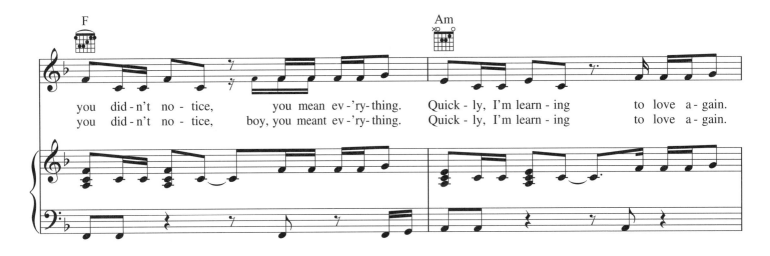

you did-n't no - tice, you mean ev-'ry-thing. Quick - ly, I'm learn - ing to love a - gain.
you did-n't no - tice, boy, you meant ev-'ry-thing. Quick - ly, I'm learn - ing to love a - gain.

All I ___ know is, ___ I'm ___ gon' be ___ o - kay. _____
All I ___ know is, ___ I'm ___ gon' be ___ o - kay. _____

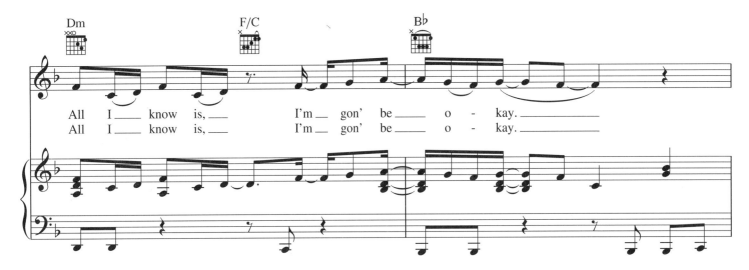

Thought I could n't live with-out you; it's gon-na hurt when it heals, _ too, _

___ oh ___ yeah. _____ (It - 'll all get bet - ter in time.) _

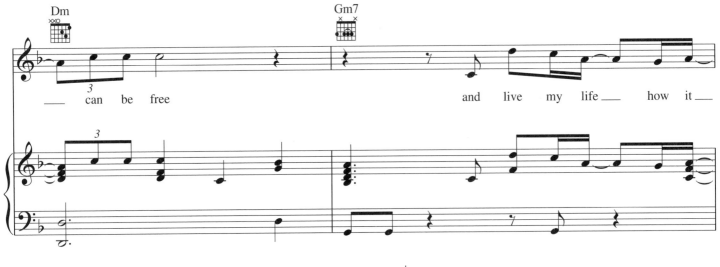

all get bet-ter in time.) ___ And e-ven though I real-ly love you,

I'm gon-na smile, 'cause I de-serve ___ to, ___ yes, I do. (It-'ll

Repeat and Fade

all get bet-ter in time.) ___ Thought I could-n't live with-out you;

Optional Ending

all get bet-ter in time.) ___

Breathe (2 AM)

Words and Music by Anna Nalick

Moderately slow, in 2

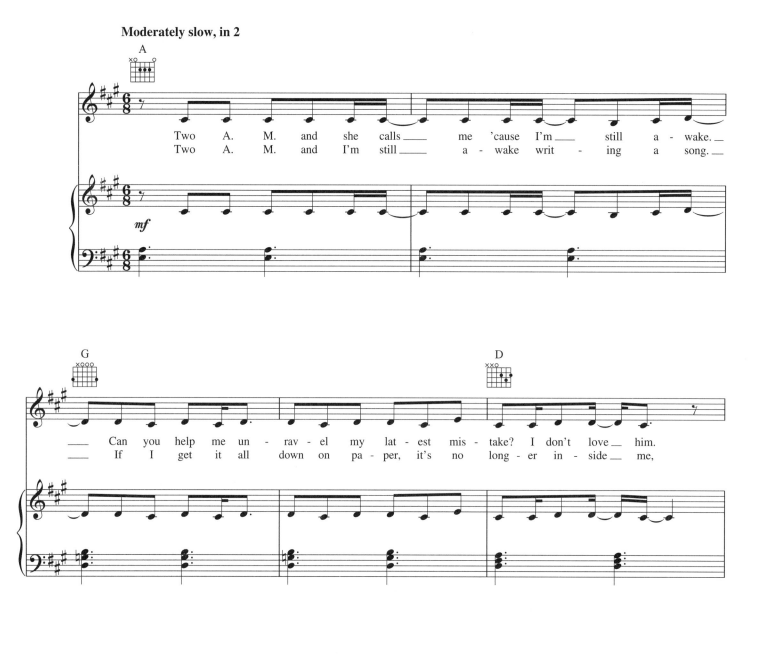

Two A. M. and she calls _____ me 'cause I'm _____ still a - wake.
Two A. M. and I'm still _____ a - wake writ - ing a song. _____

_____ Can you help me un - rav - el my lat - est mis - take? I don't love _____ him.
_____ If I get it all down on pa - per, it's no long - er in - side _____ me,

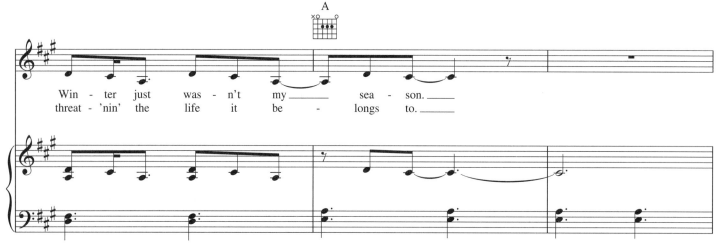

Win - ter just was - n't my _____ sea - son. _____
threat - 'nin' the life it be - longs to. _____

Yeah, we walk ___ through the doors, ___ so ac-cus - ing, their eyes, ___
And I feel ___ like I'm na - ked in front ___ of the crowd, ___

G

___ like they have an - y right at all to crit - i -
___ 'cause these words are my di - a - ry scream - in' a -

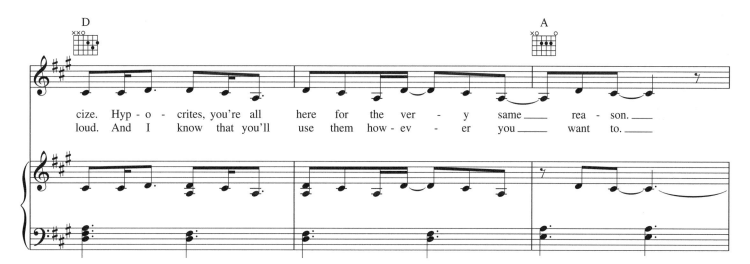

D   A

cize. Hyp-o - crites, you're all here for the ver - y same ___ rea - son. ___
loud. And I know that you'll use them how-ev - er you ___ want to. ___

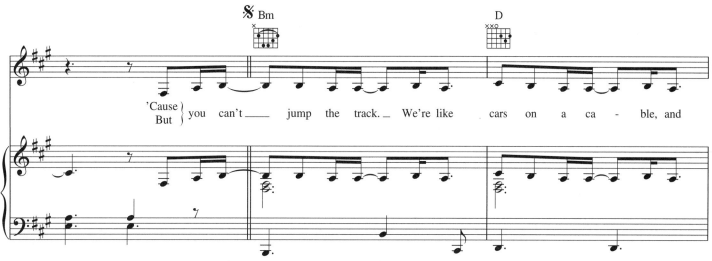

%Bm   D

'Cause } you can't ___ jump the track. ___ We're like cars on a ca - ble, and
But }

breathe. _____

To Coda I _To Coda II_

In May he turned twen-ty-one _____ on the base _____ of Fort Bliss. Just a day, _____ he sat down to the flask in his fist. Ain't been so-ber since may-be Oc-to-ber of last year. _____

Here in town, you can tell he's been down for a while, _____

but, my God, it's so beau-ti-ful when the boy smiles. Wan-na hold him,

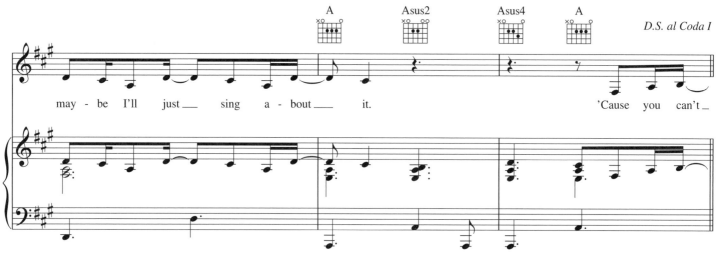

D.S. al Coda I

may-be I'll just ___ sing a-bout ___ it. 'Cause you can't ___

Coda I

There's a light _____ at each end _____ of this

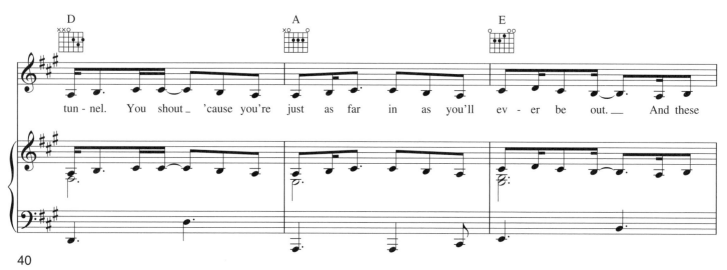

tun-nel. You shout _ 'cause you're just as far in as you'll ev-er be out. _ And these

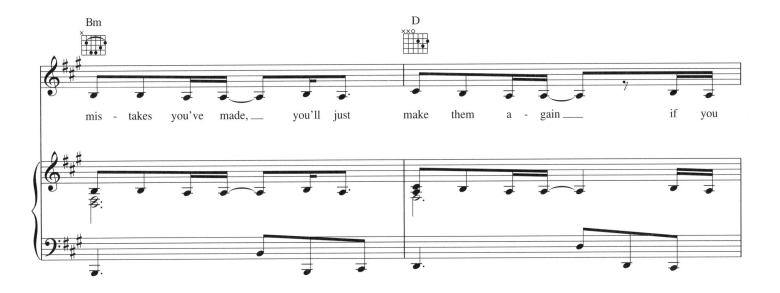

mis - takes you've made, ___ you'll just make them a - gain ____ if you

D.C. al Coda II

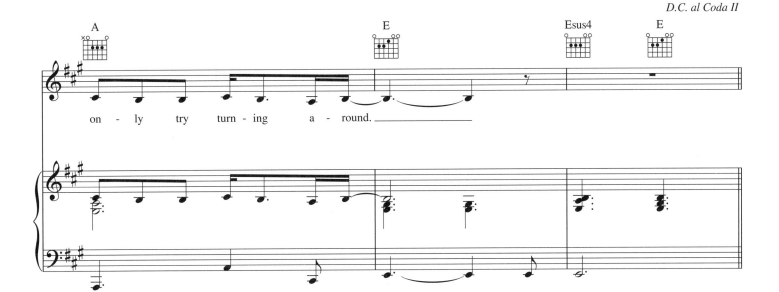

on - ly try turn - ing a - round. _____

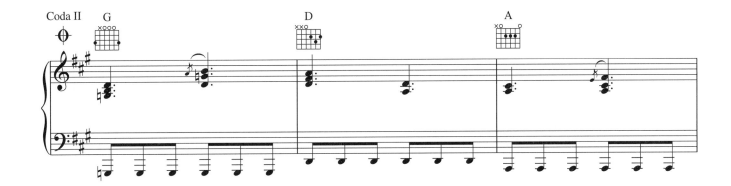

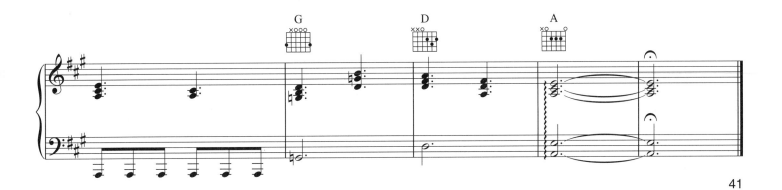

Bubble Toes

Words and Music by Jack Johnson

I'll re-mem-ber when ___ you and me, ___

mm, ___ how we used to be ___ just good friends. Would-n't give me none, ___

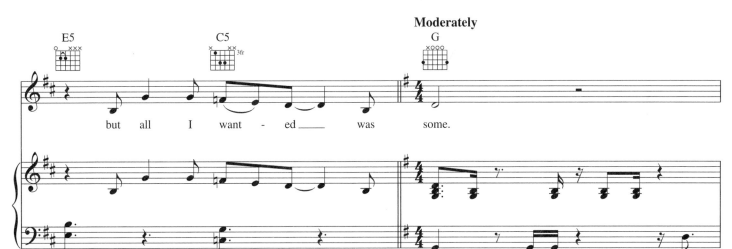

Moderately

but all I want-ed ___ was some.

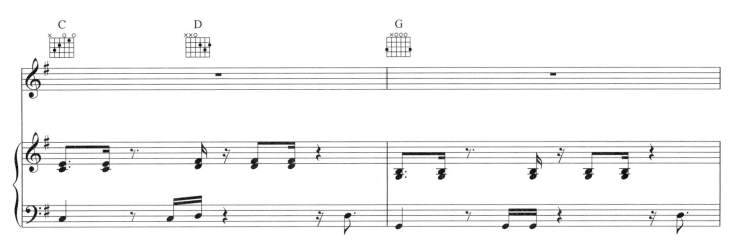

She's got - ta whole lot - ta rea - sons. She can't think of a

sin - gle one __ that can jus - ti - fy __ leav - ing. And he got none, __ but he thinks __ he got so man - y prob -

lems. Man, he got too much time __ to waste. __

His dreams are like __ com - mer - cials, but __ her dreams __

___ are pic - ture per - fect. And __ our dreams are so __ re - lat - ed, though _ they're __

of - ten un - der - es - ti - mat - ed. __

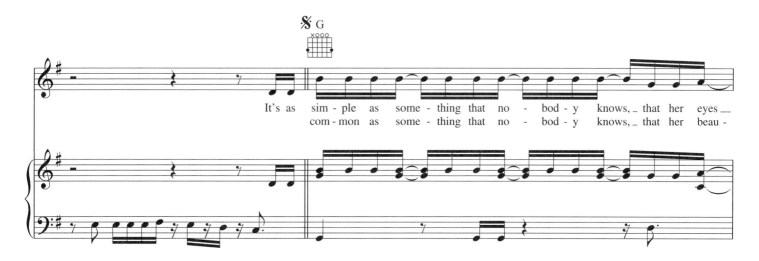

It's as sim - ple as some - thing that no - bod - y knows, _ that her eyes _
com - mon as some - thing that no - bod - y knows, _ that her beau -

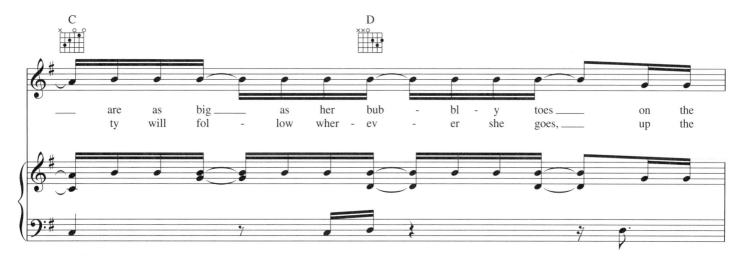

__ are as big __ as her bub - bl - y toes __ on the
ty will fol - low wher - ev - er she goes, __ up the

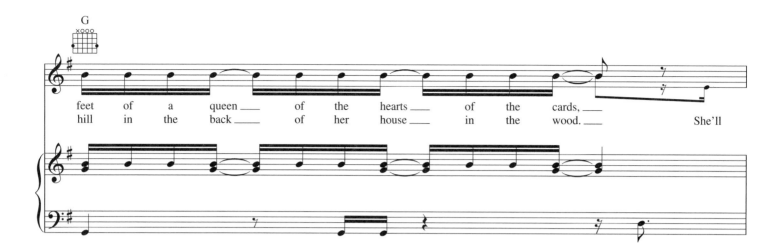

feet of a queen ___ of the hearts ___ of the cards, ___
hill in the back ___ of her house ___ in the wood. ___ She'll

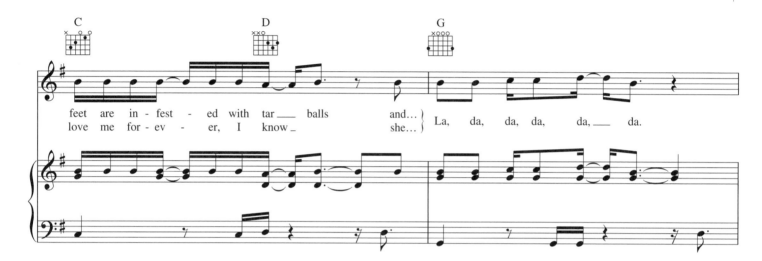

feet are in - fest - ed with tar ___ balls and... ⎫
love me for - ev - er, I know ___ she... ⎬ La, da, da, da, da, ___ da.

To Coda II

La, da, da, da, ___ da, da, ___ da. La, da, da, da, da, ___ da.

To Coda I

La, da, da, da, ___ da, da, ___ da, da.

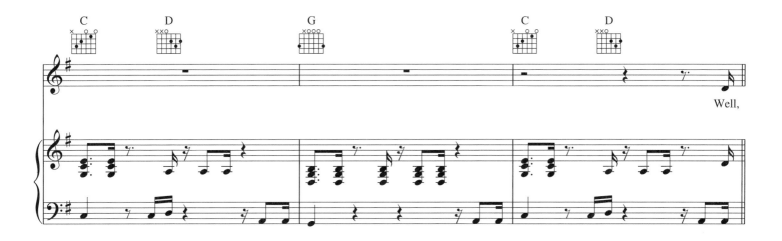

Well,

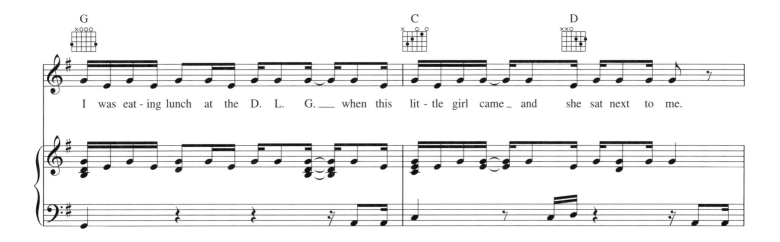

I was eat-ing lunch at the D. L. G. ___ when this lit-tle girl came ___ and she sat next to me.

Nev-er seen no-bod-y move the way she did. ___ Well, she did and she does and she'll do it a-gain. ___ When you

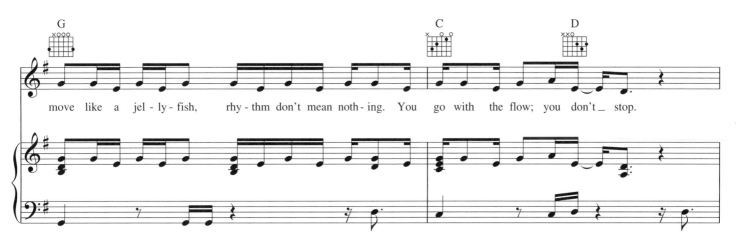

move like a jel-ly-fish, rhy-thm don't mean noth-ing. You go with the flow; you don't ___ stop.

47

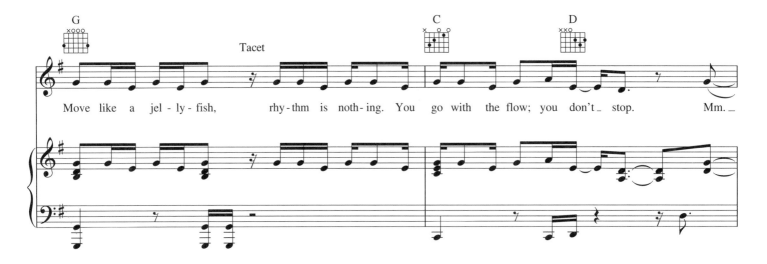

Move like a jel-ly-fish, rhy-thm is noth-ing. You go with the flow; you don't stop. Mm.

D.S. al Coda I

It's as

Coda I

da.

If

you would on-ly lis-ten, you might just real-ize what you're miss-ing. You're miss-ing me.

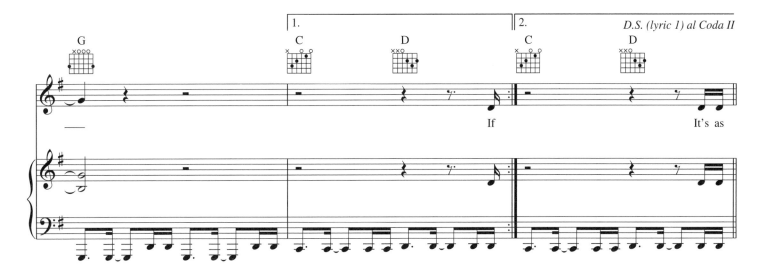

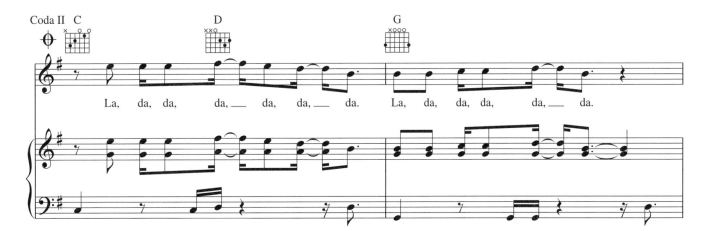

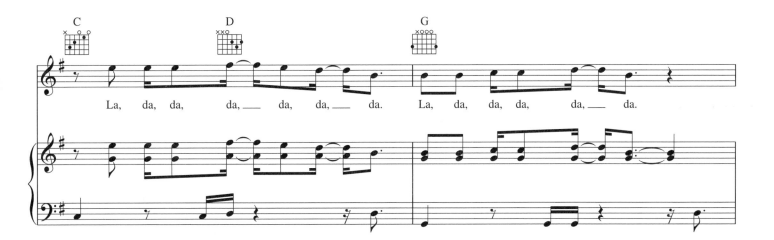

Bubbly

Words and Music by
Colbie Caillat and Jason Reeves

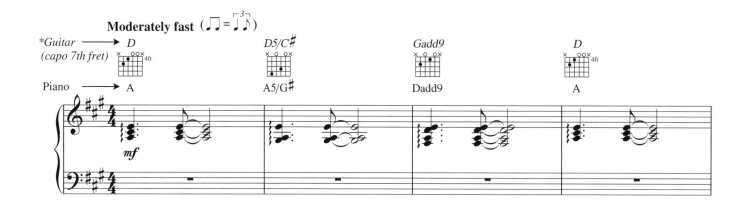

(Spoken:) Will you count me in?

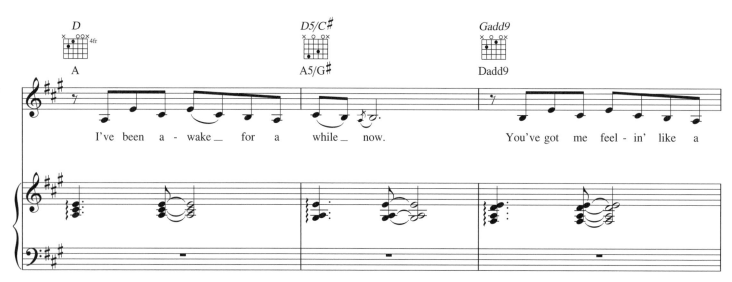

I've been a-wake for a while now. You've got me feel-in' like a

*Guitarists: Use open D tuning (low to high): D-A-D-F♯-A-D.

    Capo 7th fret (fret numbers next to chord diagrams indicate number of frets above capo).

makes me crin - kle my nose. _____ Wher - ev - er it goes, _____ I al - ways _____ know _____

that you make me smile. _____ Please stay for a while _____ now. Just take your time _____

wher - ev - er you go. _____

But

what am I gon - na say _____

when you make me feel ___ this way? _____

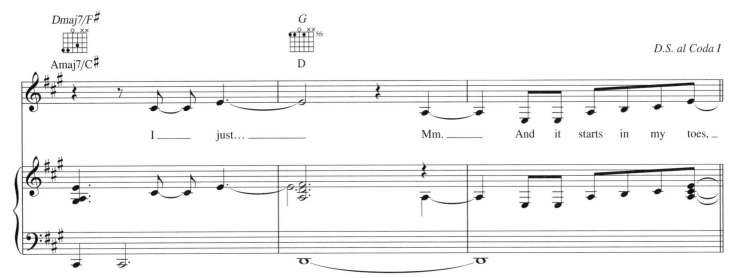

D.S. al Coda I

I _____ just… _____ Mm. _____ And it starts in my toes, _

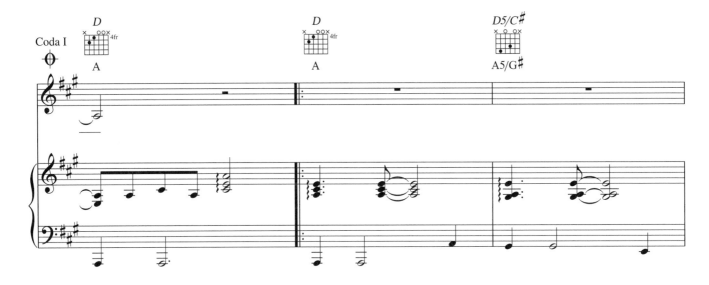

Coda I

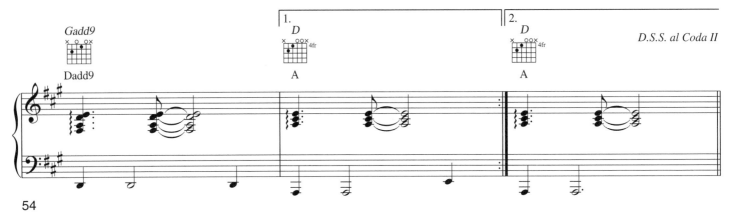

D.S.S. al Coda II

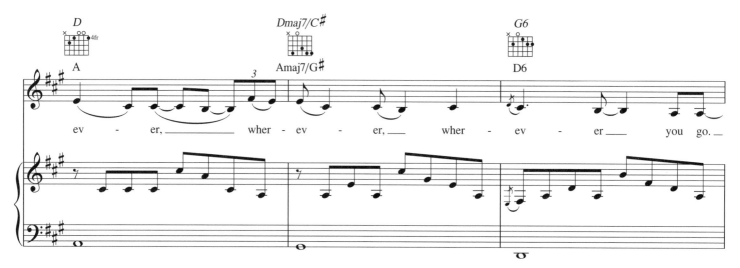

ev - er, _____ wher - ev - er, ___ wher - ev - er ___ you go. _

___ Ooh, wher - ev - er you __ go,

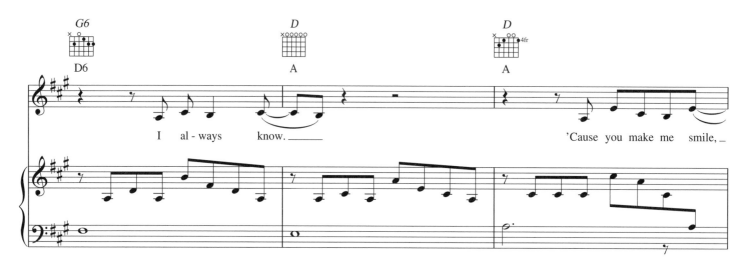

I al - ways know. _____ 'Cause you make me smile, _

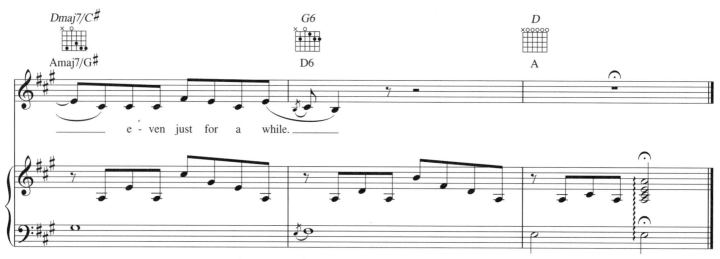

_____ e - ven just for a while. _____

Come Away With Me

Words and Music by Norah Jones

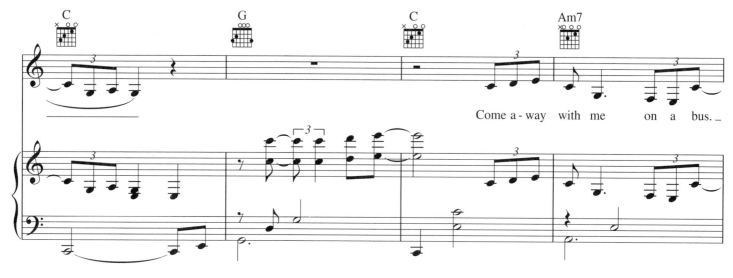

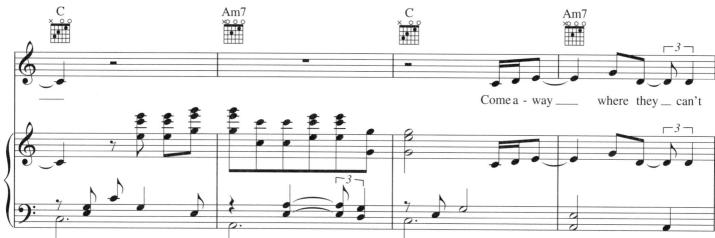

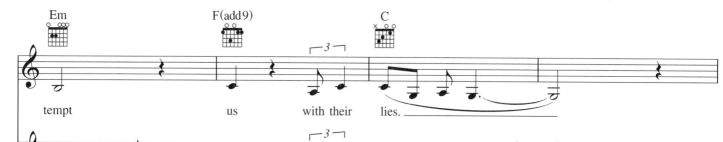

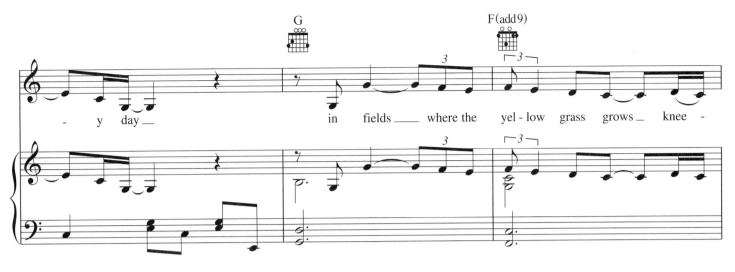

- y day ___ in fields ___ where the yel - low grass grows ___ knee -

high. So won't you ___ try ___ to come? Come a - way ___

___ with me and ___ we'll kiss on a moun - tain - top. ___

Come a - way ___ with me ___ and I'll ___ nev - er

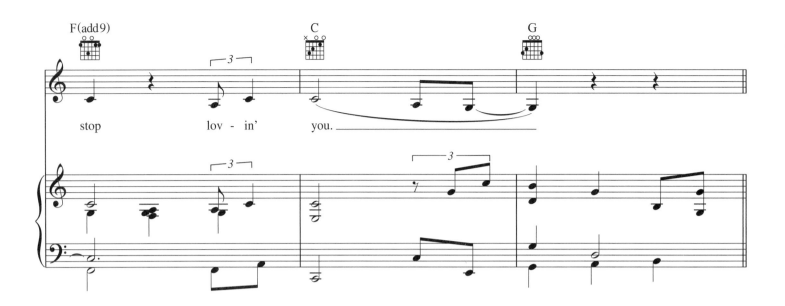

stop   lov - in'   you._____

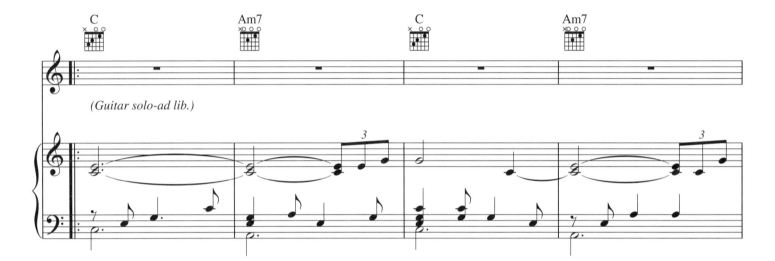

(Guitar solo-ad lib.)

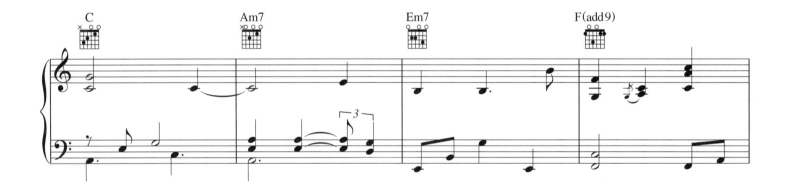

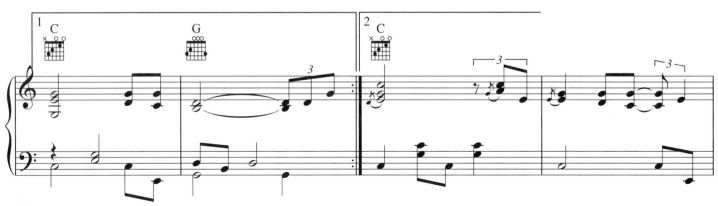

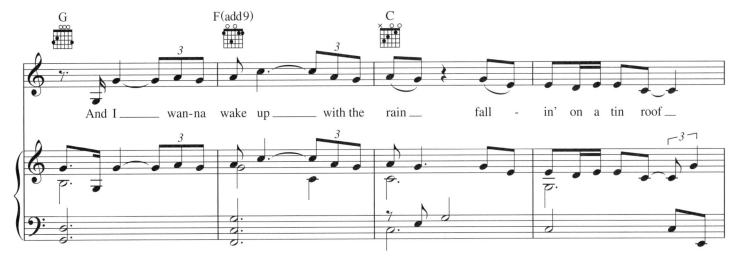

And I _____ wan-na wake up _____ with the rain ___ fall - in' on a tin roof ___

while I'm safe there in your arms. ___ So all I _____ ask is ___ for

you to come a-way with me in the night. ___

Come a - way _____ with me. _____

Complicated

Words and Music by Avril Lavigne,
Lauren Christy, Scott Spock
and Graham Edwards

Moderate Pop

Uh huh,   life's like this.

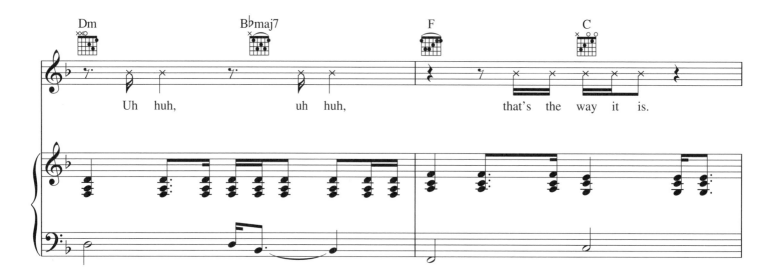

Uh huh,   uh huh,   that's the way it is.

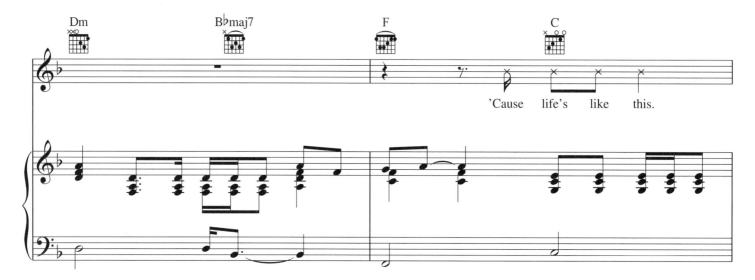

'Cause life's like this.

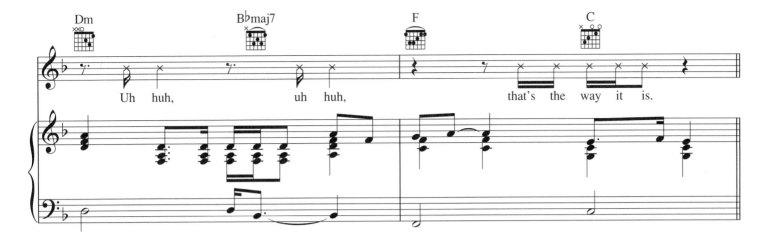

Uh huh, uh huh, that's the way it is.

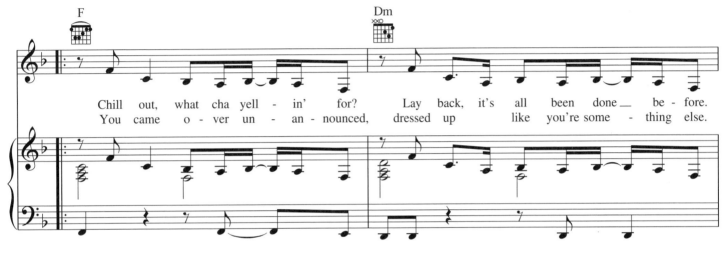

Chill out, what cha yell - in' for? Lay back, it's all been done __ be - fore.
You came o - ver un - an - nounced, dressed up like you're some - thing else.

And if you could on - ly __ let it be __ you will see. __
Where you are ain't where __ it's __ at, you see. __ You're mak - in' me __

I like you the way __ you are when we're driv - in' in __ your car
laugh out when you strike __ your pose. Take off all your prep - py clothes.
Lay back, it's all been done __ be - fore.

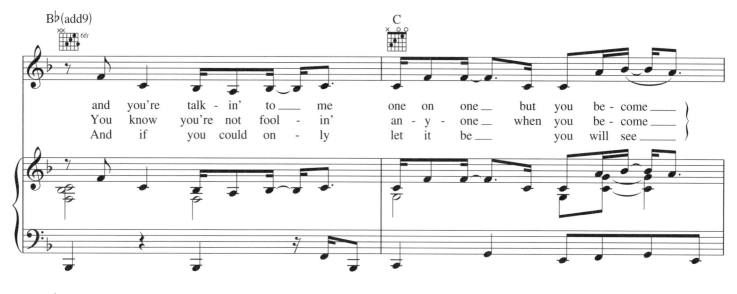

and you're talk - in' to __ me one on one __ but you be - come ____
You know you're not fool - in' an - y - one __ when you be - come ____
And if you could on - ly let it be __ you will see ____

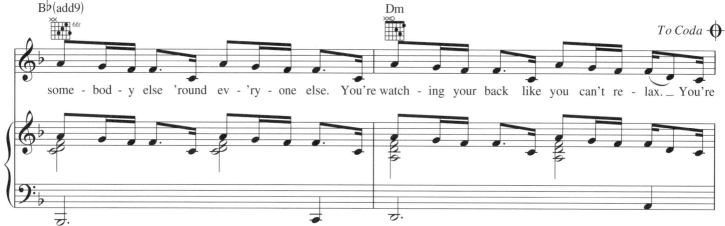

To Coda

some - bod - y else 'round ev - 'ry - one else. You're watch - ing your back like you can't re - lax. __ You're

try'n' to be cool. You look like a fool to me. _____ Tell ___ me,

why'd you have to go and make things so com - pli - cat - ed? See the way you're

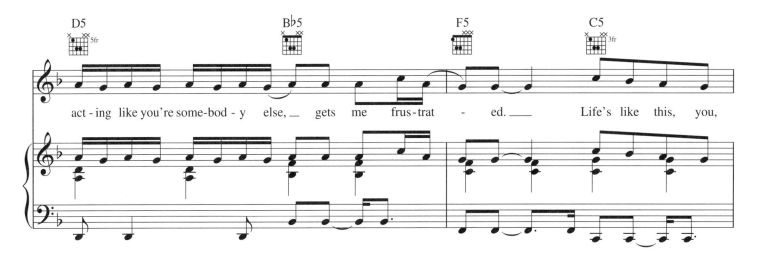

act-ing like you're some-bod-y else, __ gets me frus-trat - ed. __ Life's like this, you,

you fall __ and you crawl __ and you break __ and you take __ what you get __ and you turn __ it in-to

hon-es-ty and prom-ise me I'm nev-er gon-na find you fake __ it, _____ no, no,

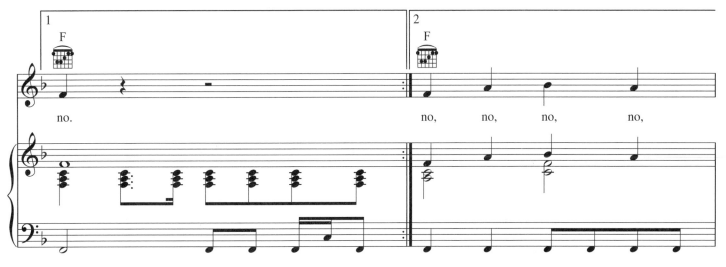

no.   no, no, no, no,

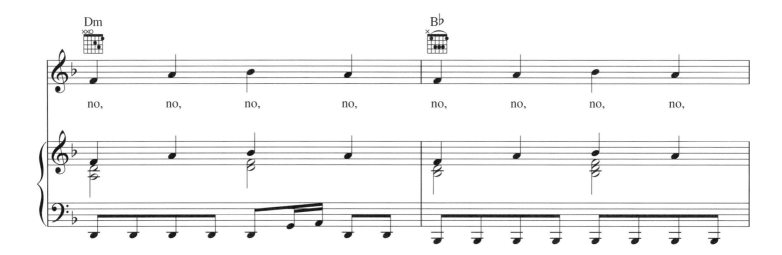

no, no, no, no, no, no, no, no,

D.S. al Coda

no, no, no, no. Chill out, what cha yell - in' for?

try'n' to be cool. You look like a fool to me. _____ Tell me _____

why'd you have to go and make things so com - pli - cat - ed? See the way you're

66

act-ing like you're some-bod-y else, __ gets me frus-trat - ed. __ Life's like this, you,

you fall __ and you crawl __ and you break __ and you take __ what you get __ and you turn __ it in - to

hon-es - ty. Prom-ise me I'm nev-er gon-na find you fake __ it, ___ no, no,

___ it, _____ no, no, _____ no.

Daughters

Words and Music by John Mayer

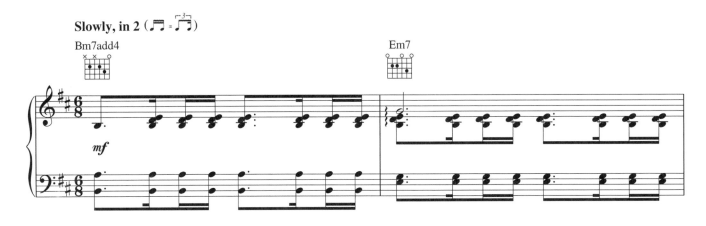

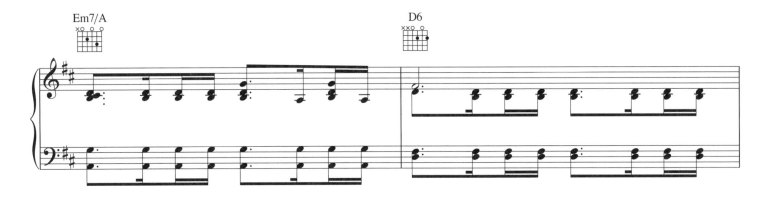

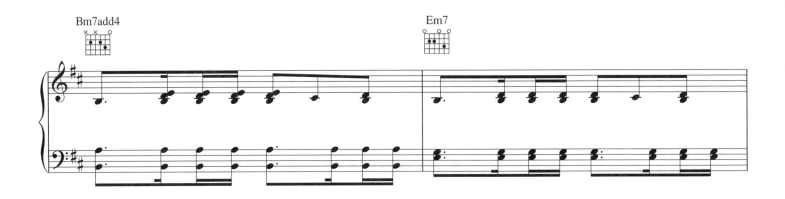

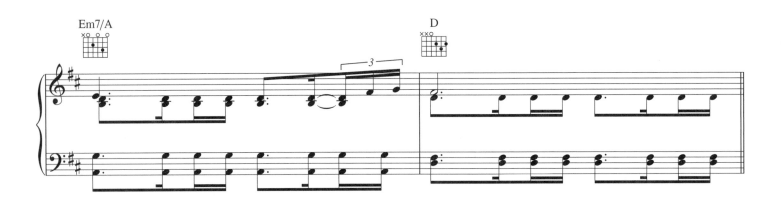

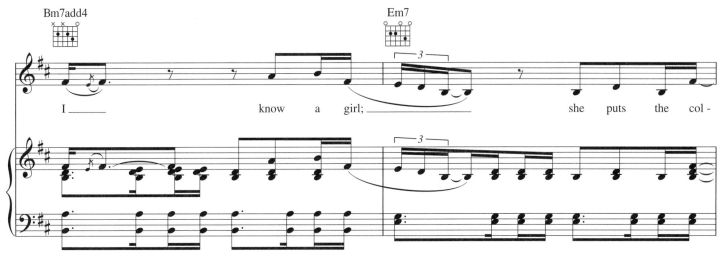

I _____ know a girl; _____ she puts the col-

or in - side of my world. _____ But

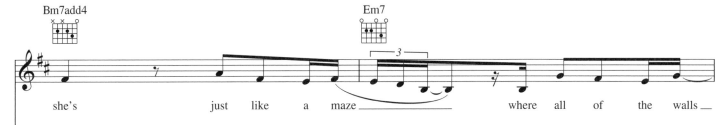

she's just like a maze _____ where all of the walls _

_ all _ con - ti - ual - ly _ change. _ And

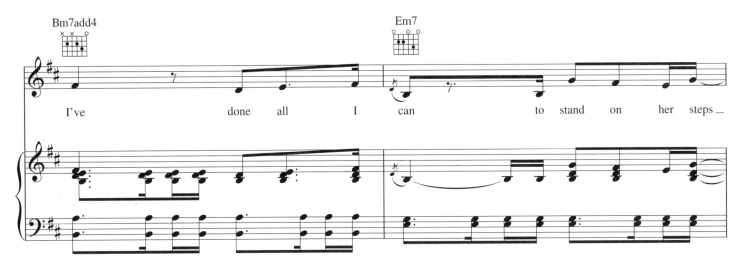

I've done all I can to stand on her steps

with my heart in my hand. Now

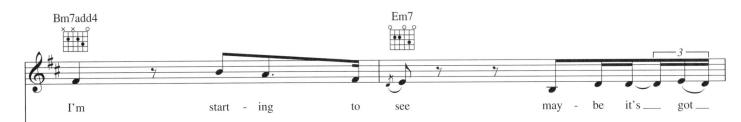

I'm start-ing to see may-be it's got

noth-ing to do with me.

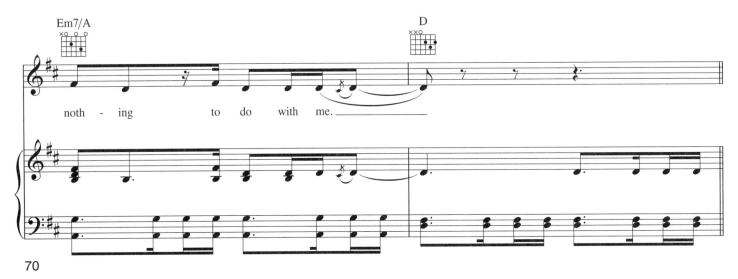

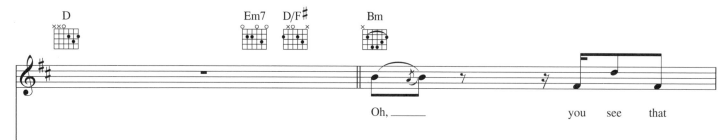

Oh, _____ you see that

skin? _____ It's the same _____ she's been stand - ing in _____

since the day she saw him

from the Motion Picture ONCE

Falling Slowly

Words and Music by Glen Hansard
and Marketa Irglova

Slowly ♩ = 69

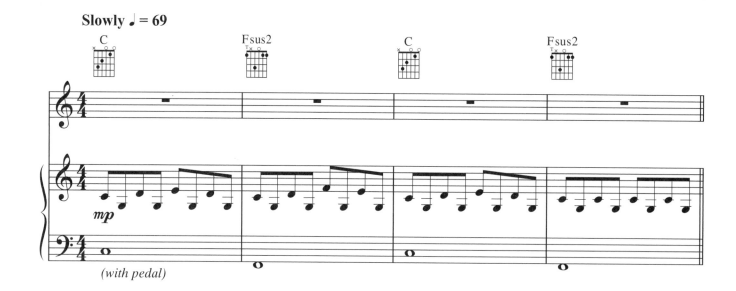

(with pedal)

Verse 1:

1. I don't know you, but I want you all the more for that.

Words fall through me and al - ways fool me and I can't re - act.

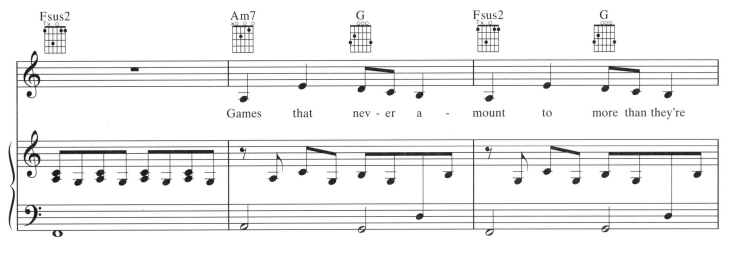

Games that nev - er a - mount to more than they're

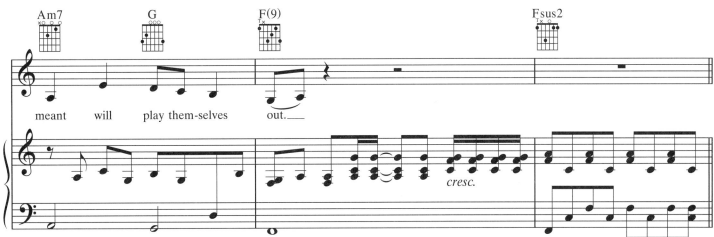

meant will play them-selves out.____

Chorus:

Take this sink - in' boat and point it home, we've still got

mf

time._____ Raise your hope - ful voice, you have a

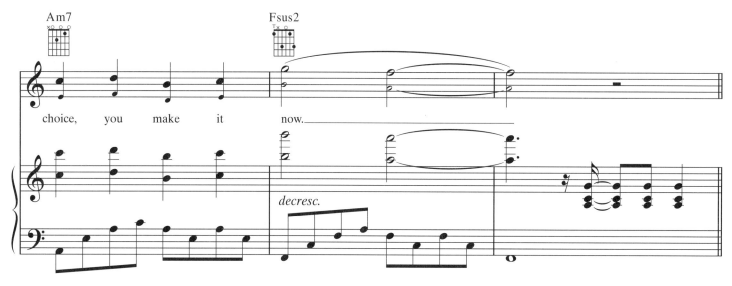

choice, you make it now.___

Verse 2:

2. Fall - ing slow - ly, eyes that know me and I can't go back.

Moods that take me and e - rase me and I'm paint - ed black.

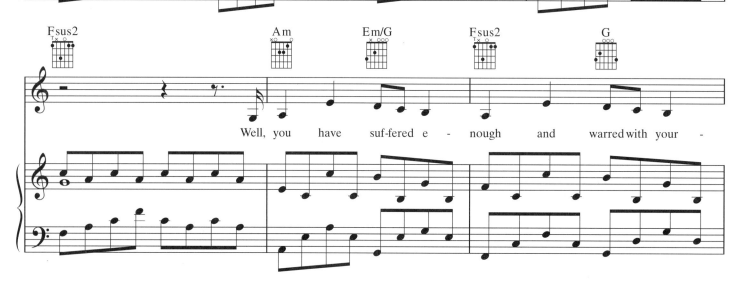

Well, you have suf-fered e - nough and warred with your -

self. It's time that you won.

Chorus:

Take this sink-in' boat and point it home, we've still got time.

Raise your hope-ful voice, you have a choice, you've made it now.

Fall-in' slow-ly,

(Strings)

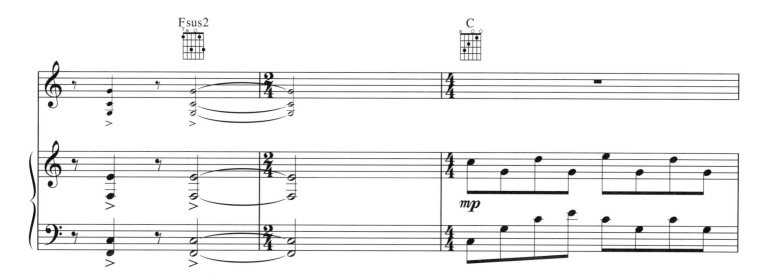

mp

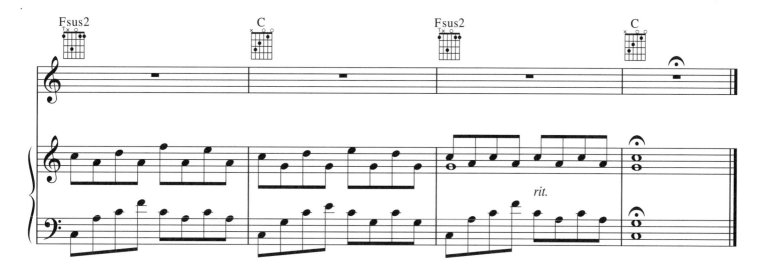

rit.

The First Cut Is The Deepest

Words and Music by Cat Stevens

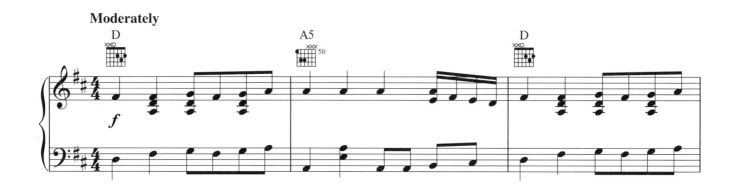

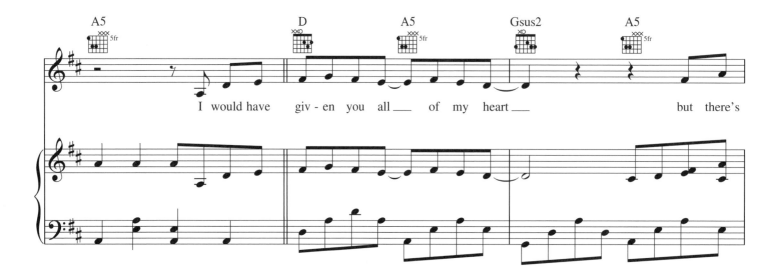

I would have giv-en you all ___ of my heart ___ but there's

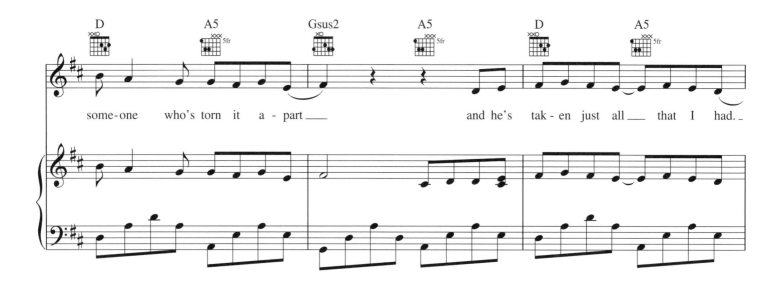

some-one who's torn it a-part ___ and he's tak-en just all ___ that I had. ___

I still want _ you by _ my _ side _

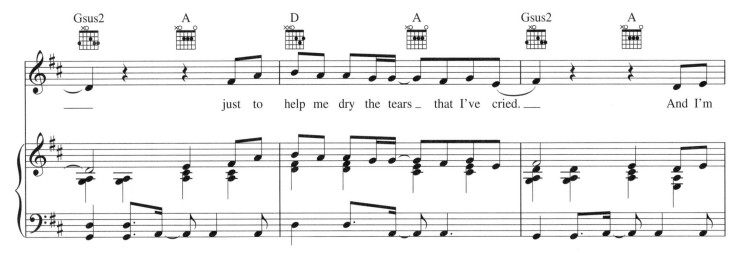

just to help me dry the tears _ that I've cried. __ And I'm

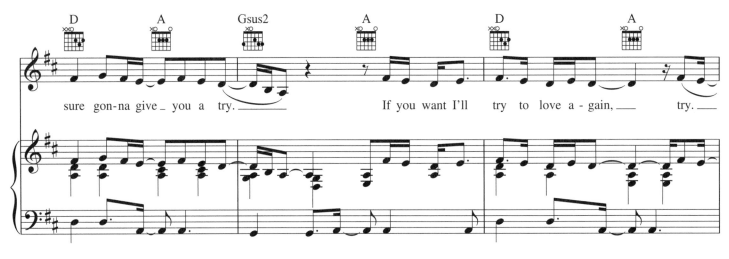

sure gon-na give _ you a try. ____ If you want I'll try to love a - gain, ___ try. __

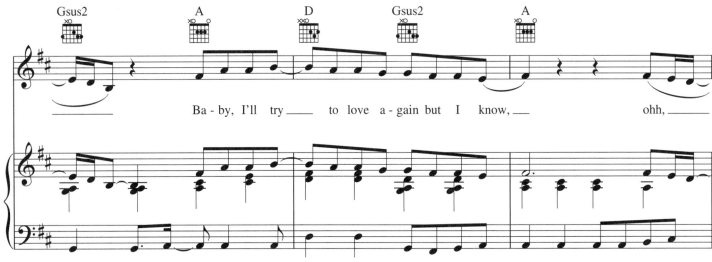

Ba - by, I'll try ___ to love a - gain but I know, ___ ohh, _____

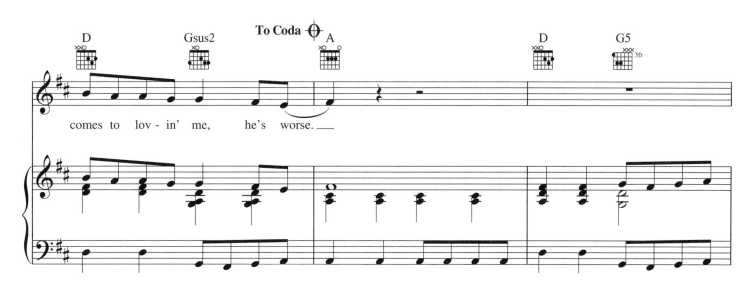

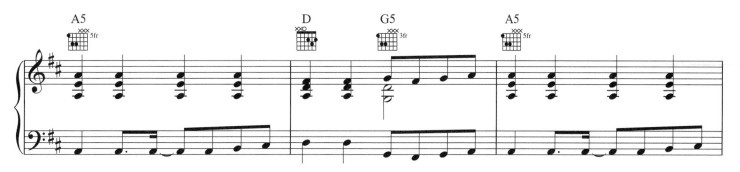

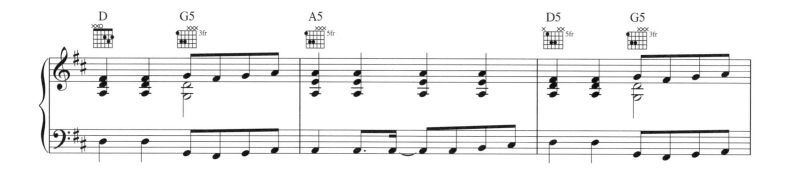

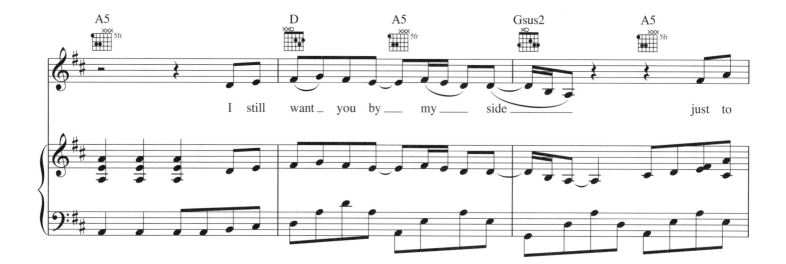

I still want_ you by__ my___ side _____ just to

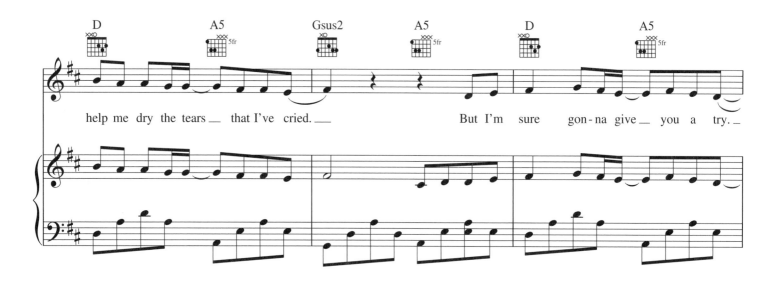

help me dry the tears _ that I've cried. ___ But I'm sure gon-na give_ you a try. _

_____ 'Cause if you want I'll try to love a-gain. Try to love a-gain.

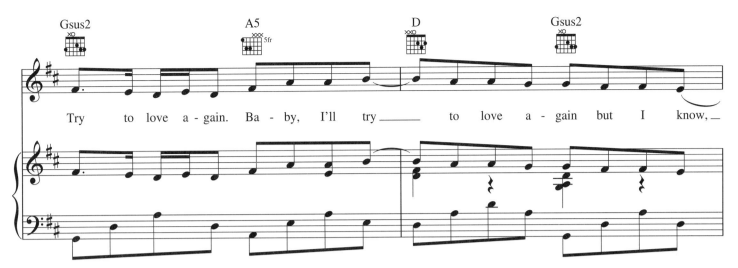

Try to love a - gain. Ba - by, I'll try _____ to love a - gain but I know, _____

_____ ohh, _____ the first cut is the deep -

D.S. al Coda

CODA

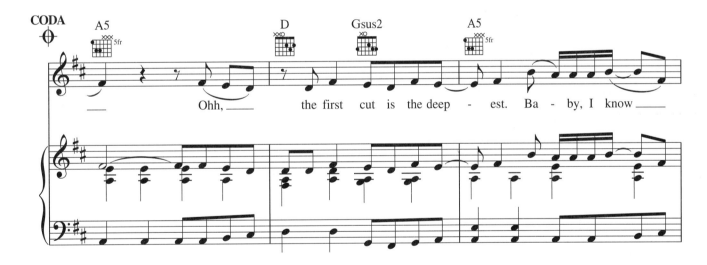

_____ Ohh, _____ the first cut is the deep - est. Ba - by, I know _____

the first cut is the deep - est. Try to love a - gain. _____

87

Follow Through

Words and Music by Gavin DeGraw

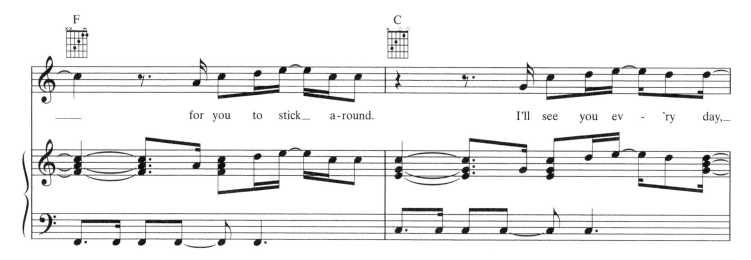

for you to stick_ a-round.   I'll see you ev - 'ry day,_

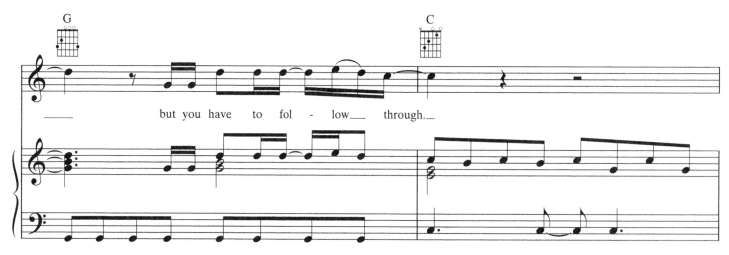

_   but you have to fol - low_ through._

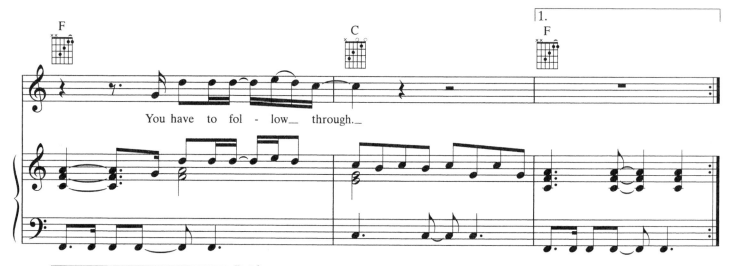

You have to fol - low_ through._

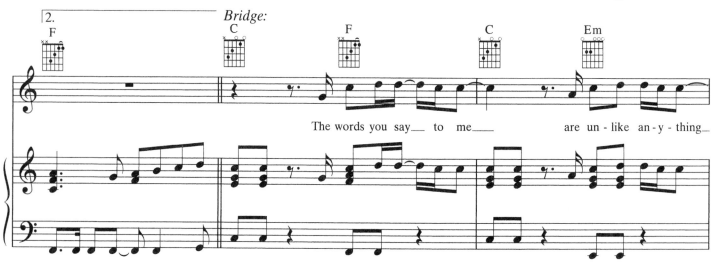

The words you say_ to me_   are un - like an - y - thing_

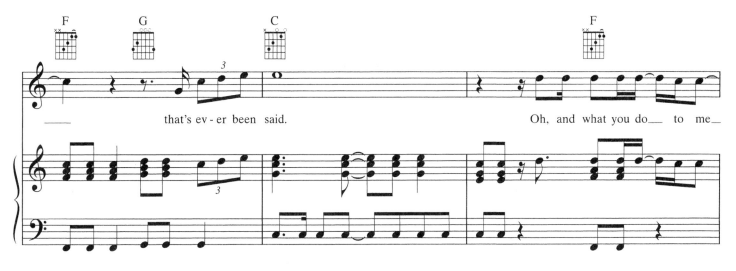

that's ev - er been said.   Oh, and what you do___ to me___

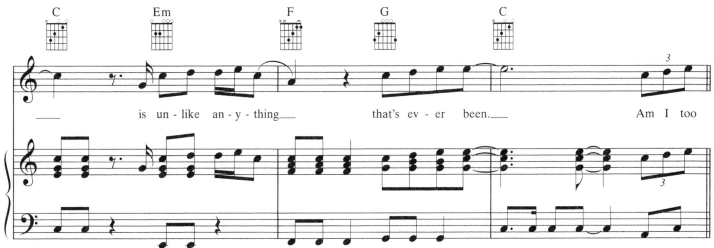

is un - like an - y - thing___   that's ev - er been.___   Am I too

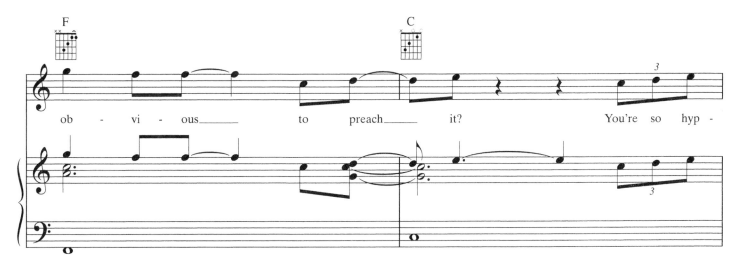

ob - vi - ous___   to preach___ it?   You're so hyp -

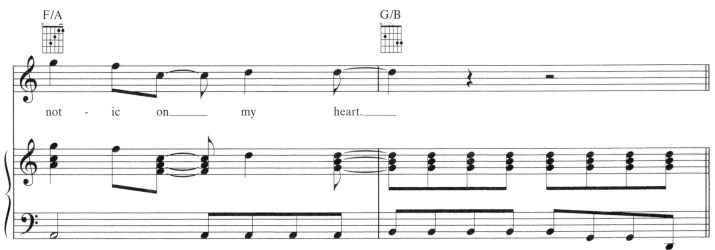

not - ic on___ my   heart.___

but you have to fol - low___ through.___

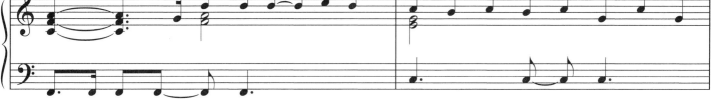

You have to fol - low through.___

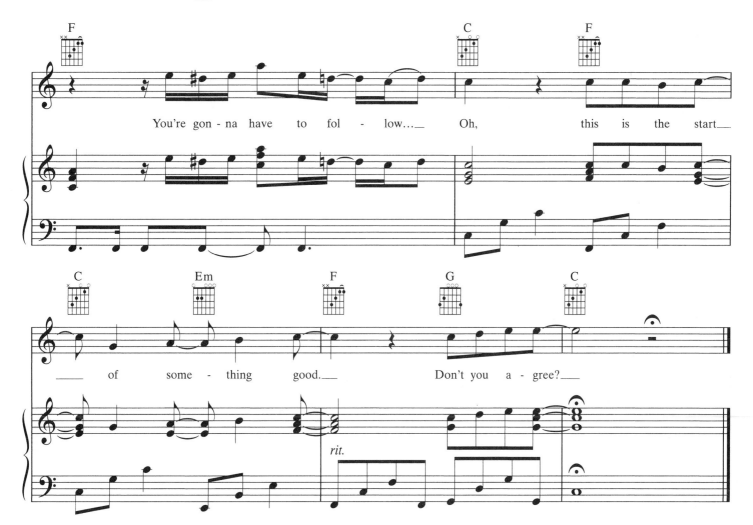

You're gon - na have to fol - low...___ Oh, this is the start___

___ of some - thing good.___ Don't you a - gree?___

rit.

Heaven

Words and Music by Henry Garza,
Joey Garza and Ringo Garza

Moderately

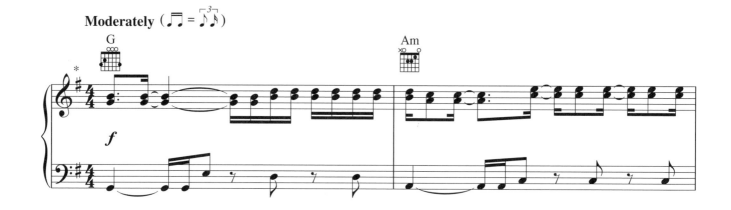

Save _____

Recorded a half step lower.

How __ far is heav - en? __ And I _____

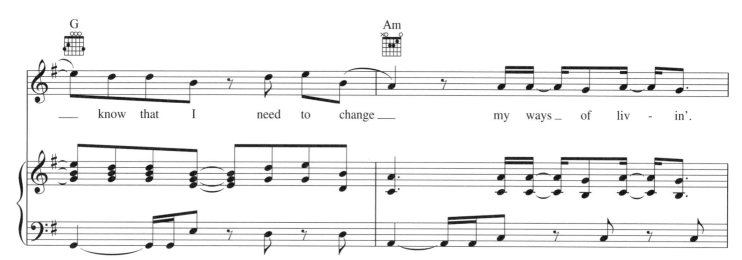

__ know that I need to change __ my ways _ of liv - in'.

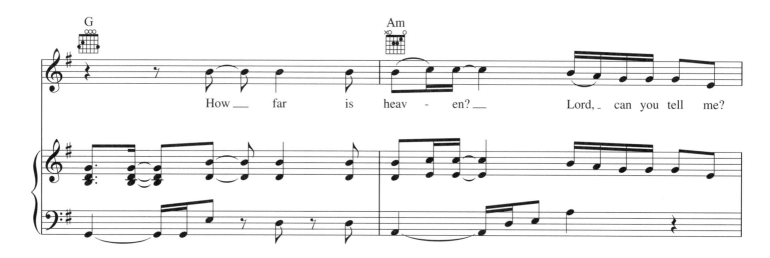

How __ far is heav - en? __ Lord, _ can you tell me?

How __ far is heav - en? __ 'Cause I just got - ta know __ how far, __

__ yeah. How __ far is heav - en? __ Yeah, ____ Lord, can you tell me?

To Coda ⊕

Guitar solo

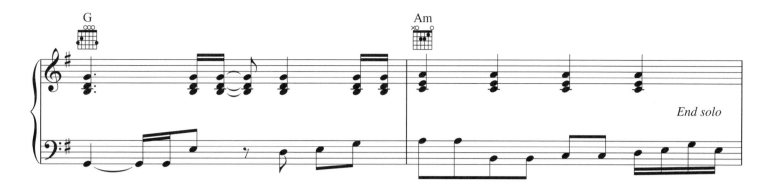

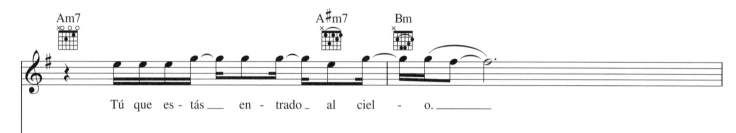

Tú que es - tás___ en - trado___ al ciel - o.___

Hech - a me___ tu ben - di - ción.___

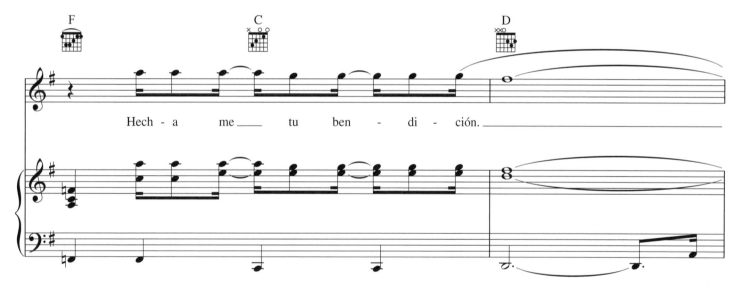

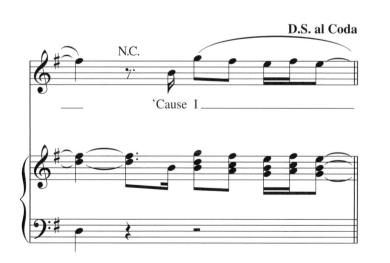

___ 'Cause I___

D.S. al Coda

N.C.

CODA

How___ far is

heav - en?___
'Cause I just got - ta know__ how far._____

I just wan - na know__ how far.___

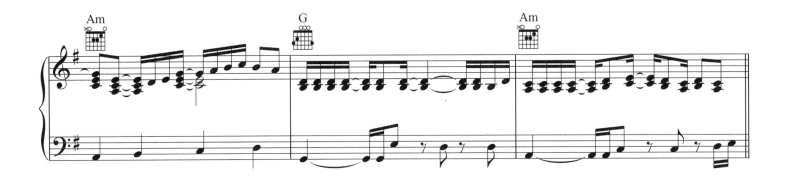

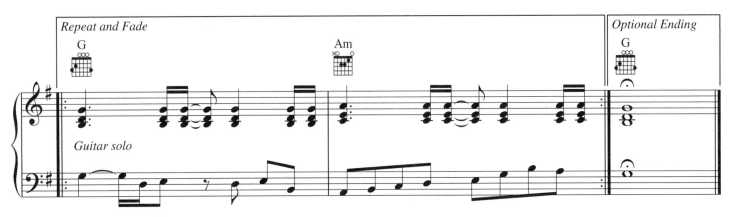

Repeat and Fade

Guitar solo

Optional Ending

I'm Missing You

Words and Music by Joshua P. Thompson, Tim Kelley,
Bob Robinson and Joe Thomas

Moderately

Play 4 times

Stand - ing here ___ look - ing out my win - dow, _____ the
Driv - ing 'round, _ thought I saw you pass _ me. _____ A

nights are long _ and my days are cold _ 'cause I don't _ have ___ you. ___
rear - view mir - ror's play - ing tricks on me, _ 'cause you fade __ a __ way. ___

How can I ___ be so damn de - mand - ing? _____ I
May - be I'm _ just hal - lu - ci - nat - ing, _____ 'cause my

know you said __ that it's o - ver now, __ but I can't __ let___ go. _____ Ev - 'ry
lone - li - ness __ got the best of me __ and my heart's __ so___ weak. _____

day I want __ to pick up the phone _____ and tell you that you're

ev - 'ry - thing __ that I need, and more. _____ If on - ly I could find you.

Chorus

Like a cold __ sum-mer af - ter - noon, ___ like the snow__ com-ing down in June, __

Here I Am

Words and Music by
Bryan Adams, Gretchen Peters
and Hans Zimmer

Moderately

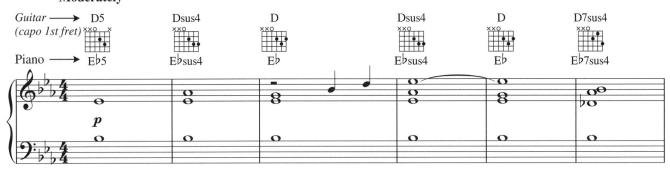

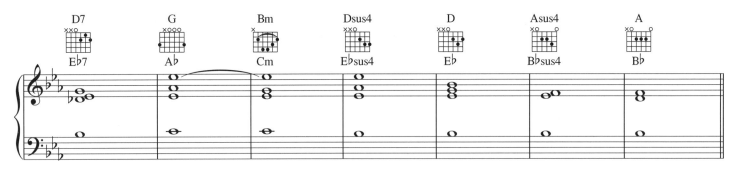

Here I am, this is me. I come in-to this world so wild ___

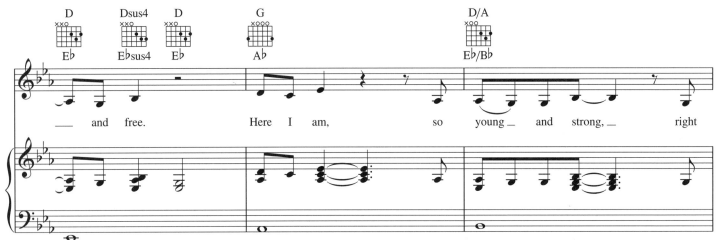

___ and free. Here I am, so young ___ and strong, ___ right

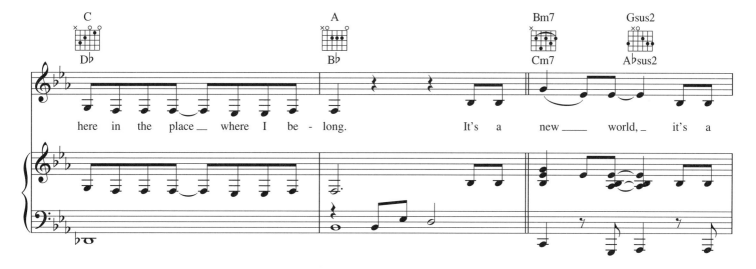

here in the place ___ where I be - long. It's a new ___ world, ___ it's a

new ___ start. ___ It's a - live with the beat - ing of ___ young ___ hearts. ___ It's a

new ___ day ___ in a new ___ land, ___ and it's wait - ing for ___ me.

Here I ___ am. ___ Oh, ___ it's a

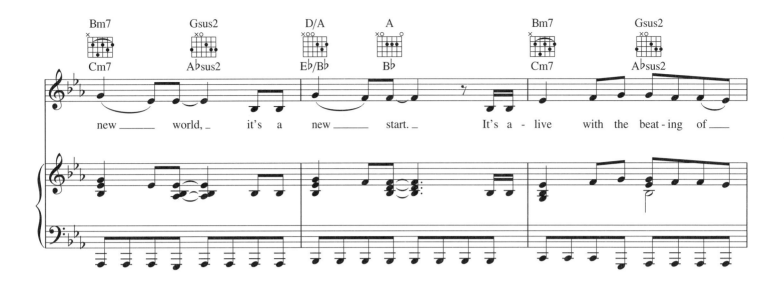

new ____ world, __ it's a new ____ start. __ It's a - live with the beat - ing of ____

young __ hearts. __ Yeah, it's a new ____ day __ in a new ____ land, __ and it's

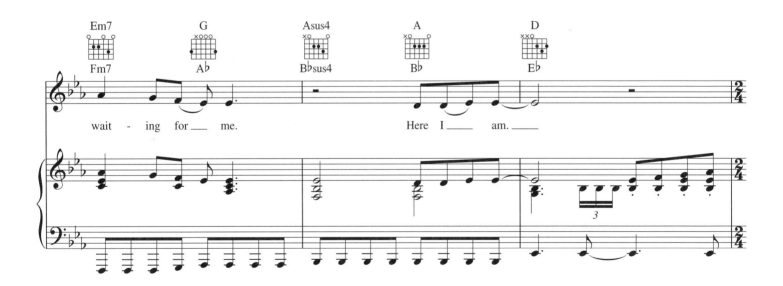

wait - ing for ____ me. Here I ____ am. ____

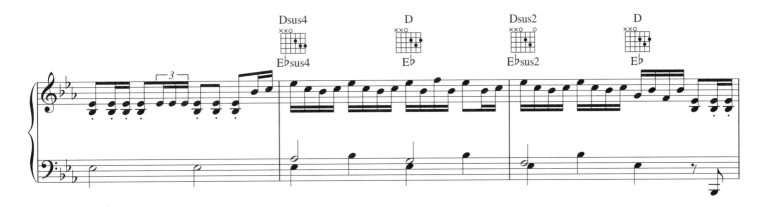

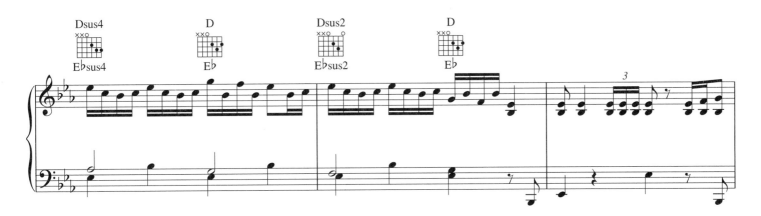

Home Sweet Home

Words and Music by
Tommy Lee and Nikki Sixx

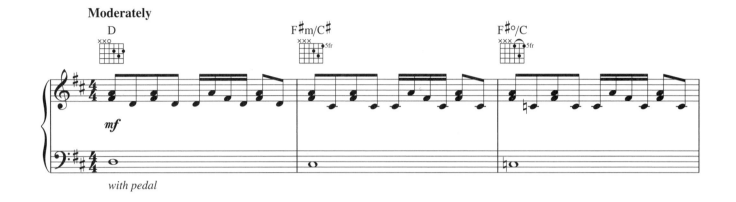

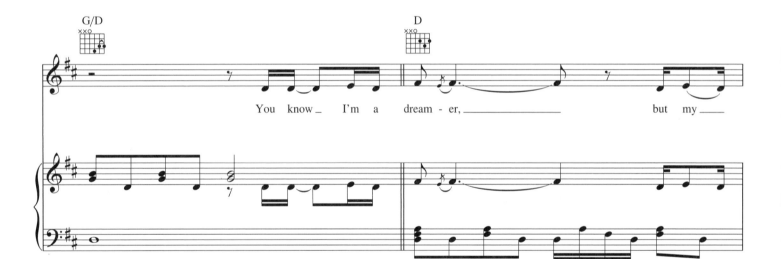

nothing, it keeps me to-geth-er — at the — seams. I'm on my

way, —— I'm on my way. —— Home sweet —

home. To - night, to - night, — I'm on my

way. —— Just set me free. —— Home sweet —

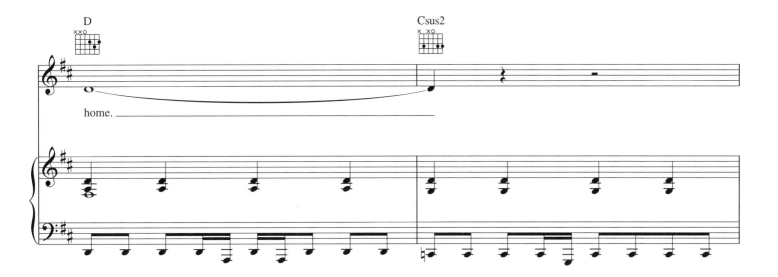

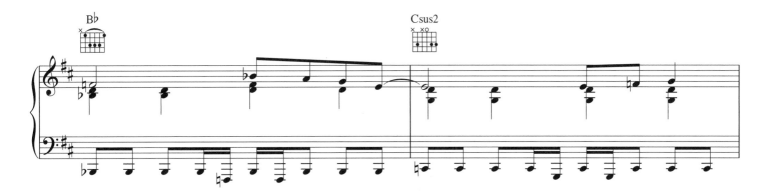

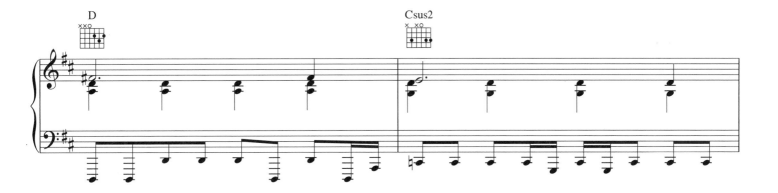

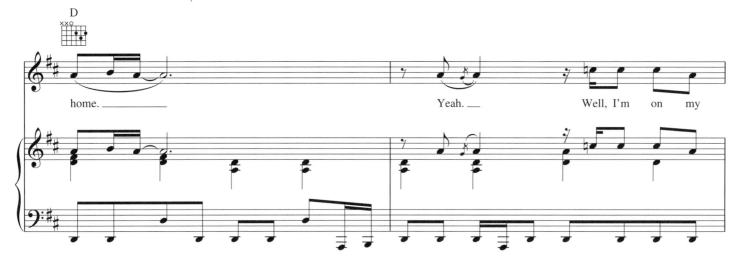

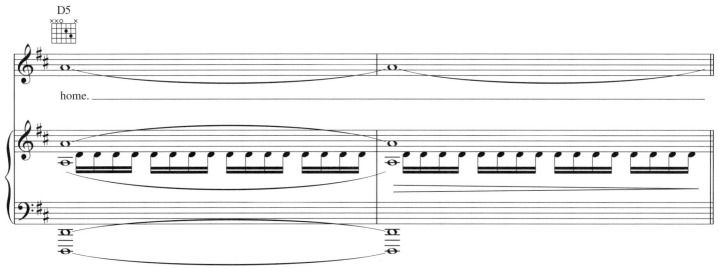

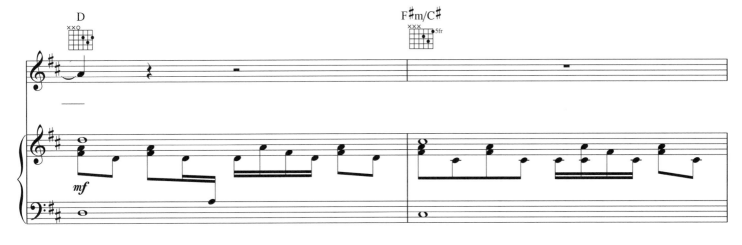

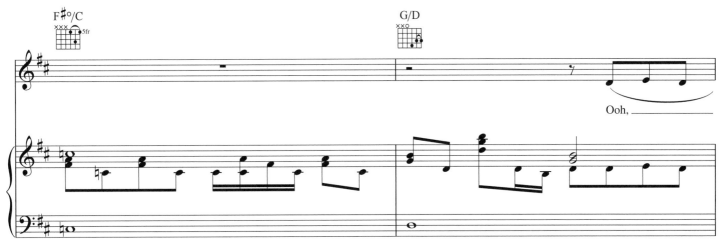

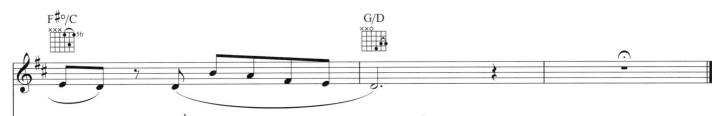

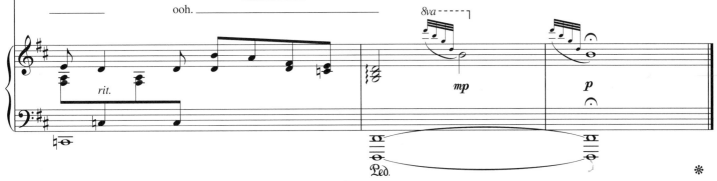

I Try

Lyrics by Macy Gray
Music by Macy Gray, Jeremy Ruzumna,
Jinsoo Lim and David Wilder

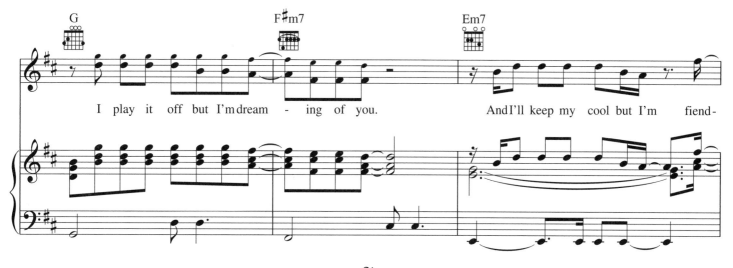

I play it off but I'm dream - ing of you. And I'll keep my cool but I'm fiend-

-in'. I try to say good - bye and I choke. I try to walk a -

way and I stum - ble. Though I try to hide it, it's clear ___ my world

crum-bles when you are not ___ near. Good - bye and I choke. I try to walk a -

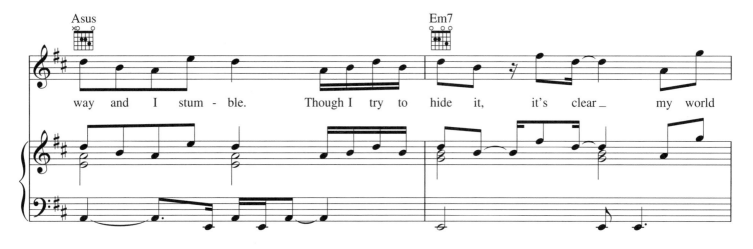

way and I stum-ble. Though I try to hide it, it's clear _ my world

crum-bles when you are not _ near. I may ap-pear to be free but _ I'm just _ a

pris-on-er of your love. And I may seem al-right and smile _____ when you

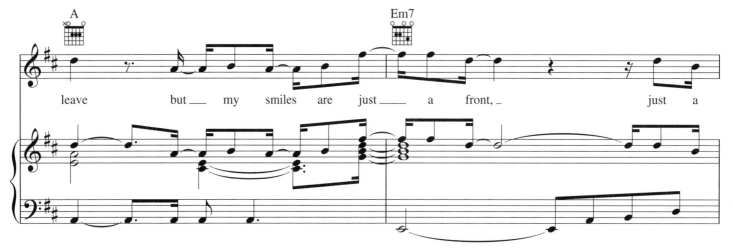

leave but _ my smiles are just _ a front, _ just a

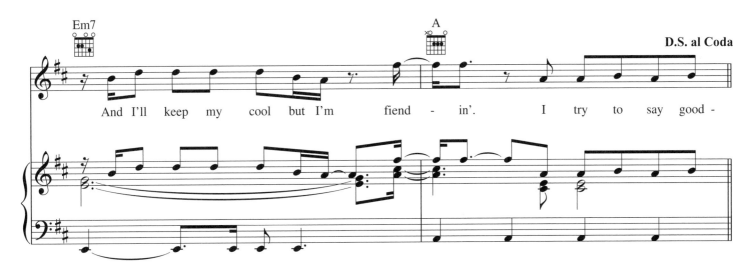

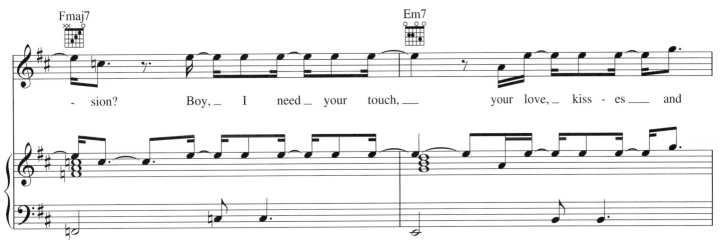

such. With all my might I try but this I can't de - ny, de - ny.

I play it off but I'm dream - ing of you.

And I'll keep my cool but I'm fiend - in'. I try to say good -

bye and I choke. Try to walk a - way and I stum - ble. Though I try to

hide it, it's clear, __ my world crum-bles when you are not __ near. Good-

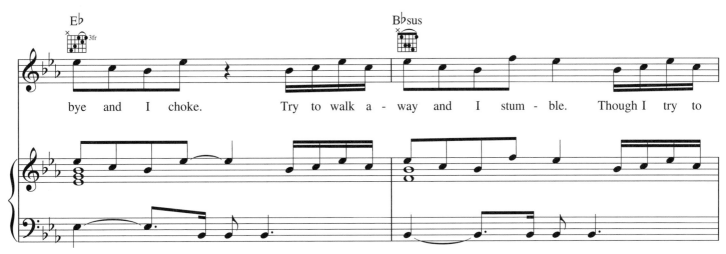

bye and I choke. Try to walk a - way and I stum - ble. Though I try to

hide it, it's clear, __ my world crum-bles when you are not __ near.

Repeat and Fade

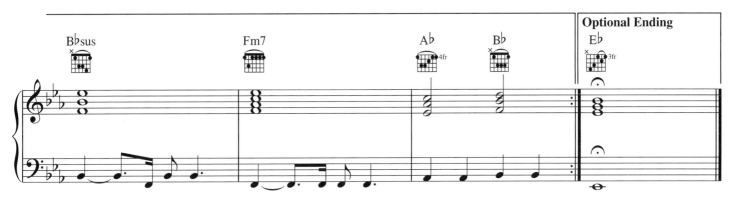

Optional Ending

I Want It That Way

Words and Music by
Martin Sandberg and Andreas Carlsson

that ___ way. ___ } Tell me why. ___ Ain't noth-in' but a heart - ache. ___ Tell me
that ___ way. ___ }

why. ___ Ain't noth-in' but a mis - take. ___ Tell me why. ___ I nev-er wan-na

D.S. al Coda
(take 2nd ending)

hear you say _____ I want __ it that __ way. __ Am I __   that way. __

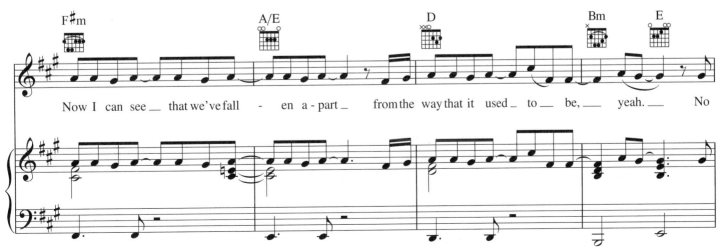

Now I can see ___ that we've fall - en a-part ___ from the way that it used to __ be, ___ yeah. ___ No

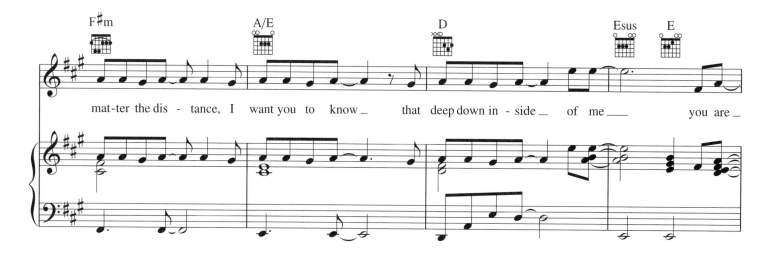

mat-ter the dis - tance, I want you to know ___ that deep down in - side ___ of me ___ you are ___

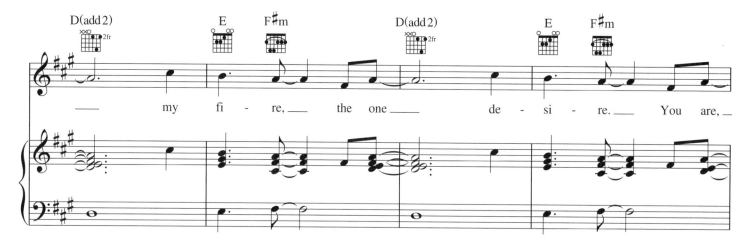

___ my fi - re, ___ the one ___ de - si - re. ___ You are,

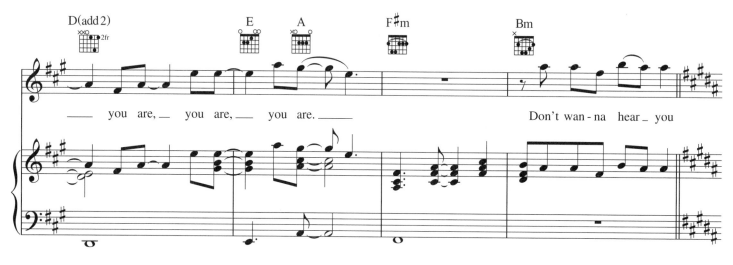

___ you are, ___ you are, ___ you are. ___ Don't wan - na hear ___ you

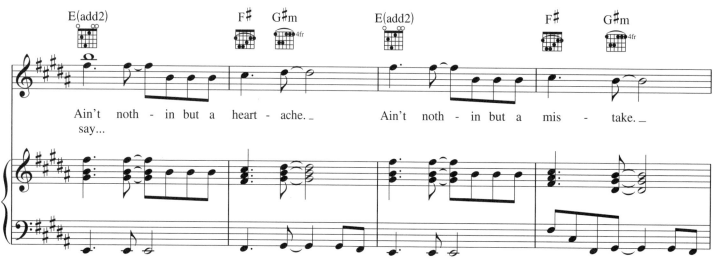

Ain't noth - in but a heart - ache. ___ Ain't noth - in but a mis - take. ___
say...

I nev-er wan-na hear you say _____ I want it that __ way. __ Tell me

why. __ Ain't noth-in' but a heart - ache. __ Tell me why. __ Ain't noth-in' but a

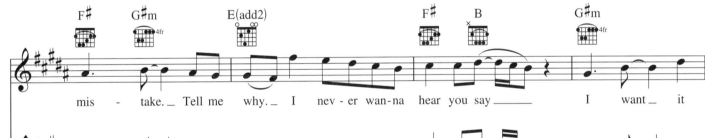

mis - take. Tell me why. __ I nev-er wan-na hear you say _____ I want __ it

that __ way. Tell me that __ way. 'Cause I want __ it that __ way.

rit.

I'm Yours

Words and Music by Jason Mraz

Moderately slow, with a Reggae feel

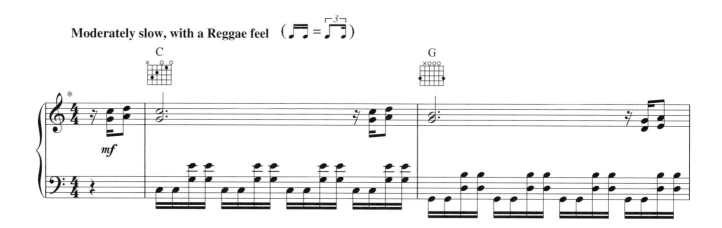

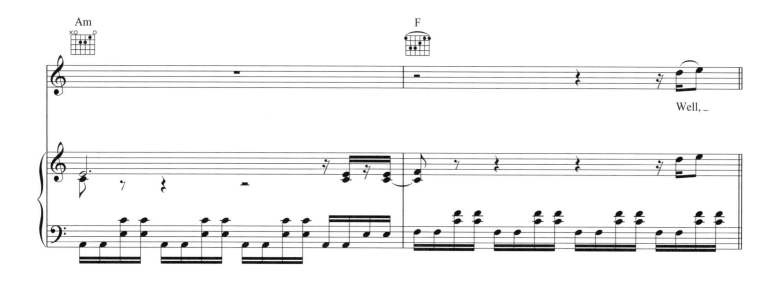

Well, _

you done   done _ me in; you bet I   felt __ it.   I   tried to be chill, _ but you're so hot that I   melt - ed.   I

*Recorded a half step lower.

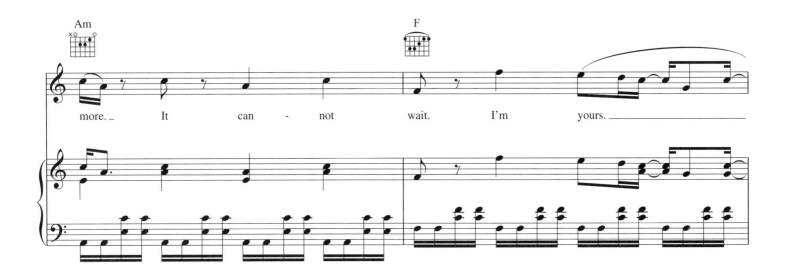

more. _ It can - not wait. I'm yours. ____

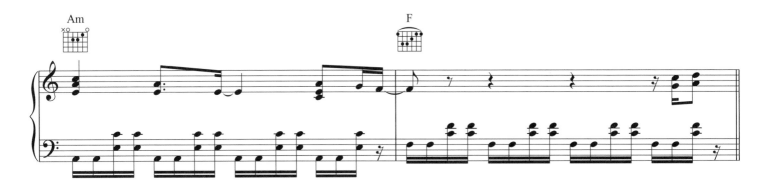

Well, o - pen up your mind and see __ like me. __ O - pen up your plans and, damn, _ you're free.

128

Look in - to your heart __ and you'll __ find love, love, _____ love, love.

Lis - ten to the mu - sic of the mo - ment; peo - ple dance __ and ___ sing. We're just one big fam - i - ly, __

__ and it's our god - for - sak - en right to be loved, __ loved, ___ loved, loved,

loved. _____ So ___ I ___ won't hes - i - tate no more, __ no _____

more. __ It can - not wait. I'm sure. ____ There's no

need __ to com - pli - cate. Our __ time __ is ____

short. __ This is our fate. I'm yours. ____ *Scat sing...*

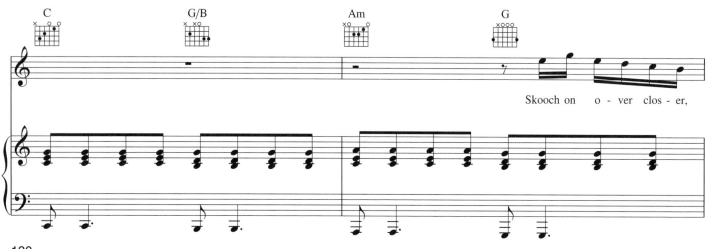

Skooch on o - ver clos - er,

dear,   and I will nib - ble your ear. _____   *Scat sing...*

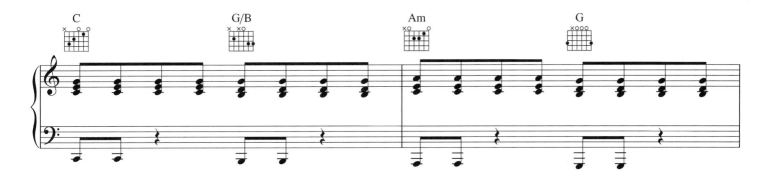

I've been spend - ing

way too long _ check-ing my tongue in the mir - ror   and bend-ing o - ver back-wards just to try to see it clear-er. But

my breath fogged _ up the glass, _ and so I drew a new face _ and I laughed. _____ I

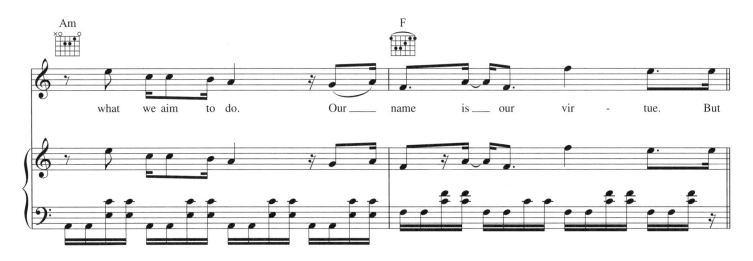

guess what I'll be say-ing is there ain't no bet-ter rea-son to rid your-self of van-i-ties and just go with the sea-sons. It's

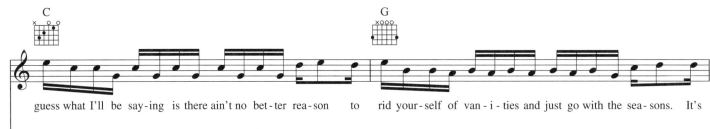

what we aim to do. Our _____ name is ___ our vir - tue. But

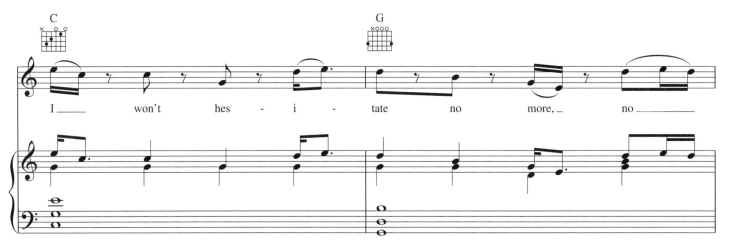

I _____ won't hes - i - tate no more, _ no

more. ___ It can - not wait. I'm yours. _____

O - pen up your mind ___ and see like me. ___ O - pen up your plans ___ and, damn, __ you're __ free. __

(I won't hes - i - tate no more, no

___ Look in - to your heart ___ and you'll __ find __ that the sky __ is yours. _____ So

more. It can - not wait. I'm sure. _____ No

please don't, please don't, please don't... There's no need _ to com - pli - cate 'cause our time _

need to com - pli - cate. Our time is

_ is short. _ This is, this is, this is our fate. I'm yours. _____ *Scat sing...*

short. _ This is our fate. I'm yours.) _____

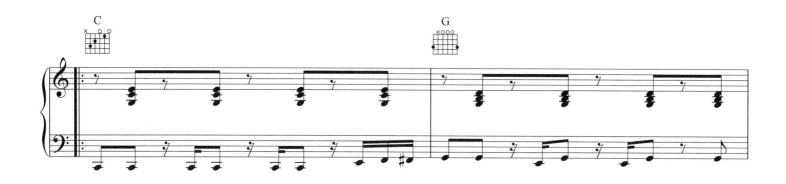

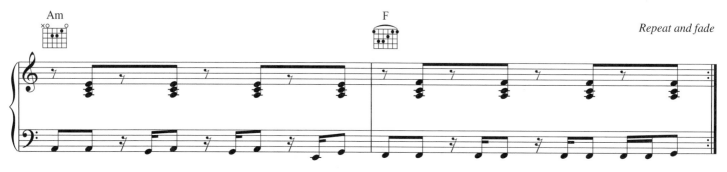

Repeat and fade

If I Ain't Got You

Words and Music by Alicia Keys

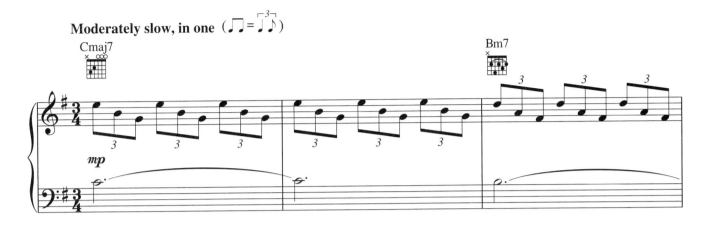

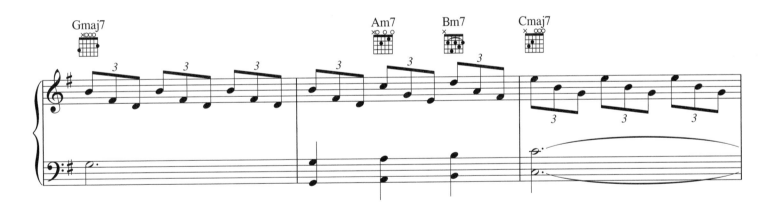

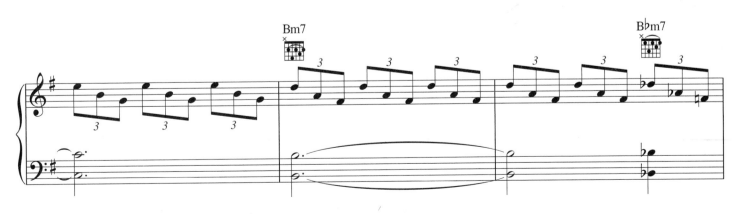

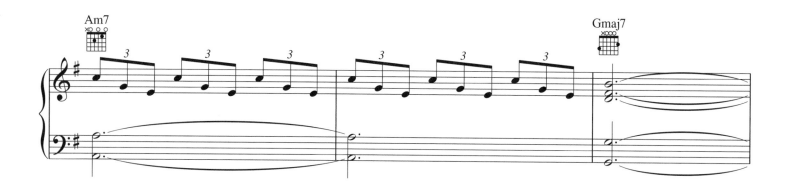

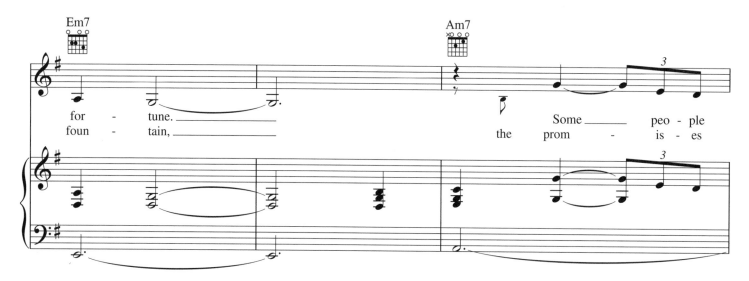

Some _____ peo - ple live for the
Some _____ peo - ple search for a

for - tune. _____
foun - tain, _____

Some _____ peo - ple
the prom - is - es

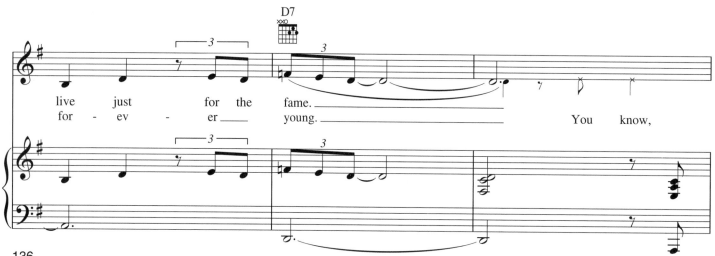

live just for the fame. _____
for - ev - er _____ young. _____

You know,

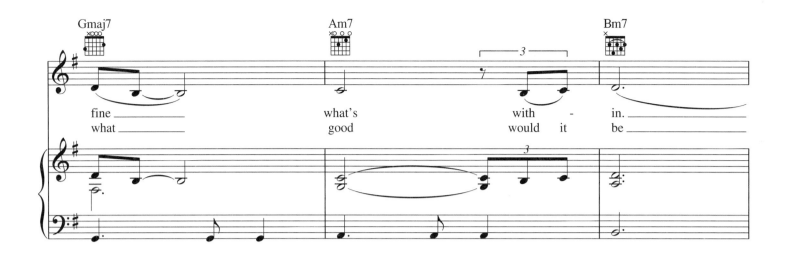

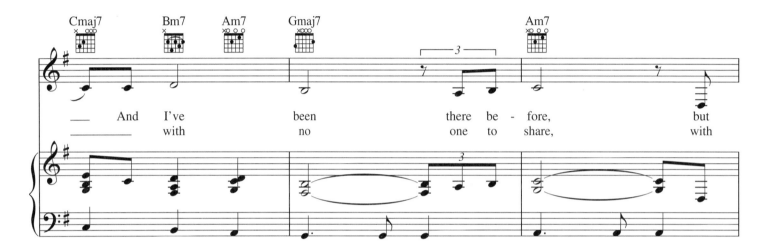

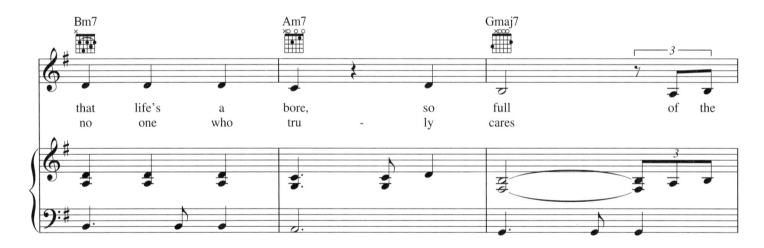

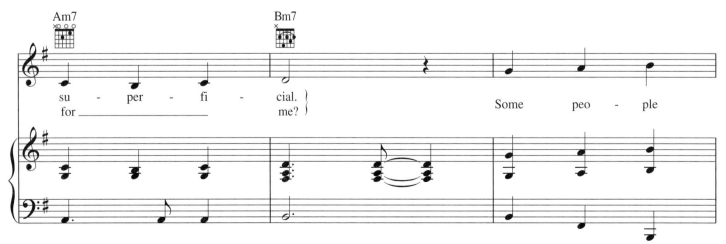

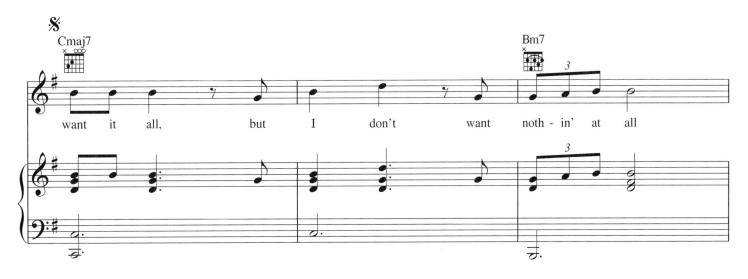

want it all, but I don't want noth-in' at all

if it ain't you, ___ ba - by, if I ain't got

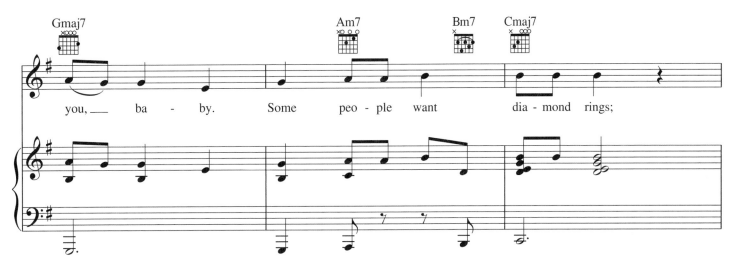

you, ___ ba - by. Some peo - ple want dia - mond rings;

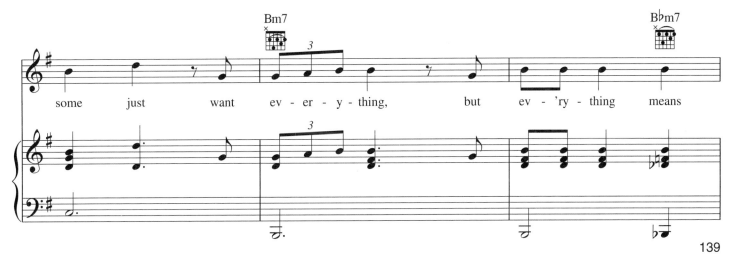

some just want ev - er - y - thing, but ev - 'ry - thing means

139

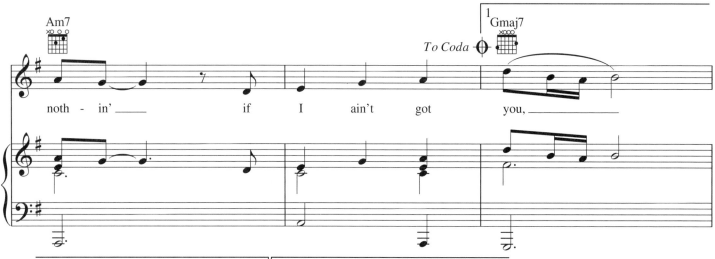

noth - in' _____ if I ain't got you, _____

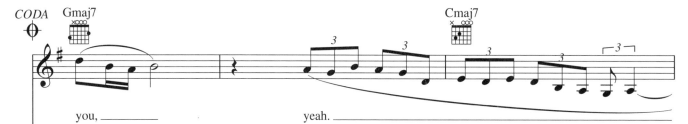

yeah. _____ you, _____ you, _____ you. _____ Some peo - ple

you, _____ yeah.

If I ain't got you with me,

ba - by. ___ Said, noth-in' in this

whole wide world don't mean a thing ___ if I ain't got you with me,

ba - by. ___

Freely

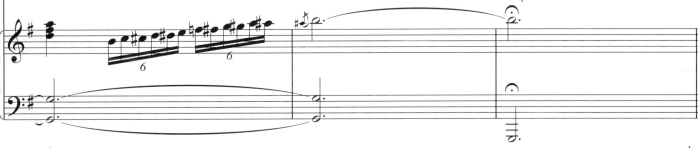

If I Were A Boy

Words and Music by
Toby Gad and Brittany Carlson

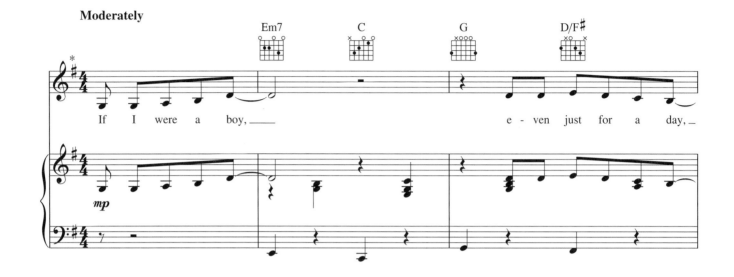

Moderately

If I were a boy, _____ e - ven just for a day, _____

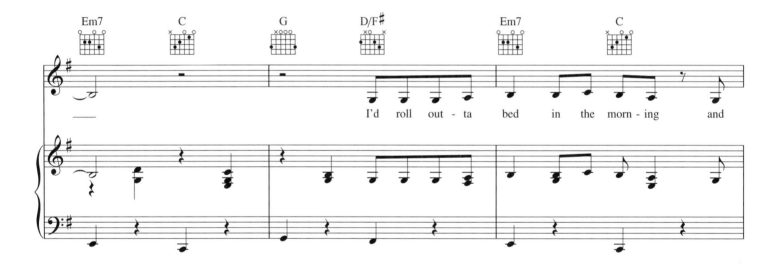

_____ I'd roll out-ta bed in the morn-ing and

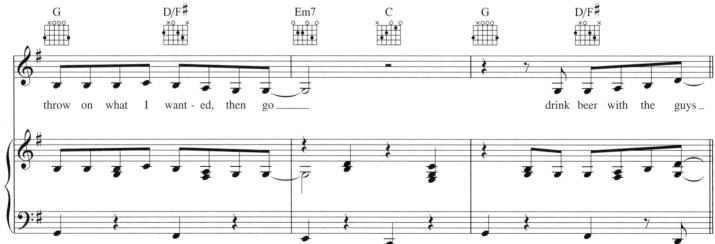

throw on what I want-ed, then go _____ drink beer with the guys _____

*Recorded a half step lower.

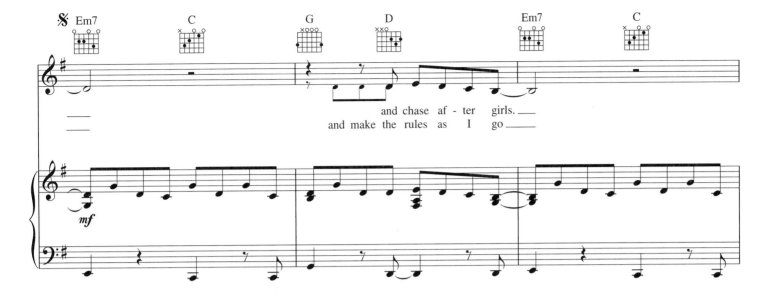

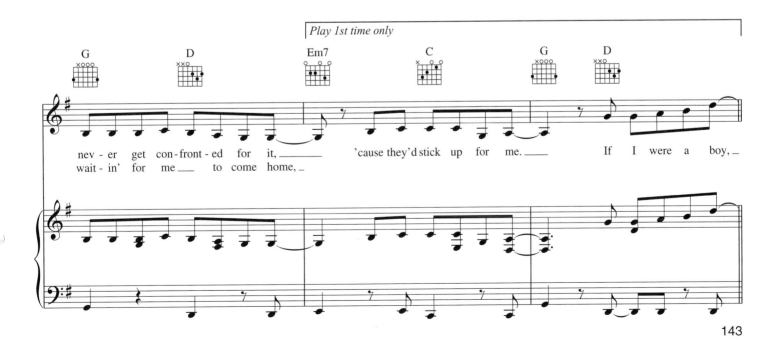

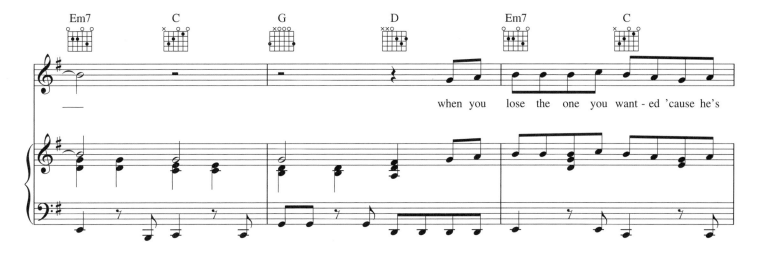

when you lose the one you want-ed 'cause he's

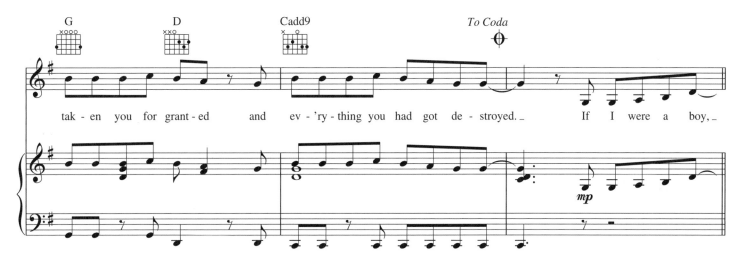

To Coda

tak-en you for grant-ed and ev-'ry-thing you had got de-stroyed. _ If I were a boy, _

I would turn off my phone, ___

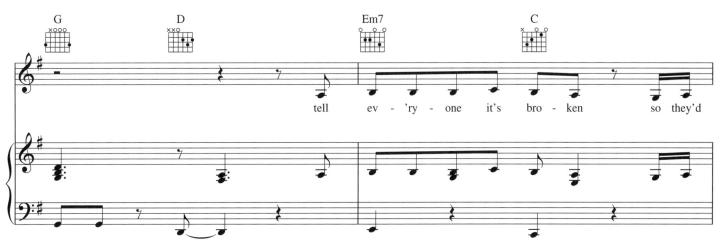

tell ev-'ry-one it's bro-ken so they'd

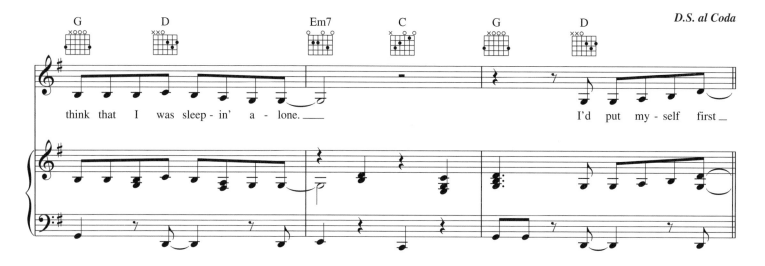

think that I was sleep - in' a - lone. ____ I'd put my - self first ____

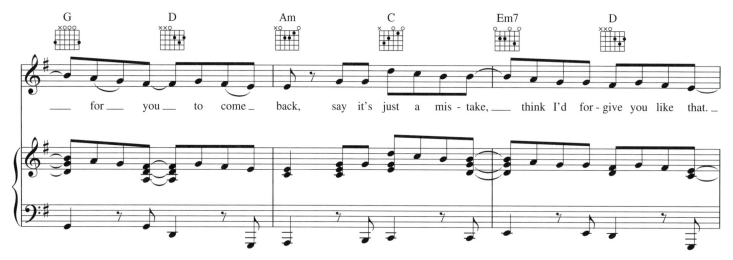

____ It's a lit - tle too late ____

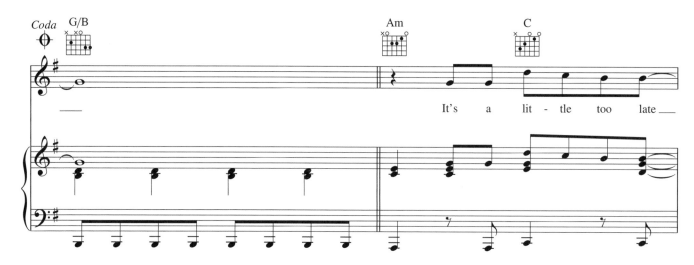

____ for ____ you ____ to come ____ back, say it's just a mis - take, ____ think I'd for - give you like that. ____

____ If you thought I would wait _____ for you, you thought

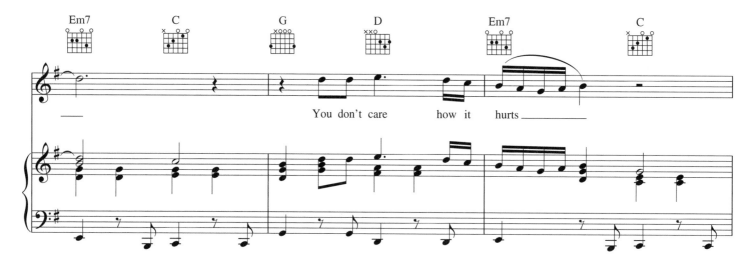

You don't care how it hurts ____

un - til you lose the one you want - ed 'cause you've

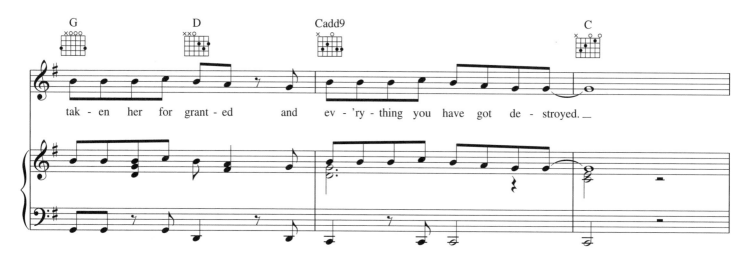

tak - en her for grant - ed and ev - 'ry - thing you have got de - stroyed. __

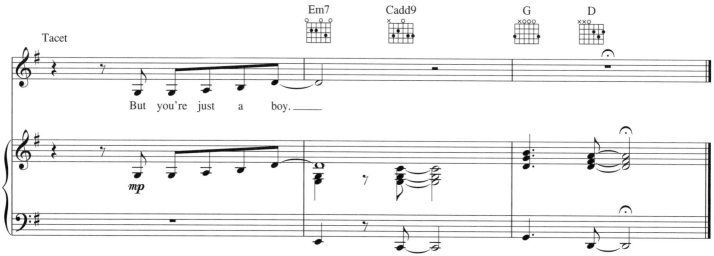

Tacet

But you're just a boy. ____

If You're Gone

Written by Rob Thomas

Moderately

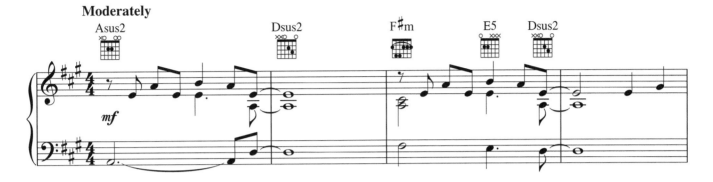

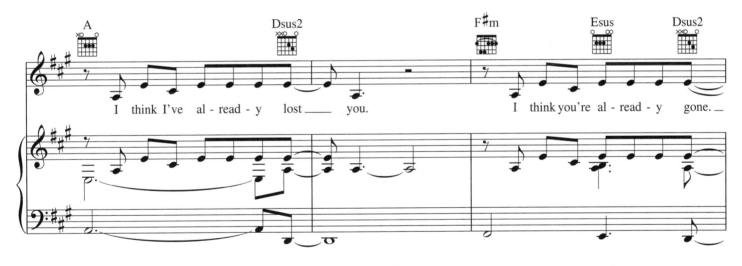

I think I've al-read-y lost ___ you. I think you're al-read-y gone. ___

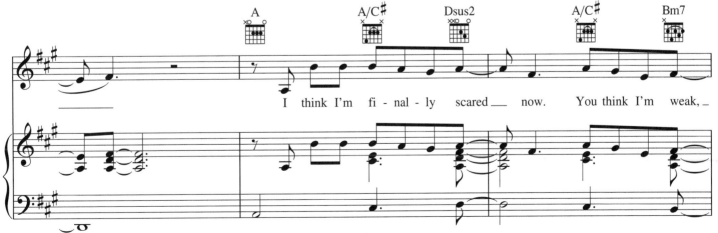

I think I'm fi-nal-ly scared ___ now. You think I'm weak, ___

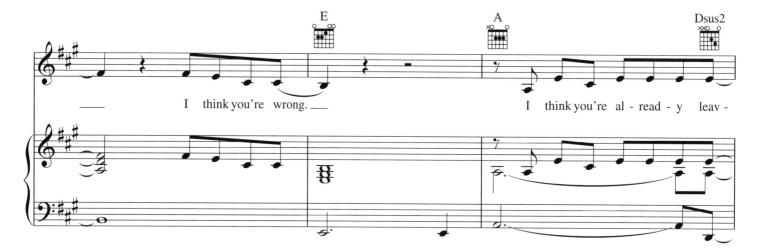

I think you're wrong. ___ I think you're al - read - y leav -

- ing, feels like your hand is on ___ the door. ___

I thought this place was an em - pire. Now I'm re - laxed. ___ I can't be sure. ___

And I think you're so mean. ___ I think we should try. ___

I think I could need ___ this in my life ___ and I think I'm scared. ___

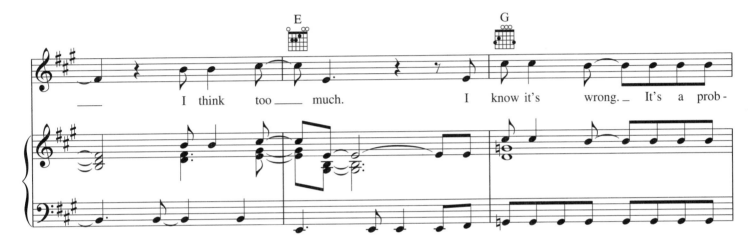

I think too ___ much. I know it's wrong. ___ It's a prob-

lem I'm deal-ing. If you're gone, _____ may-be it's time ___ to come ___ home. ___

There's an aw - ful lot of breath - ing room, ___

but I ___ can hard-ly move. ___ If you're gone, ___

___ ba - by, you need ___ to come ___ home, ___ come ___

___ home. There's a lit - tle ___ bit of ___ some-thing me ___ in ev - 'ry-thing in ___

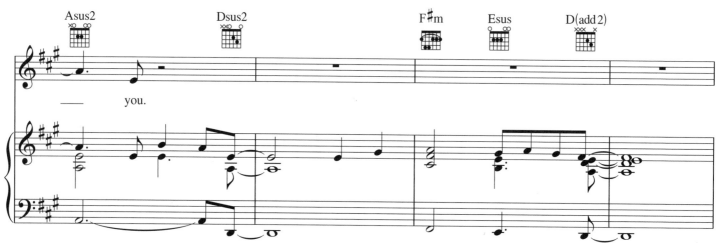

___ you.

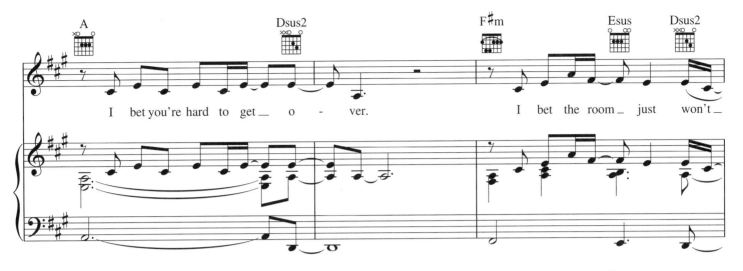

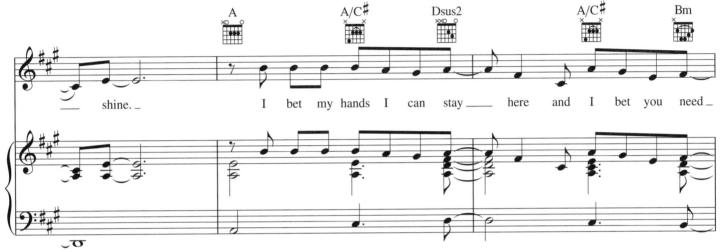

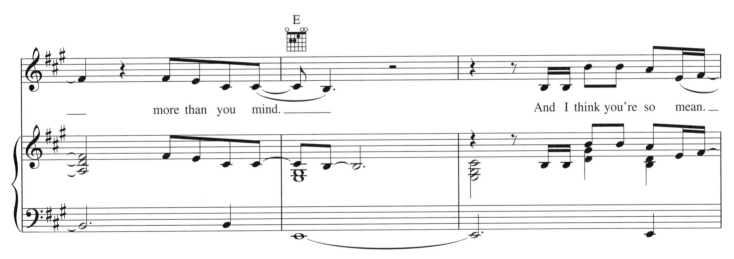

I think I'm just scared that I know too much.

D.S. al Coda

can't re-late and that's a prob-lem I'm feel-ing. If you're gone,

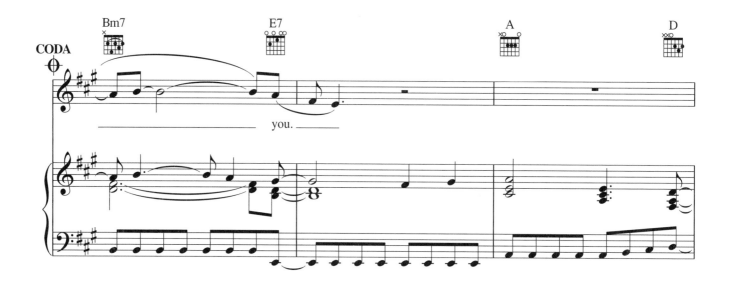

CODA

you.

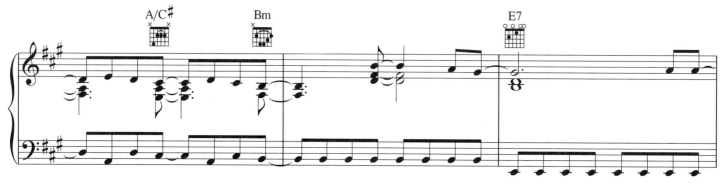

lem I'm deal-ing. If you're gone, _____ then may-be it's time __ to come home. __

__ Well, there's an aw-ful lot of breath-ing room, __

__ but I __ can hard-ly move. __ You know, __ if you're gone, __

hell, ___ ba-by, you need ___ to come ___ home, __

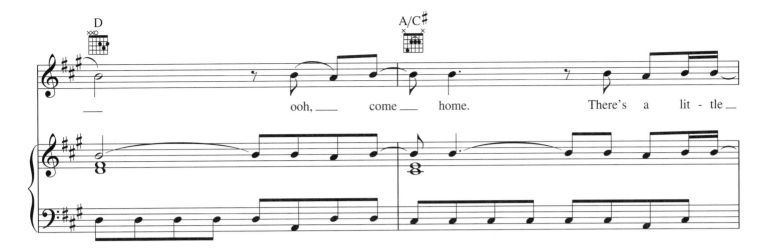

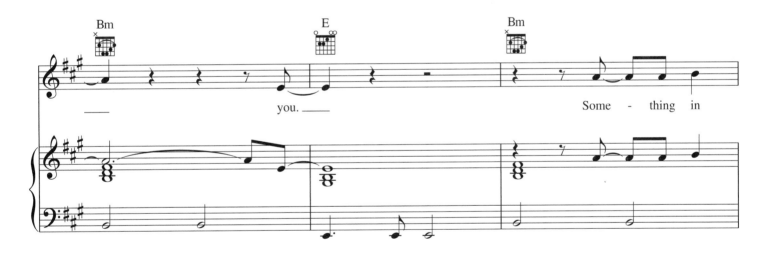

In My Daughter's Eyes

Words and Music by James Slater

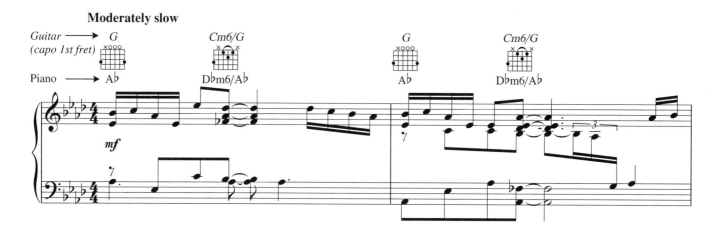

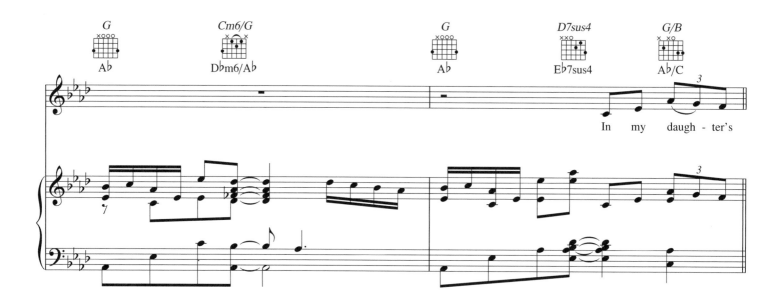

strong and wise, _ and I know ___ no fear. But the truth _ is
turns to light _ and the world ___ is at peace. This mir - a - cle ___ God

plain to see, ___ she was sent ___ to res - cue me. ___ I see who __ I __
gave to me ___ gives me strength _ when I am weak. ___ I find rea - son _

___ wan - na be ___ in my daugh - ter's ___ eyes.
___ to be - lieve ___ in my daugh - ter's _

In my daugh - ter's ___ eyes. And when she wraps her

hand a - round my fin - ger al - ways puts a smile __ in __ my heart. __ Ev -'ry - thing be -

comes a lit - tle clear - er. I re - al - ize what life __ is all a - bout. It's hang - ing on when your

heart has had __ e - nough. It's giv - ing more when you feel __ like giv - ing up. __ I've

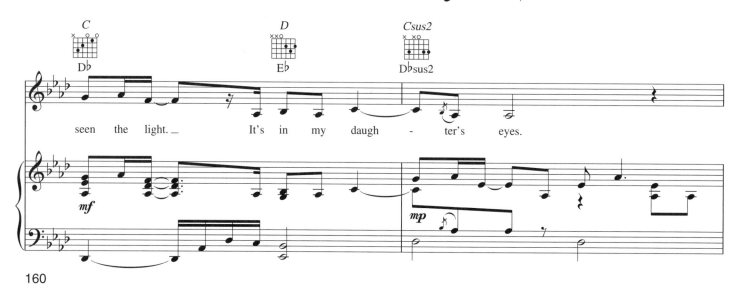

seen the light. __ It's in my daugh - ter's eyes.

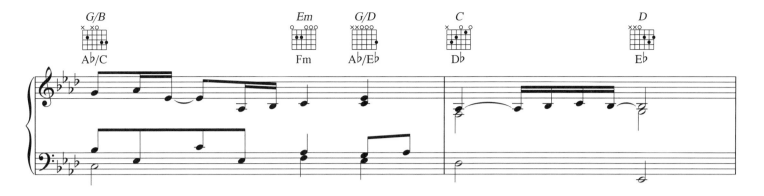

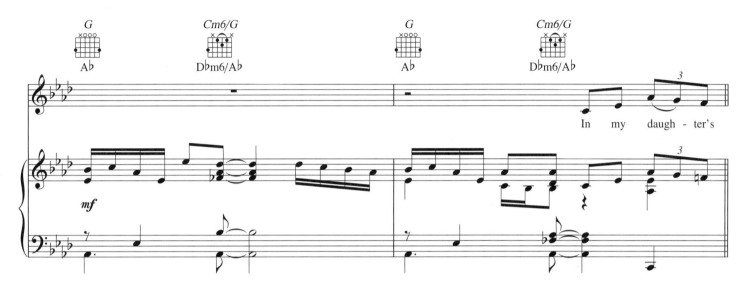

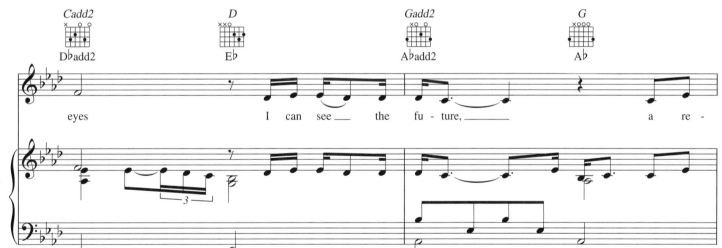

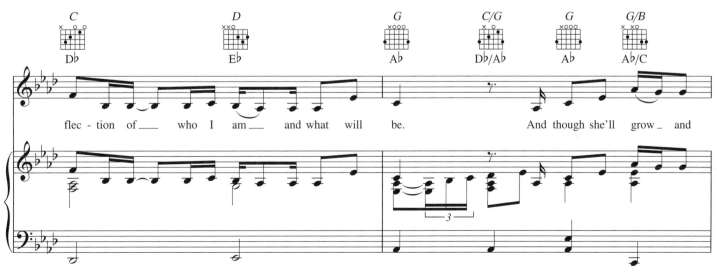

some-day leave, __ may - be raise __ a fam - i - ly, when I'm gone __ I

hope you'll see how hap - py she made __ me, for I'll be

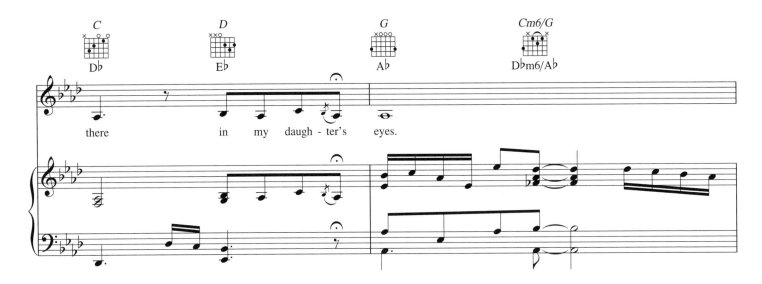

there in my daugh - ter's eyes.

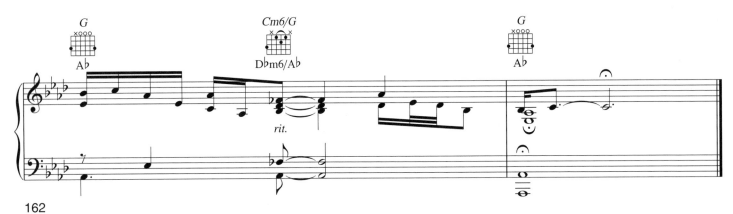

Landslide

Words and Music by Stevie Nicks

Moderately flowing

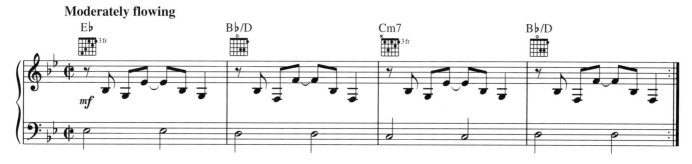

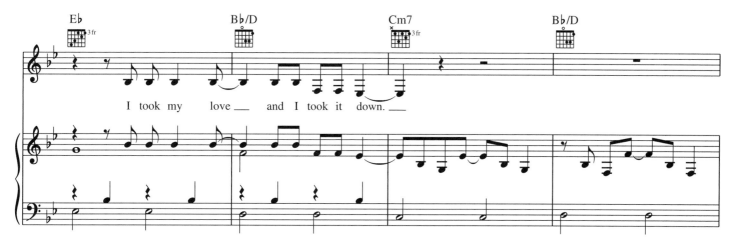

I took my love __ and I took it down. __

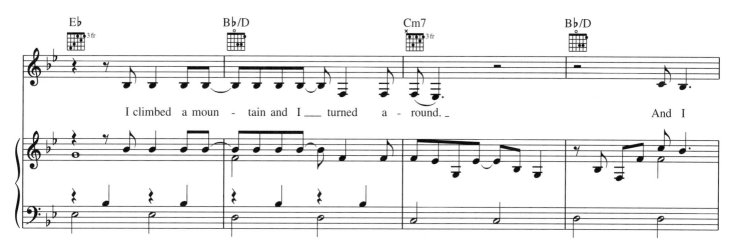

I climbed a moun - tain and I __ turned a - round. __ And I

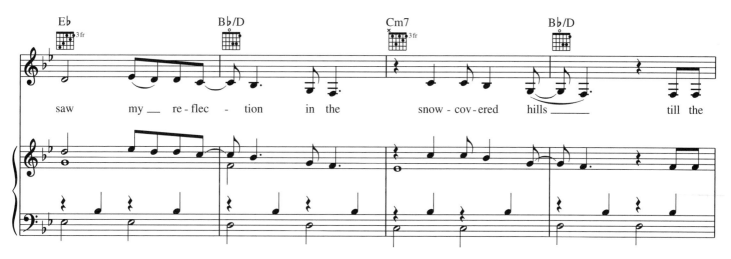

saw my __ re - flec - tion in the snow - cov - ered hills __ till the

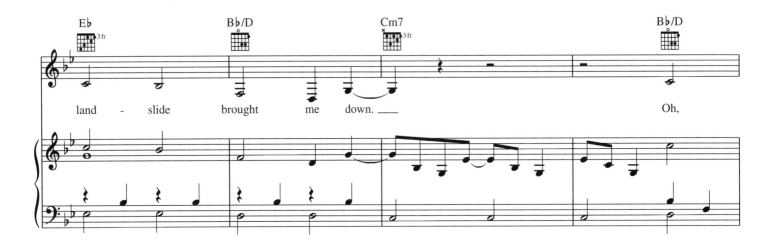

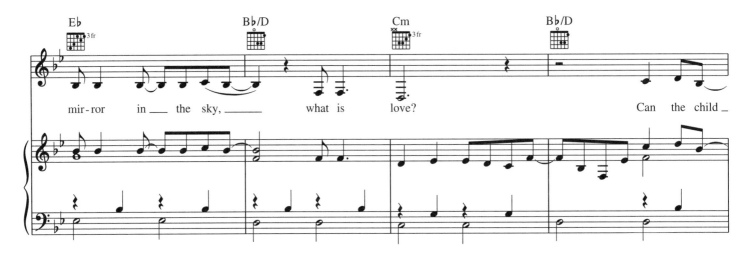

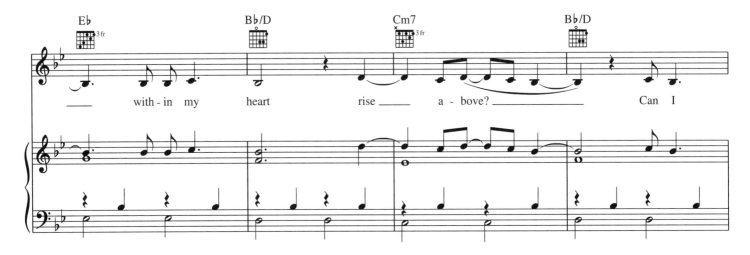

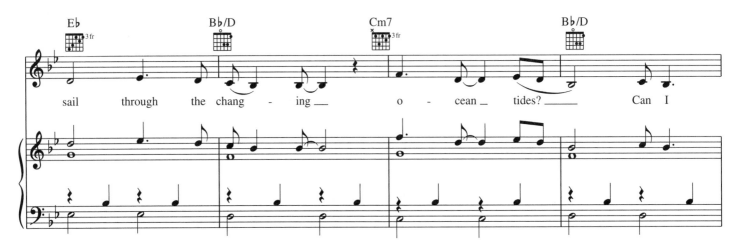

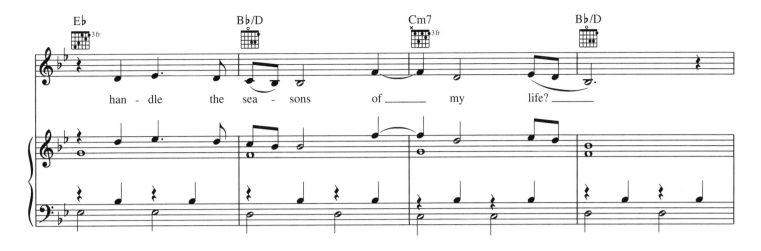

han - dle the sea - sons of _____ my life? _____

Mm mm, I don't know. Mm mm, _____

_____ mm mm. Well, I've _____

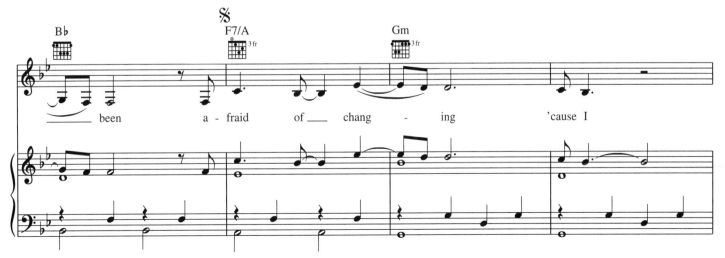

_____ been a - fraid of _____ chang - ing 'cause I

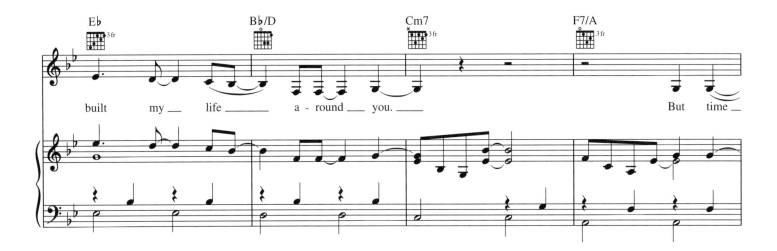

built my ___ life ___ a - round ___ you. ___   But time ___

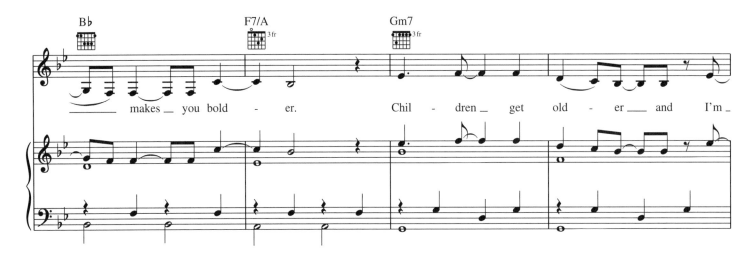

___ makes ___ you bold - er. Chil - dren ___ get old - er ___ and I'm ___

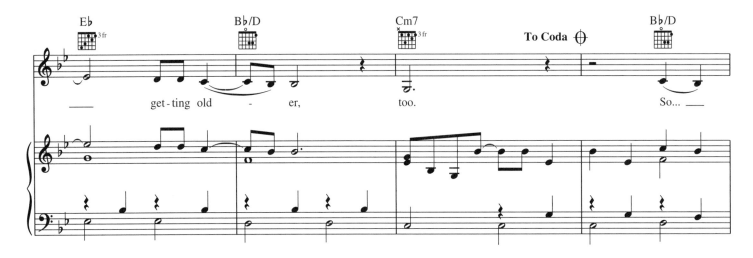

___ get - ting old - er, too. So... ___

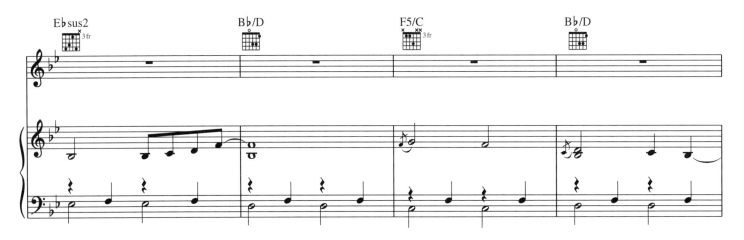

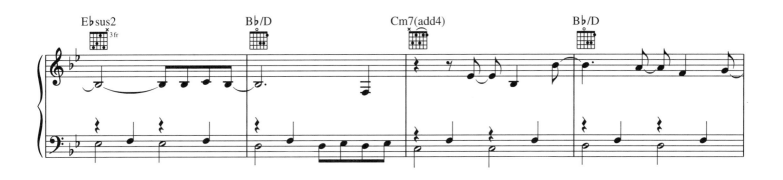

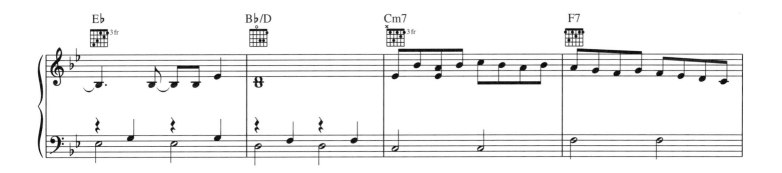

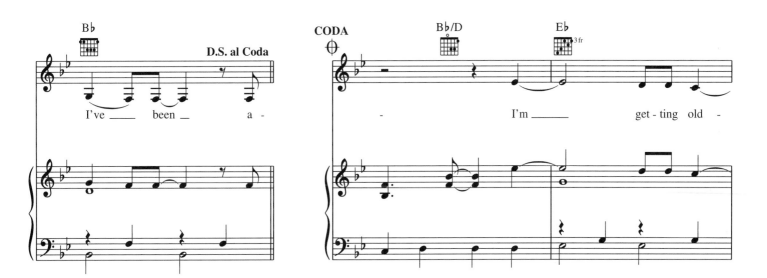

167

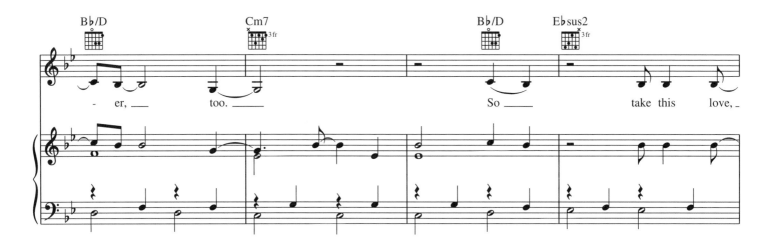

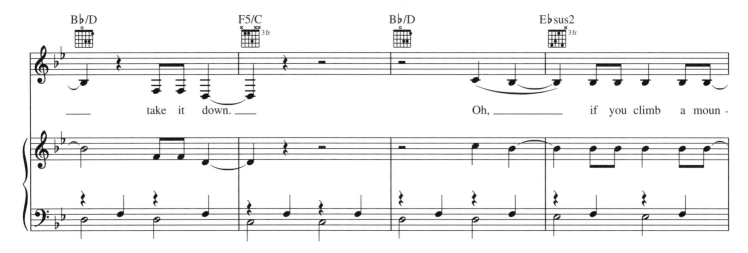

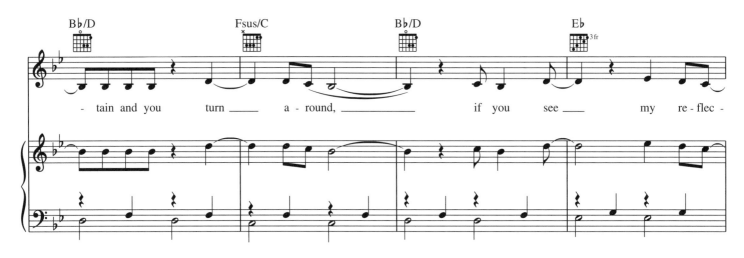

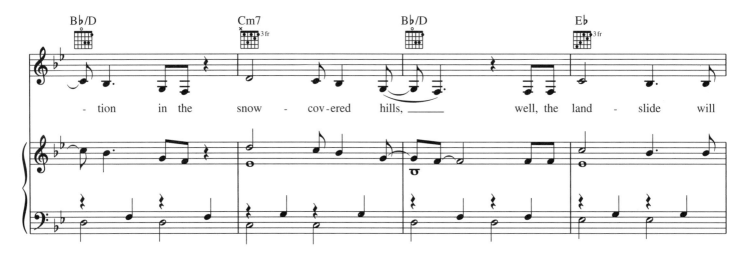

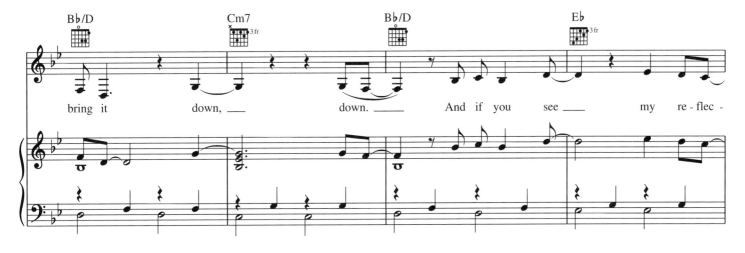

bring it down, ___ down. ___ And if you see ___ my re - flec -

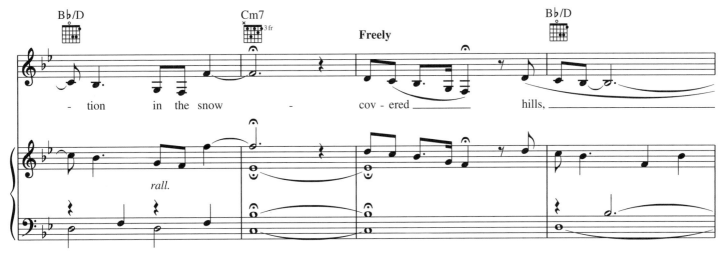

Freely

- tion in the snow - cov - ered ___ hills, ___

Tempo 1

___ well, may - be ___ the land - slide 'll bring it down. ___ Well, ___

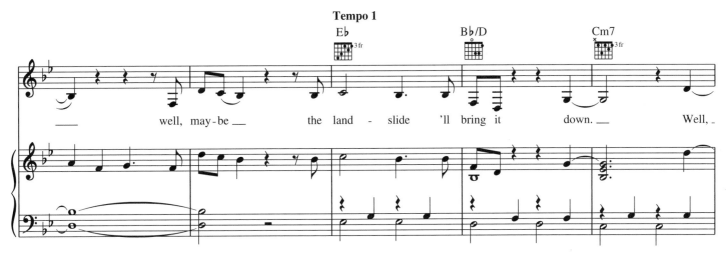

___ well, ___ the land - slide 'll bring it down. ___

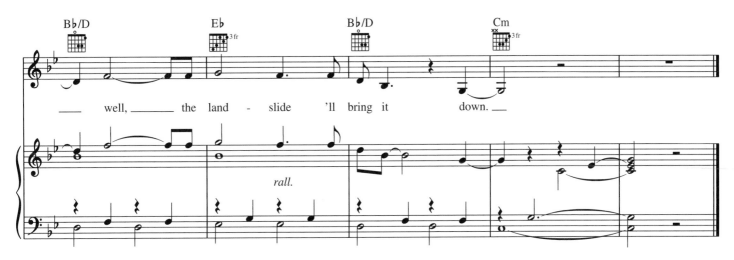

It's My Life

Words and Music by Jon Bon Jovi,
Martin Sandberg and Richie Sambora

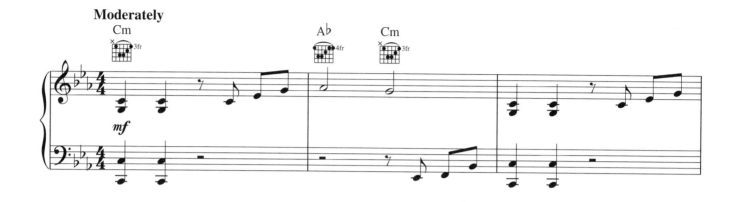

This ain't a song ___ for the bro - ken - heart - ed.
this is for the ones who stood their ground.

No si - lent prayer for
For Tom - my and Gi - na who

I just wan - na live ___ while I'm ___ a - live. ___

It's my life. My heart is like an o - pen high - way.

Like Frank - ie said, "I did ___ it my way." ___ I just wan - na

live while I'm ___ a - live. ___ It's my

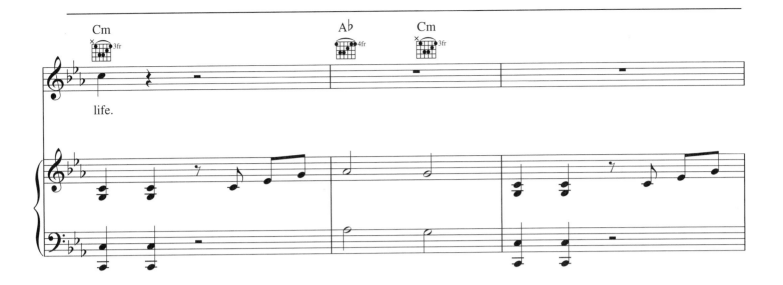

life.

Yeah, It's my life. _____

Guitar solo

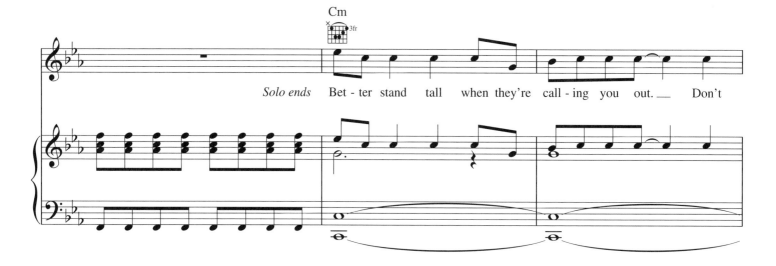

Solo ends Bet-ter stand tall when they're call-ing you out.___ Don't

bend, don't break, ba-by, don't back down. It's my___

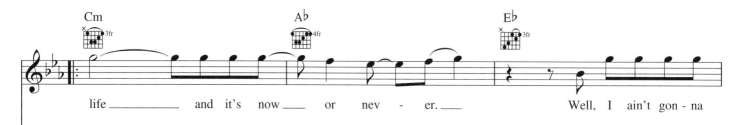

life_____ and it's now___ or nev - er.___ Well, I ain't gon-na

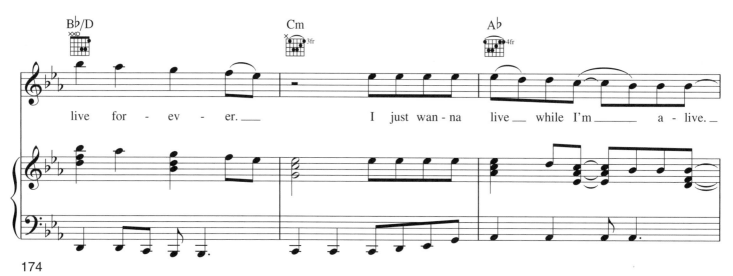

live for - ev - er.___ I just wan-na live___ while I'm_____ a - live.___

It's my life. My heart is like an o-pen high-way. Like Frank-ie said, "I did it my way." I just wan-na live while I'm a-live.

It's my It's my life.

Lost Without U

Words and Music by
Robin Thicke and Sean Hurley

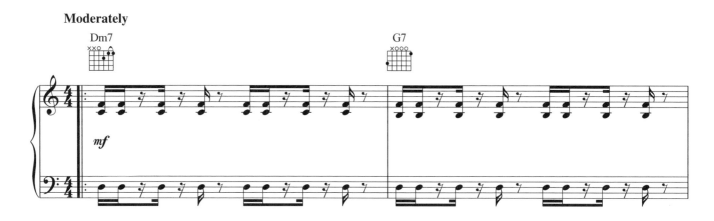

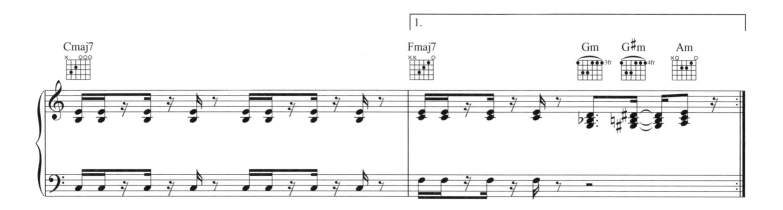

Lost with-out u. Can't help___ my-

self. How does __ it feel 2 know that I

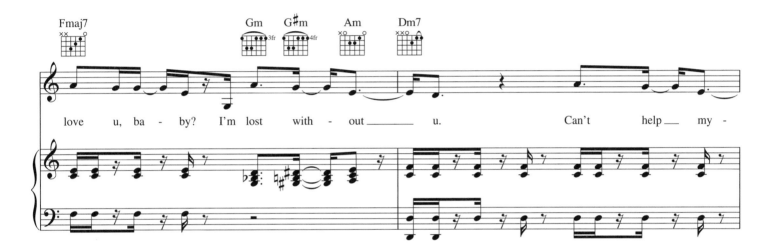

love u, ba - by? I'm lost with - out _____ u. Can't help __ my -

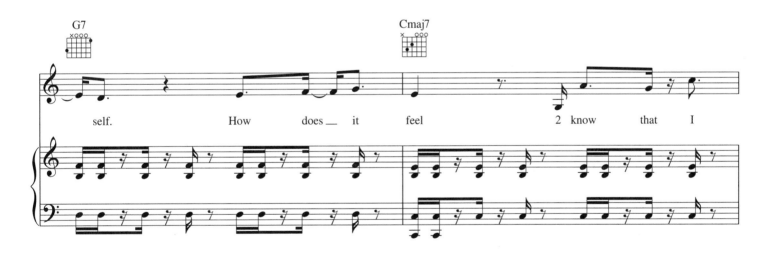

self. How does __ it feel 2 know that I

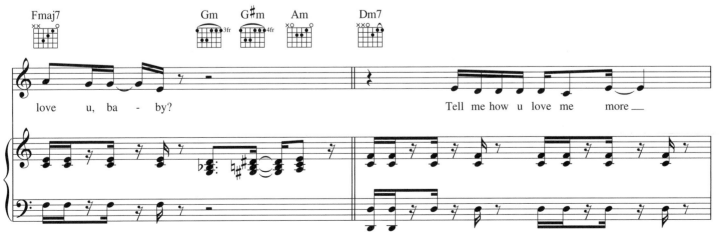

love u, ba - by? Tell me how u love me more __

and how u think I'm sex - y, babe, ___ that u don't want no - bod - y else. U don't want

this guy, u don't want that guy. U wan - na touch your - self ___ when u see ___ me.

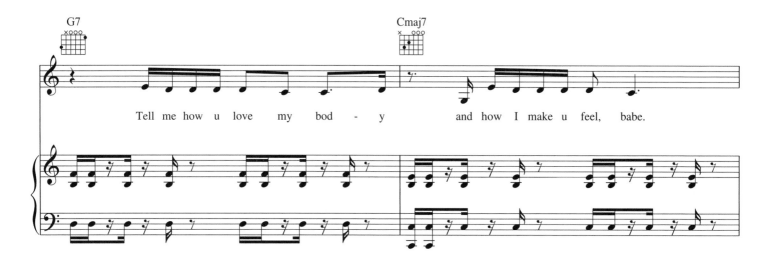

Tell me how u love my bod - y and how I make u feel, babe.

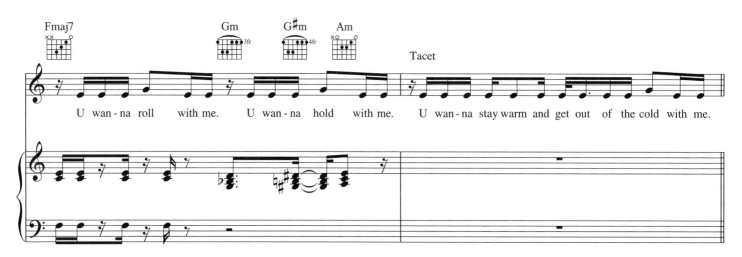

U wan - na roll with me. U wan - na hold with me. U wan - na stay warm and get out of the cold with me.

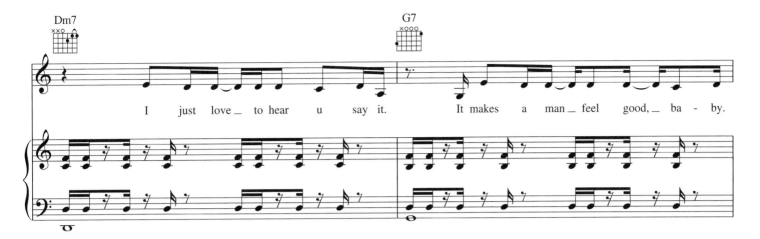

I just love_ to hear u say it. It makes a man_ feel good,_ ba - by.

Tell me u de - pend on me. I need 2 hear it. I'm lost with - out

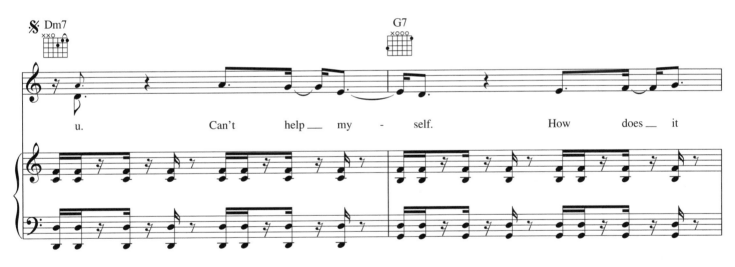

u. Can't help___ my - self. How does__ it

feel 2 know that I love u, ba - by? I'm lost with - out____

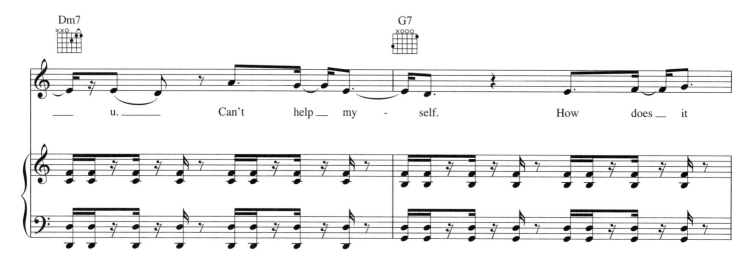

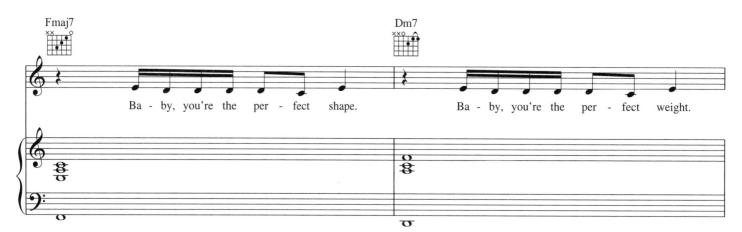

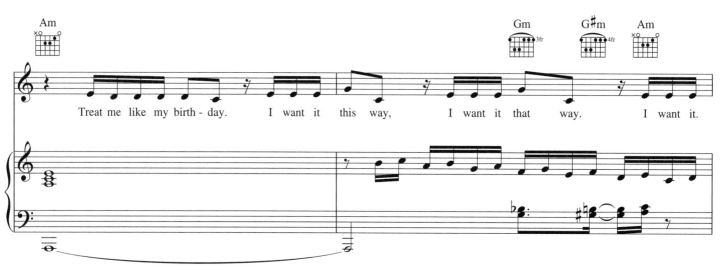

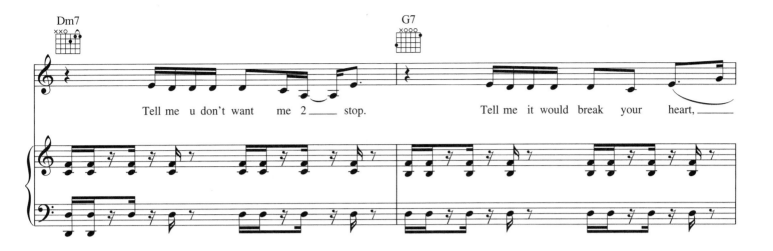

Tell me u don't want me 2___ stop. Tell me it would break your heart,___

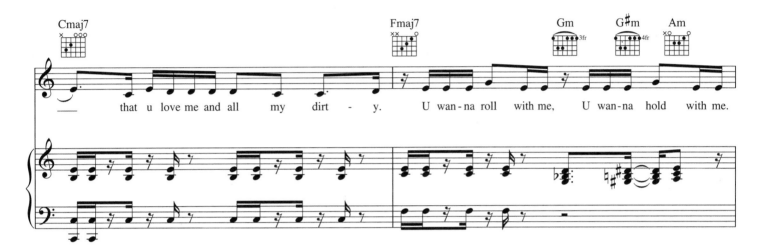

___ that u love me and all my dirt - y. U wan-na roll with me, U wan-na hold with me.

U wan-na make fires and get Nor-we-gian wood with me. I just love___ 2 hear___ u say it.

D.S. al Coda

Tacet

It makes a man___ feel good,___ ba - by. I'm lost with - out___

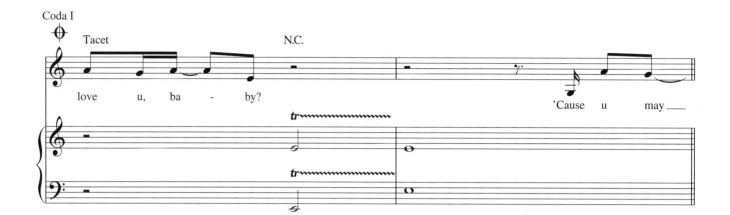

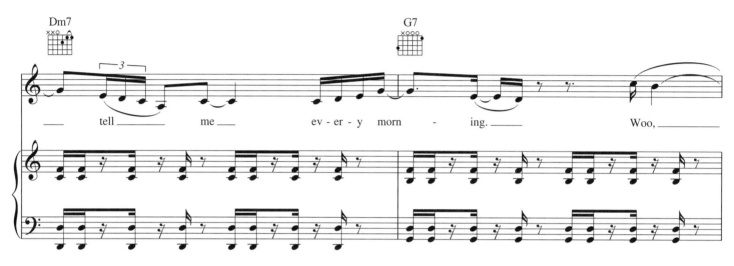

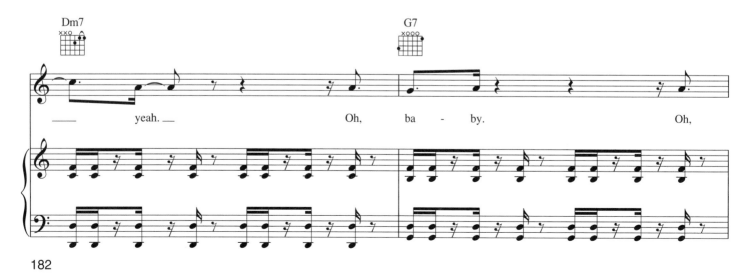

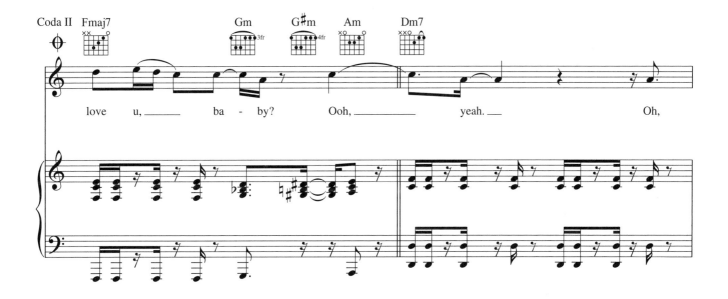

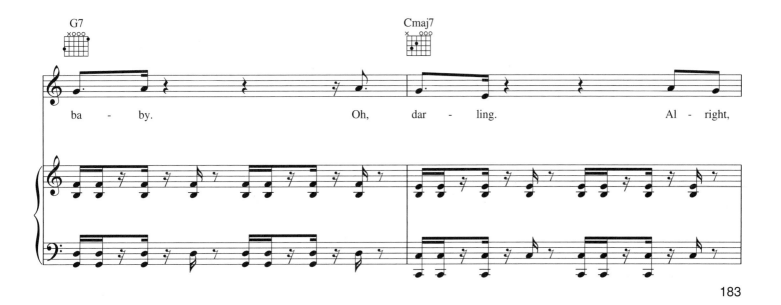

183

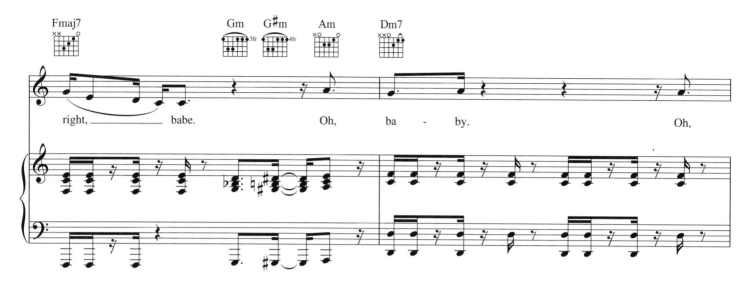

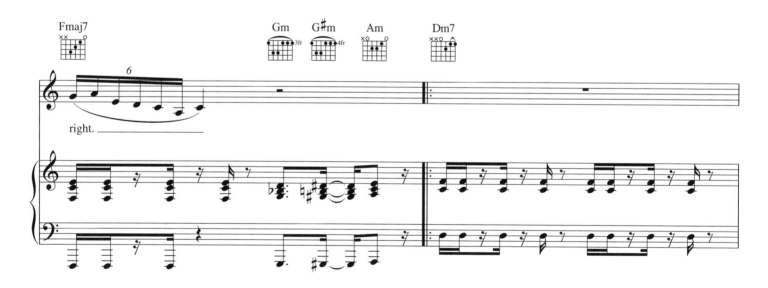

Repeat and fade

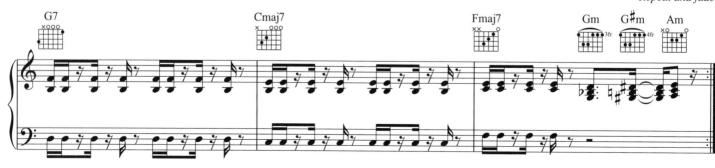

184

The Middle

Words and Music by
James Adkins, Thomas D. Linton,
Richard Burch and Zachary Lind

Moderately fast

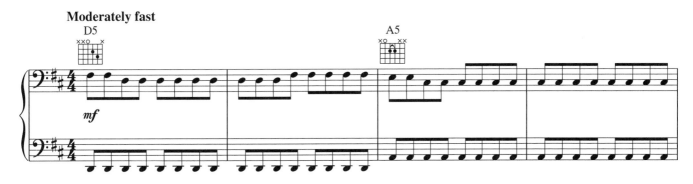

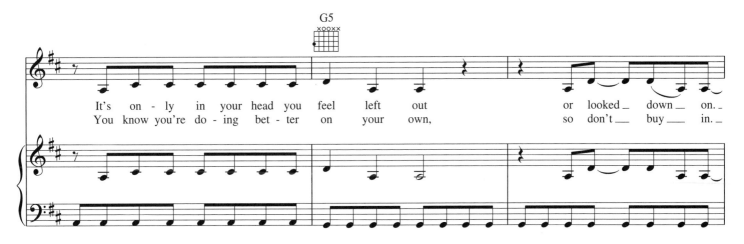

1.3. Hey,   don't write your-self   off   yet.
2. Hey,   you know they're all the same.

It's on-ly in your head you feel left out   or looked down on.
You know you're do-ing bet-ter on your own,   so don't buy in.

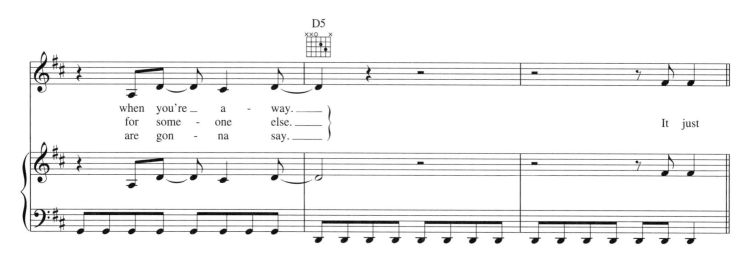

186

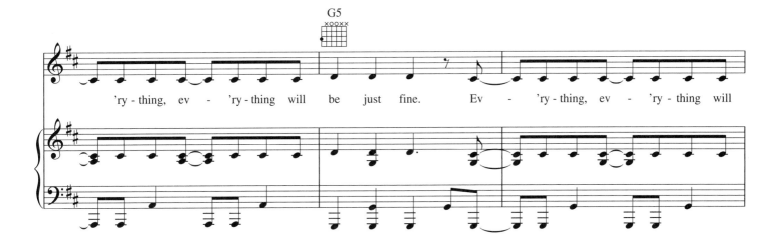

'ry - thing, ev - 'ry - thing will be just fine. Ev - 'ry - thing, ev - 'ry - thing will

To Coda 1.

be all right, all right. right. It just

2.

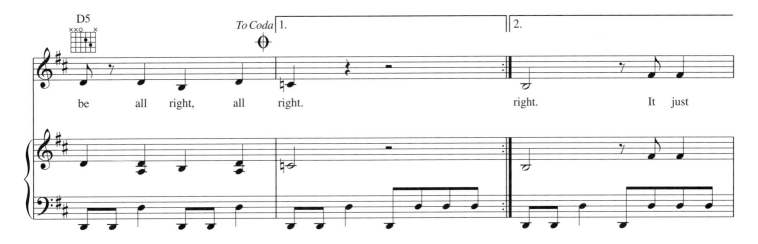

takes some time. Lit - tle girl, you're in the mid - dle of the ride. Ev -

'ry - thing, ev - 'ry - thing will be just fine. Ev - 'ry - thing, ev - 'ry - thing will

be   all   right,   all   right.

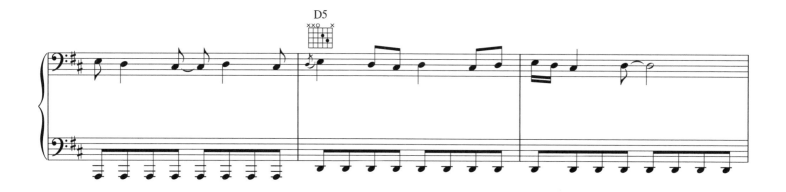

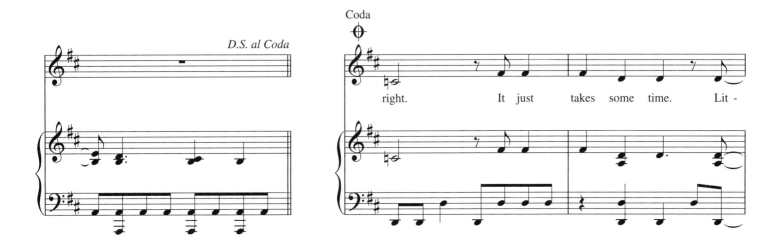

D.S. al Coda

Coda

right. It just takes some time. Lit -

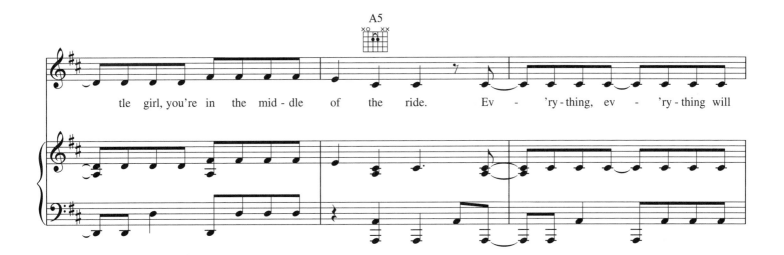

tle girl, you're in the mid - dle of the ride. Ev - 'ry - thing, ev - 'ry - thing will

be just fine. Ev - 'ry - thing, ev - 'ry - thing will be all right.

Love Song

Words and Music by Sara Bareilles

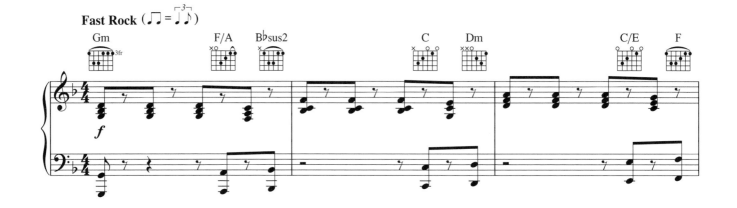

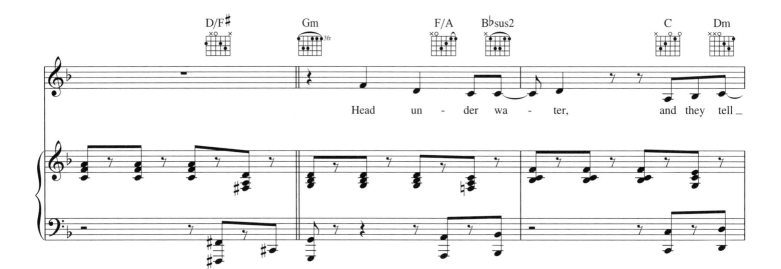

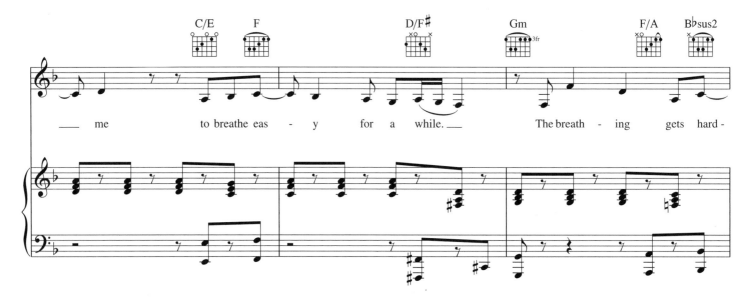

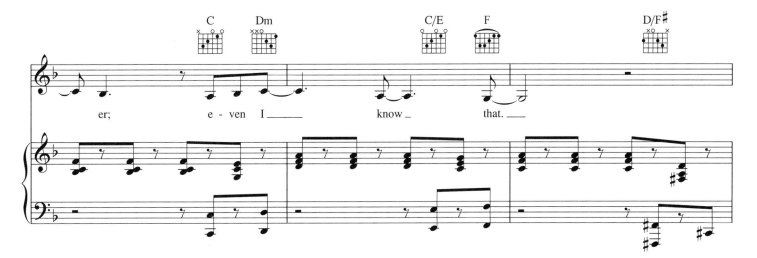

er; e - ven I _____ know _ that. _

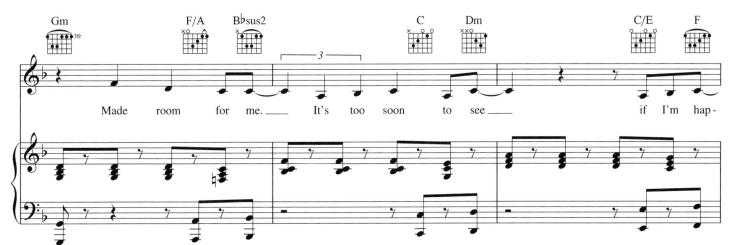

Made room for me. _____ It's too soon to see _____ if I'm hap-

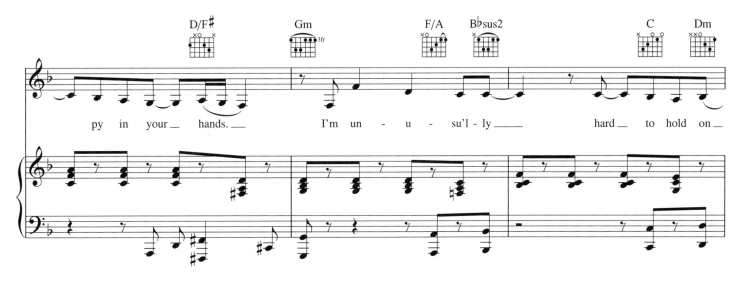

py in your _ hands. _ I'm un - u - su'l - ly _____ hard _ to hold on _

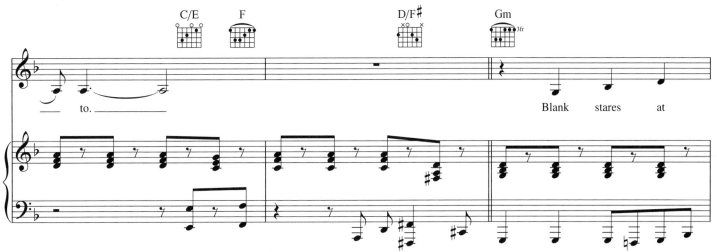

_ to. _____ Blank stares at

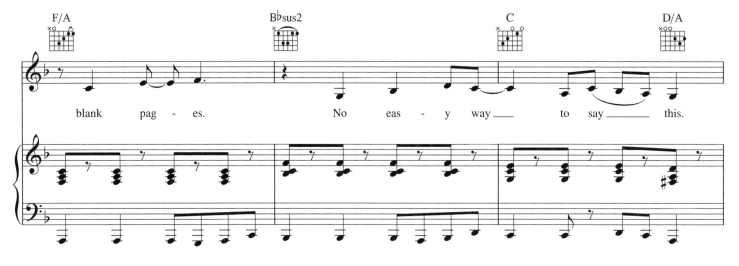

blank pag - es.　　No eas - y way ___ to say ___ this.

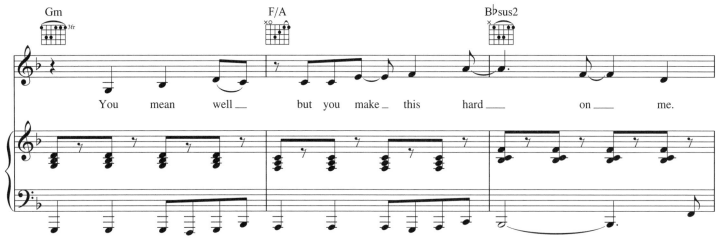

You mean well ___ but you make ___ this hard ___ on ___ me.

I'm not gon - na write you a love song ___ 'cause you ask ___ for it, 'cause you need _
love song, ___ 'cause you ask ___ for it, 'cause you need _

___ one. }
___ one? }
You see, ___ I'm not gon - na write you a love song ___ 'cause you tell _

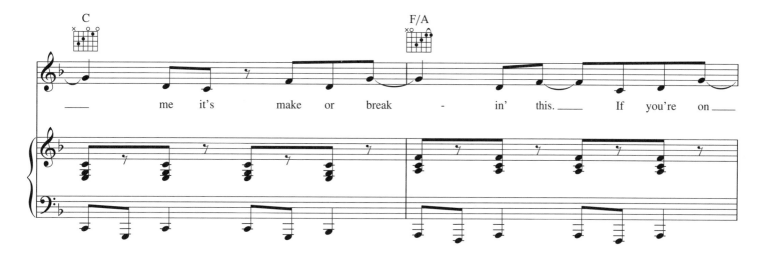

me it's make or break - in' this. ___ If you're on ___

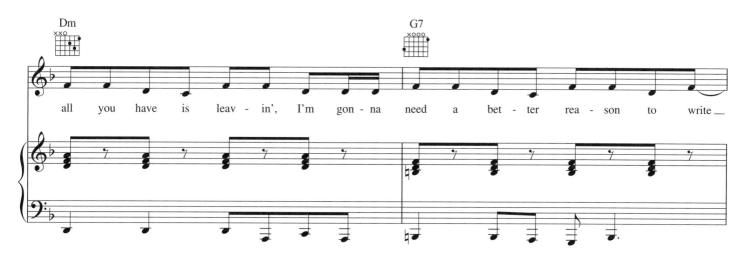

your way, ___ I'm not gon-na write you to stay. ___ If

all you have is leav-in', I'm gon-na need a bet-ter rea-son to write ___

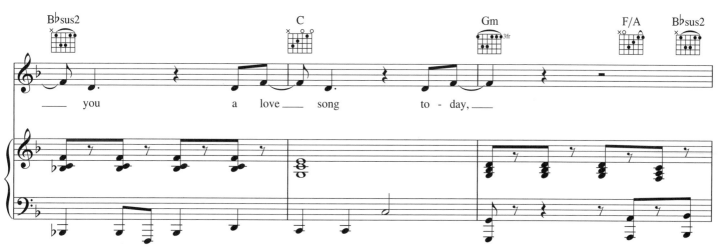

___ you a love ___ song to - day, ___

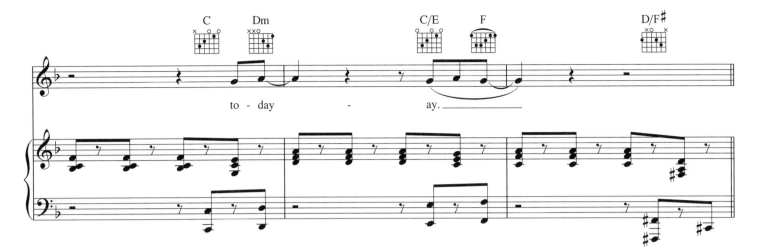

to - day - ay. _____

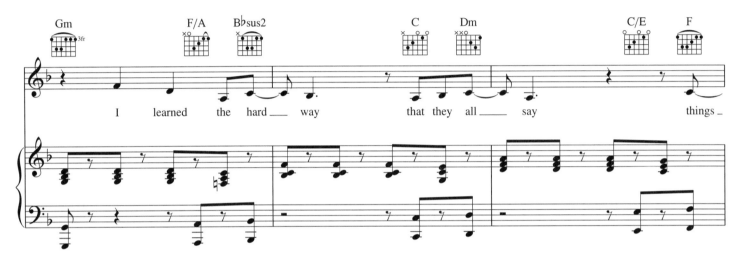

I learned the hard ___ way that they all ___ say things ___

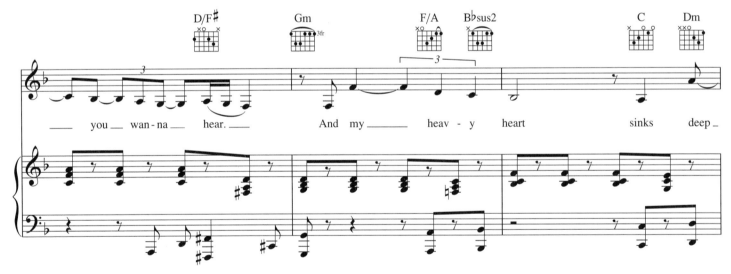

___ you wan - na ___ hear. ___ And my _____ heav - y heart sinks deep ___

___ down ___ un - der ___ you ___ and your twist - ed

194

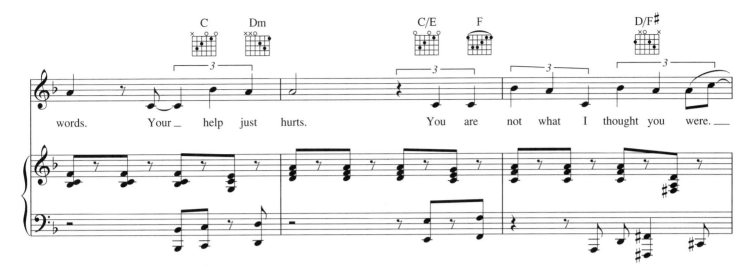

words. Your help just hurts. You are not what I thought you were.

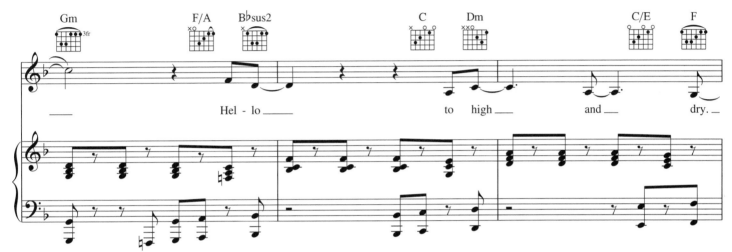

Hel - lo to high and dry.

Con - vinced me to please you.

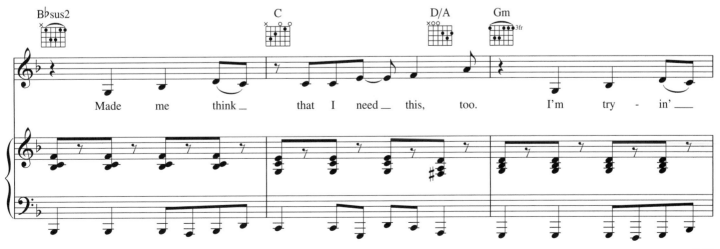

Made me think that I need this, too. I'm try - in'

D.S. (lyric 1) al Coda I

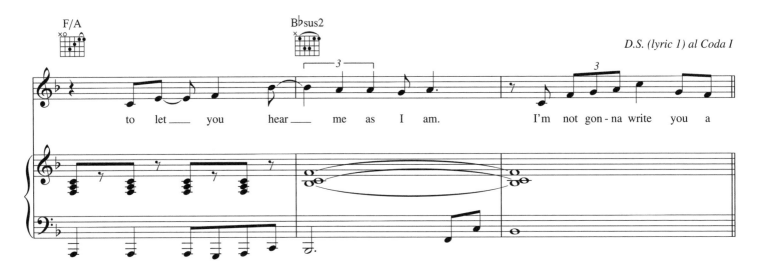

to let ___ you hear ___ me as I am. I'm not gon-na write you a

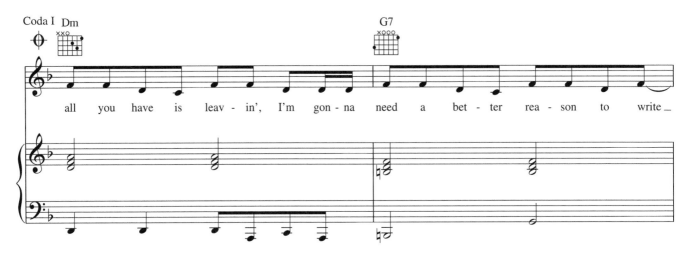

all you have is leav-in', I'm gon-na need a bet-ter rea-son to write ___

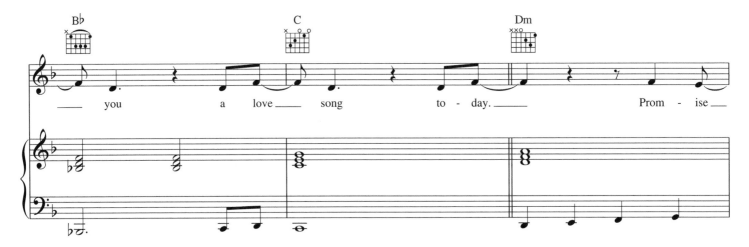

___ you a love ___ song to - day. ___ Prom - ise ___

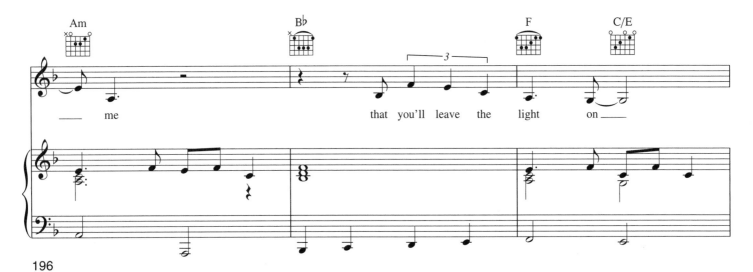

___ me that you'll leave the light on ___

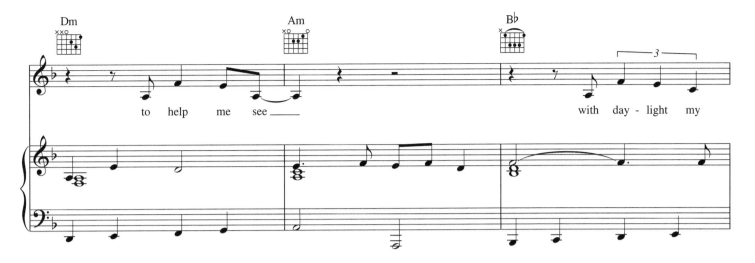

to help me see _____ with day-light my

guide, gone. _____ 'Cause I be-lieve _____ there's a way _____

_____ you can love me, be-cause I say _____ I won't write you a love _____

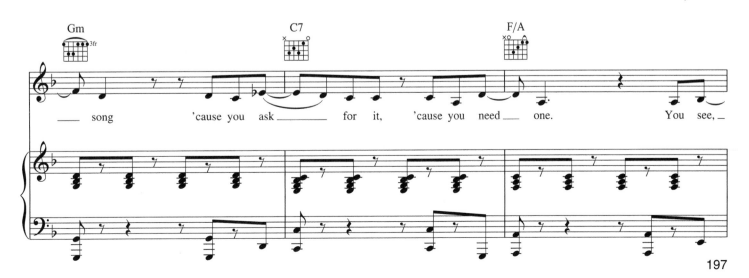

_____ song 'cause you ask _____ for it, 'cause you need _____ one. You see, _____

I'm not gon-na write you a love song ___ 'cause you tell ___

D.S. (lyric 2) al Coda II

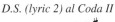

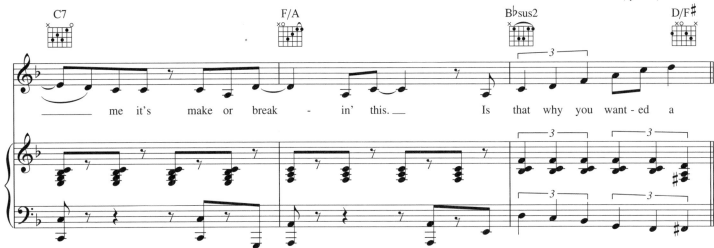

me it's make or break - in' this. ___ Is that why you want - ed a

Coda II

___ If your heart is no - where in it, I don't

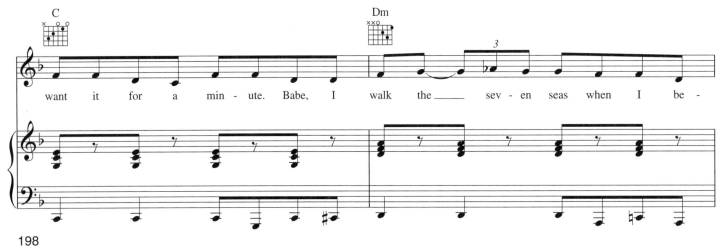

want it for a min - ute. Babe, I walk the ___ sev - en seas when I be -

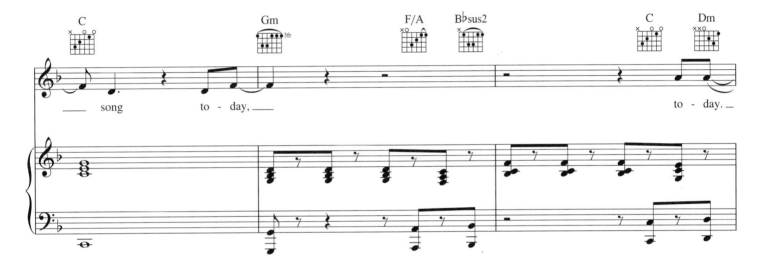

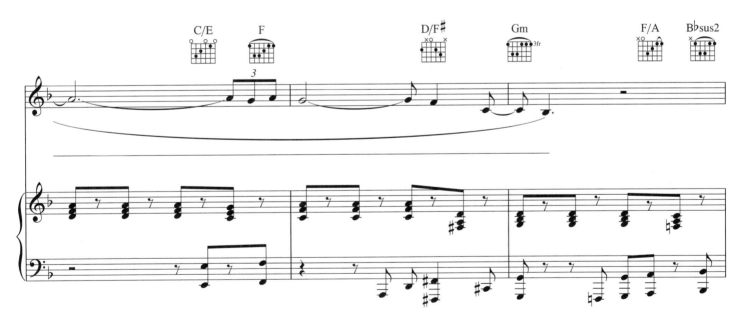

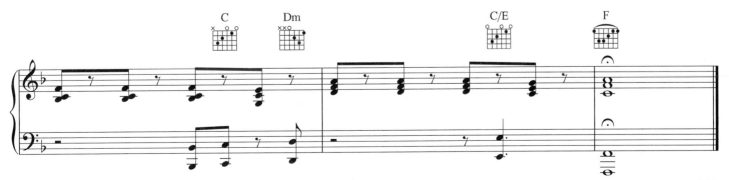

Mr. Brightside

Words and Music by Brandon Flowers,
Dave Keuning, Mark Stoermer
and Ronnie Vannucci

Lyrics:

Com-in' out of my cage ___ and I've been do-in' just fine. Got-ta, got-ta be down ___ be-cause I want it all. It start-ed out with a kiss. ___ How did it end up like this? It was on-ly a kiss. ___ It was on-ly a kiss. ___

* *Recorded a half step lower.*

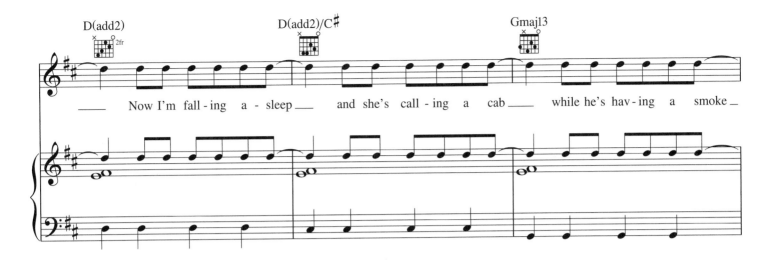

Now I'm fall-ing a-sleep ___ and she's call-ing a cab ___ while he's hav-ing a smoke ___

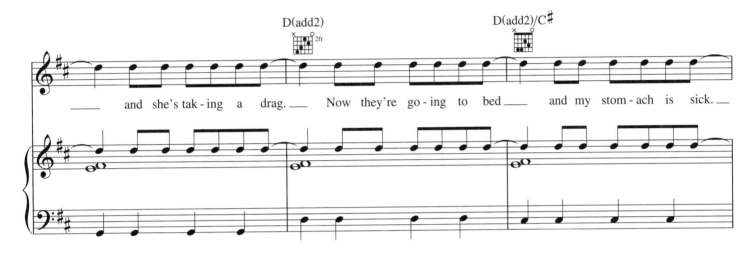

___ and she's tak-ing a drag. ___ Now they're go-ing to bed ___ and my stom-ach is sick. ___

___ And it's all in my head ___ but she's touch-ing his chest now.

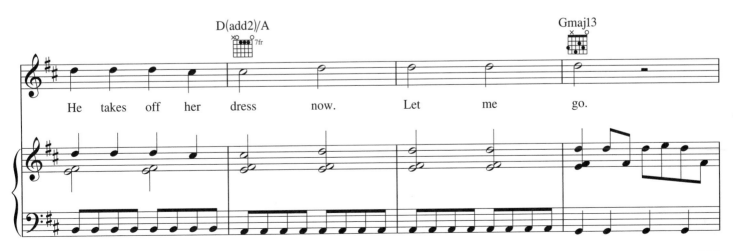

He takes off her dress now. Let me go.

I just can't look. It's kill - ing me and

tak - ing ___ con - trol.

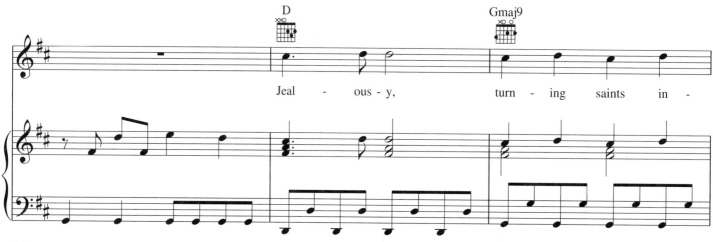

Jeal - ous - y, turn - ing saints in -

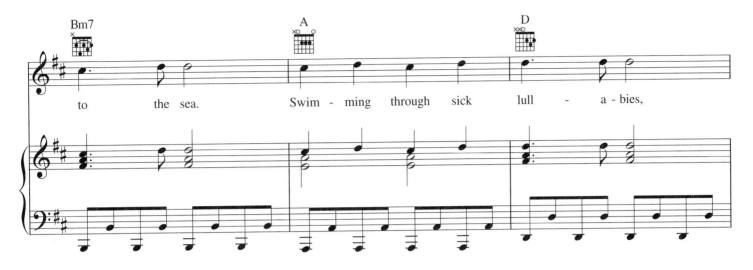

to the sea. Swim-ming through sick lull - a - bies,

chok - ing on your al - i - bis, but it's just the

price I pay. Des - ti - ny is call - ing me. O - pen up my

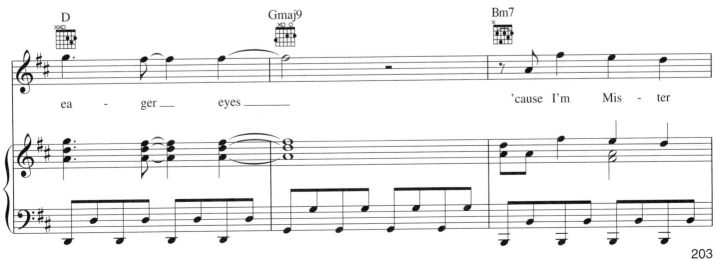

ea - ger __ eyes _____ 'cause I'm Mis - ter

Bright - side.

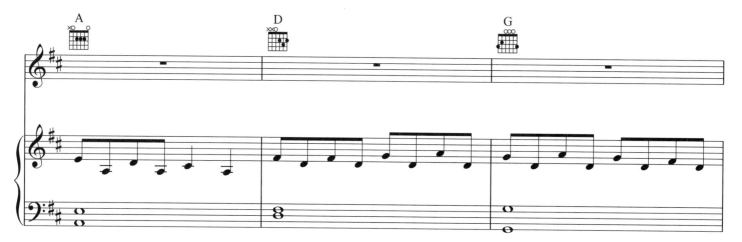

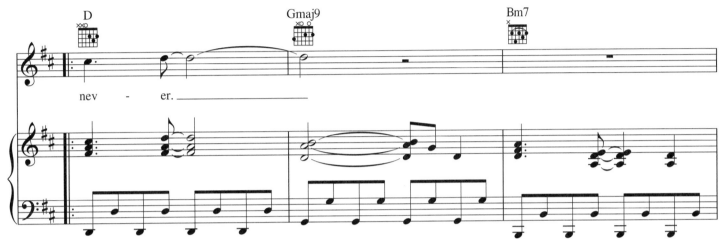

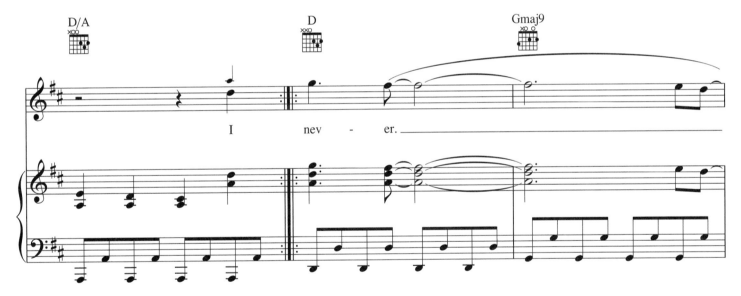

A Moment Like This

Words and Music by
John Reid and Jorgen Kjell Elofsson

Original key: C♯ minor. This edition has been transposed up one half-step to be more playable.

tell me that ___ you don't ___ think I'm cra - zy

when I tell you love ___ has come here and ___ now. ___ A mo - ment like this. ___

___ Some peo - ple wait ___ a life - time for a mo - ment like this. ___

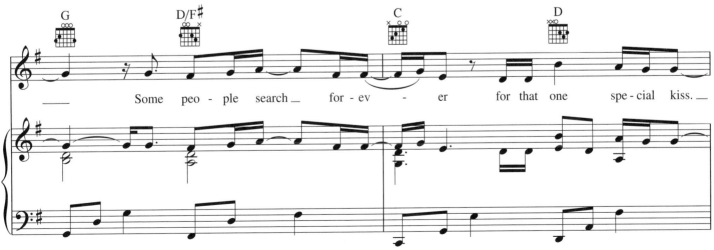

___ Some peo - ple search ___ for - ev - er for that one spe - cial kiss. ___

Oh, I can't be - lieve __ it's hap - pen - ing __ to me. _____ Some

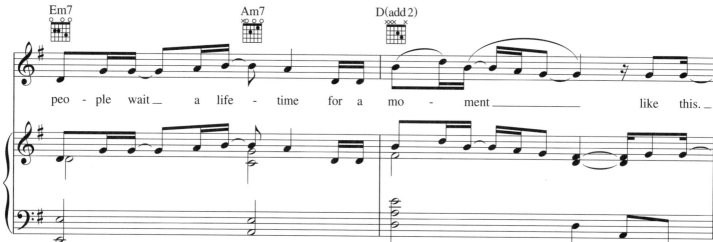

peo - ple wait __ a life - time for a mo - ment _____ like this. __

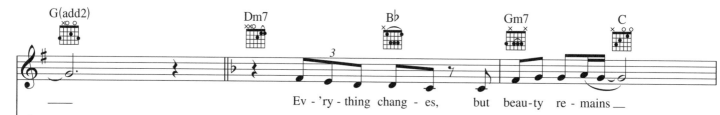

Ev - 'ry - thing chang - es, but beau - ty re - mains __

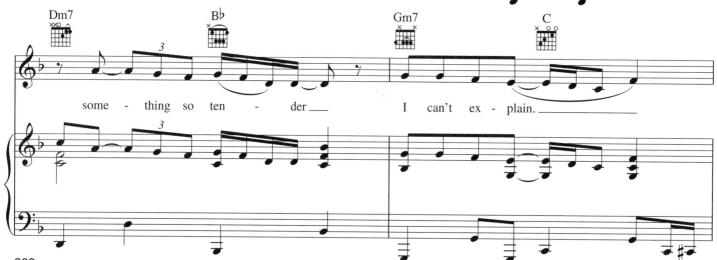

some - thing so ten - der __ I can't ex - plain. _____

208

Some peo - ple search _ for - ev - er for that one spe - cial kiss. _

_ Oh, I can't be - lieve _ it's hap - pen - ing _ to me. _____ Some

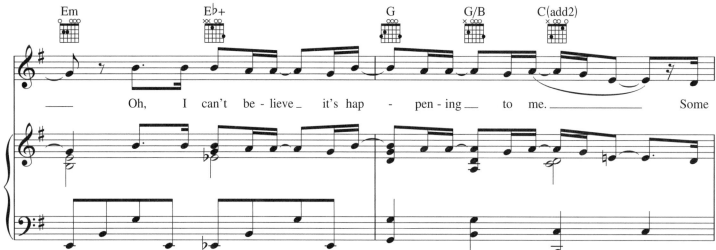

peo - ple wait _ a life - time for a mo - ment _ like this. _

_ Could _ this be _ the great - est love _ of

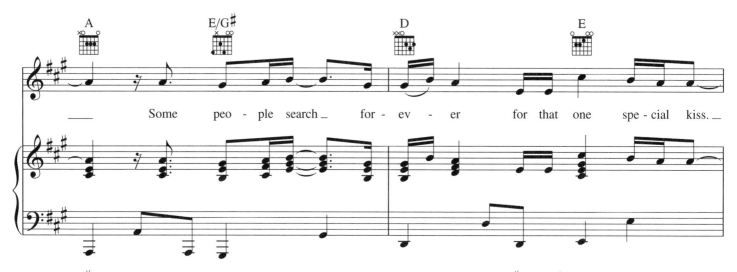

Some peo-ple search for-ev-er for that one spe-cial kiss.

Oh, I can't be-lieve it's hap-pen-ing to me. Some

peo-ple wait a life-time for a mo-ment like this.

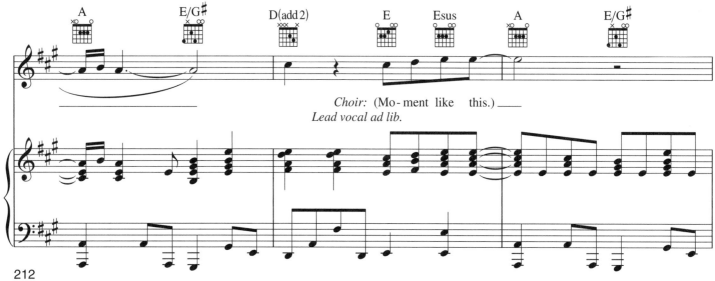

Choir: (Mo-ment like this.)
Lead vocal ad lib.

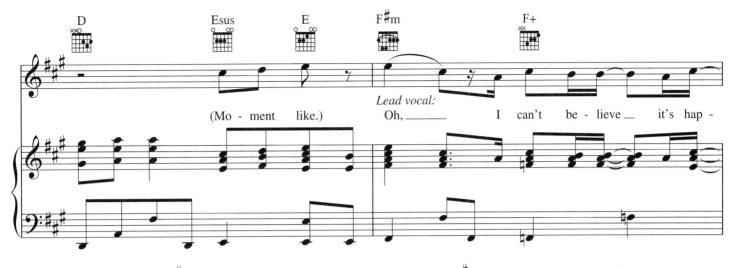

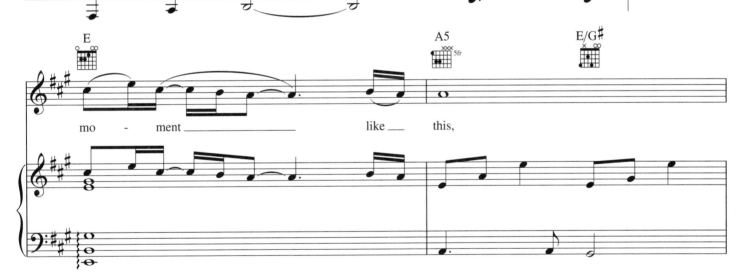

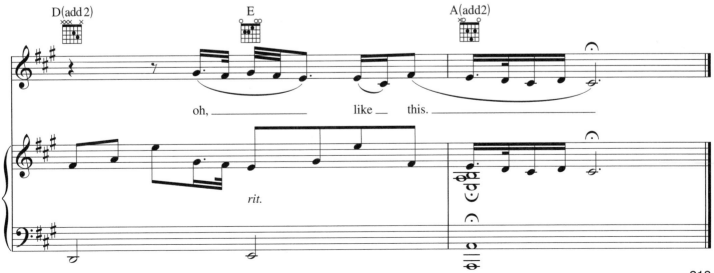

New Soul

Words and Music by Yael Naim
and David Donatien

Lyrics:

1. I'm a new soul, I came to this strange world hop-ing I could
young soul in this ver-y strange world, hop-ing I could

learn a bit 'bout how to give and take.__ But since I came here, felt the joy and
learn a bit 'bout what is true and fake.__ But why all this__ hate? Try to com-mu-

the fear, find-ing my-self mak-ing ev-'ry pos-si-ble mis-take.__
ni-cate, find-ing trust and love is not al-ways eas-y to make.__ La la

Chorus:

la la, la la la la la la la la la la la, la la la, la la la. La la la la, la la la la la la, la la la la la, la la la, la la la. 2. See I'm a la. Ooh.

216

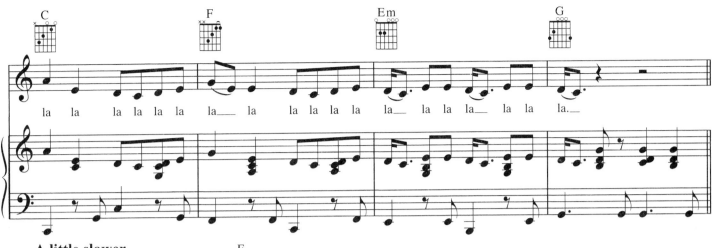

la la la la la la la la la la la la la la la la la.

A little slower

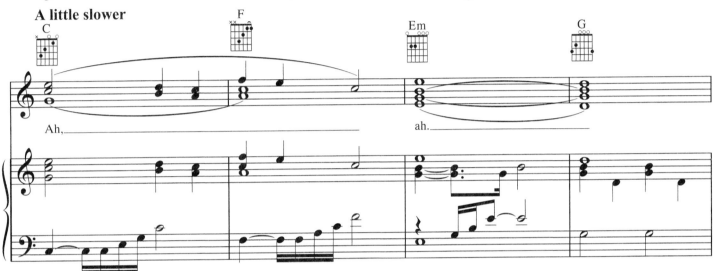

Ah, ah.

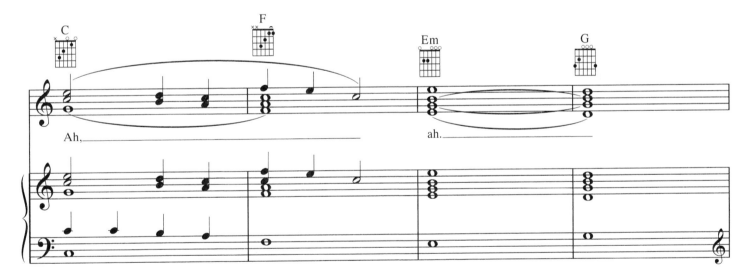

Ah, ah.

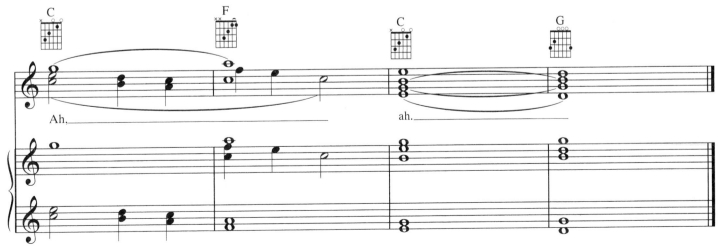

Ah, ah.

219

No Such Thing

Words by John Mayer
Music by John Mayer
and Clay Cook

Moderately fast

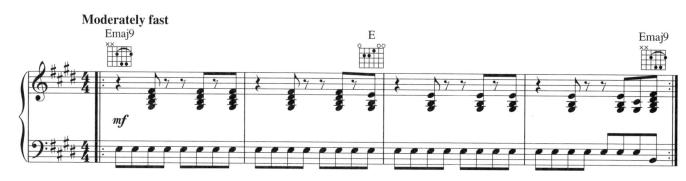

"Wel - come to the real __ world," she said to me con - de - scend -

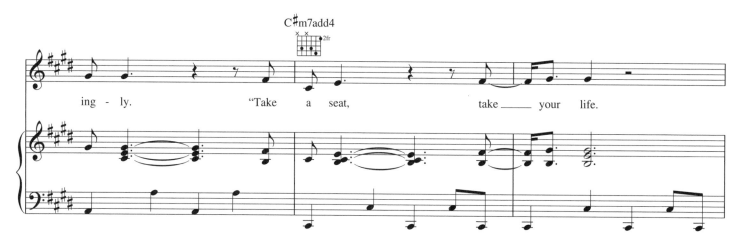

ing - ly. "Take a seat, take _____ your life.

Plot it out __ in black ___ and white." ___   Well, I

never lived the dreams of the prom___ kings ___ and the dra - ma queens._ I'd like to think the

best of me ____ is still hid - ing up my __ sleeve. ____ They

love to tell you "Stay in - side the lines." ____

But some - thing's bet - ter

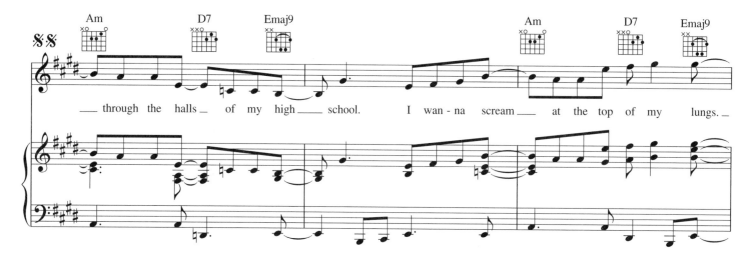

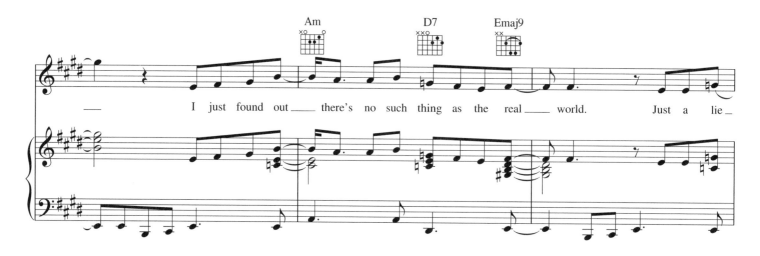

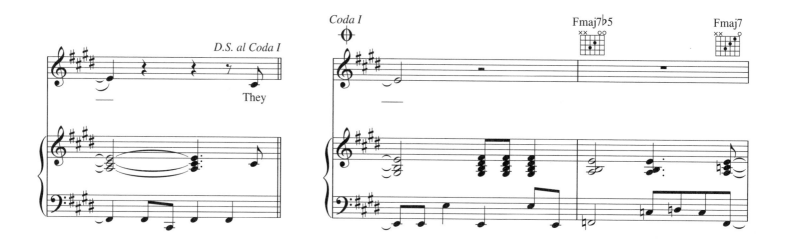

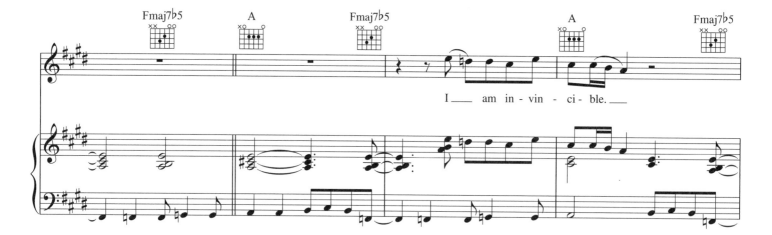

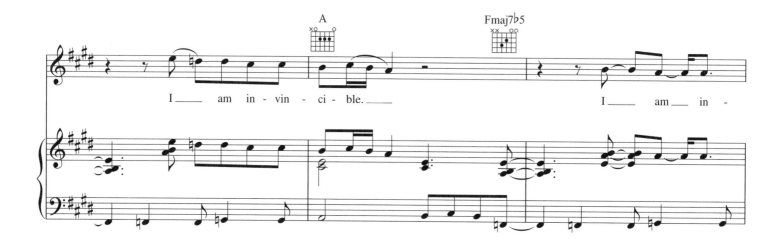

224

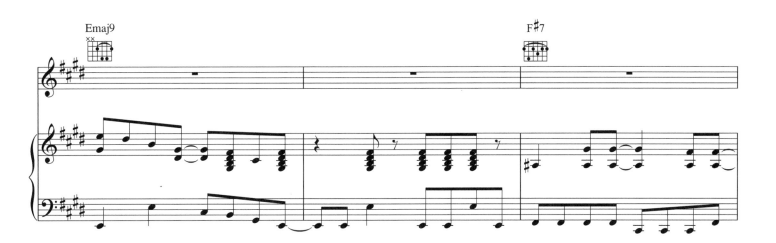

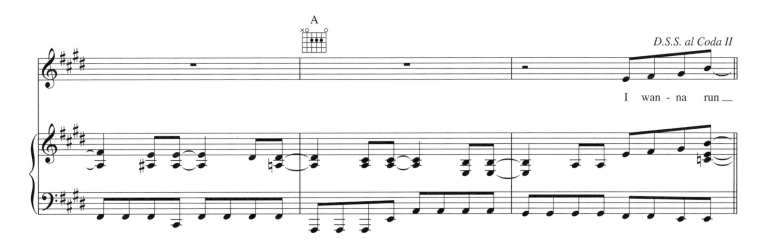

I wan - na run __

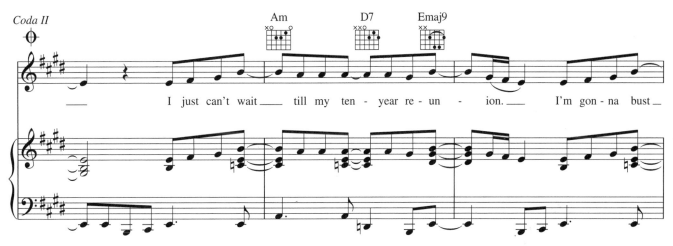

__ I just can't wait __ till my ten - year re - un - ion. __ I'm gon - na bust __

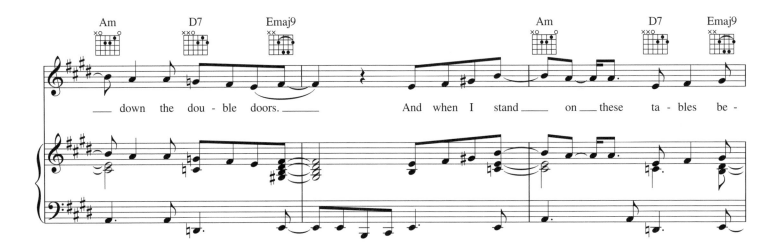

_____ down the dou - ble doors. _____ And when I stand _____ on _____ these ta - bles be -

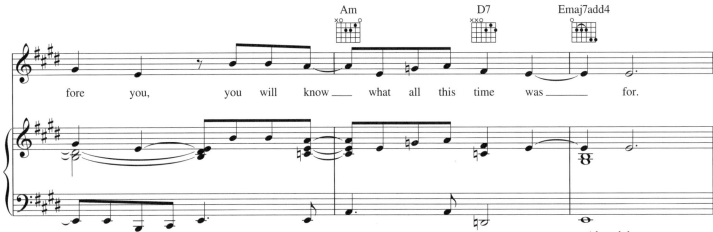

fore you, you will know _____ what all this time was _____ for.

with pedal

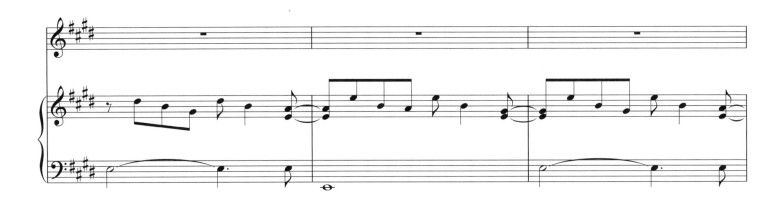

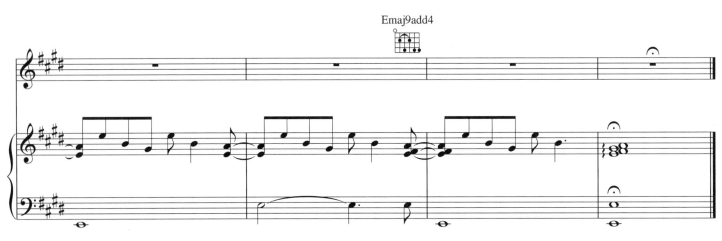

226

Oops!...I Did It Again

Words and Music by
Martin Sandberg and Rami Yacoub

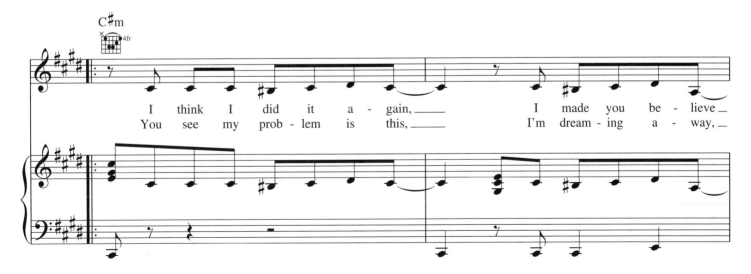

we're more than just friends. ___ Oh, ba - by,
wish - ing that he - roes, they tru - ly ex - ist.

it might seem like a crush, ___ but it does - n't mean
I cry watch - ing the days, ___ can't you see I'm a fool ___

that I'm se - ri - ous. ___ 'Cause to
in so man - y ways? ___ But to

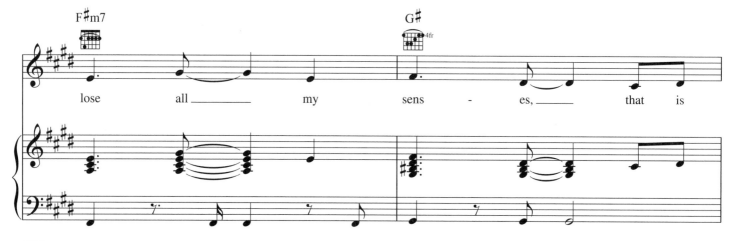

lose all ___ my sens - es, ___ that is

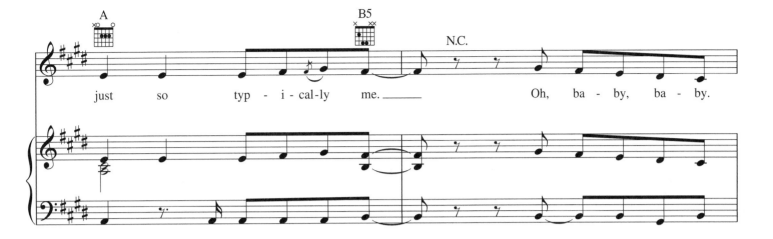

just so typ-i-cal-ly me. _____ Oh, ba-by, ba-by.

Oops!... I did it a-gain, _____ I played with your heart, _

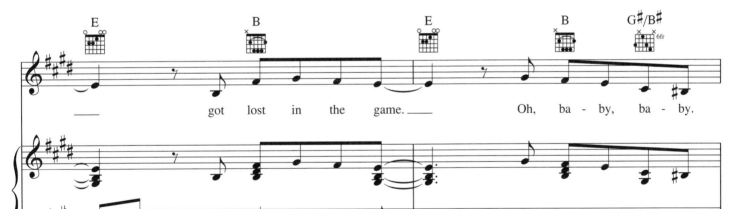

_____ got lost in the game. _____ Oh, ba-by, ba-by.

Oops!... You think I'm in love, _____ that I'm sent from a-bove. _

I'm not that in-no-cent.

not that in-no-cent.

Yeah,

yeah, yeah, yeah, yeah, yeah.

Yeah,

yeah, yeah, yeah, yeah, yeah.

(Spoken:) *"All Aboard!"* *"Britney,*

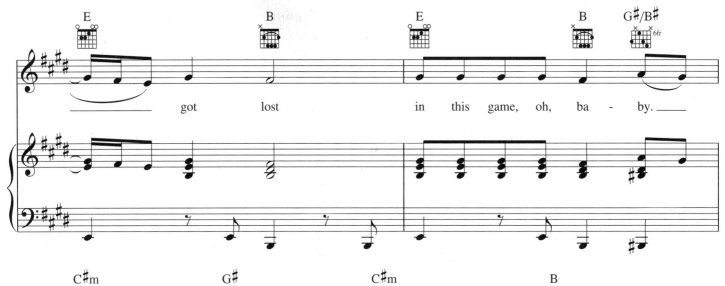

got lost in this game, oh, ba - by. ____

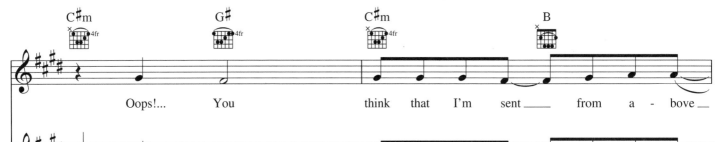

Oops!... You think that I'm sent ____ from a - bove ____

____ I'm not that in - no - cent.

Oops!... I did it a - gain, ____ I played with your heart, _

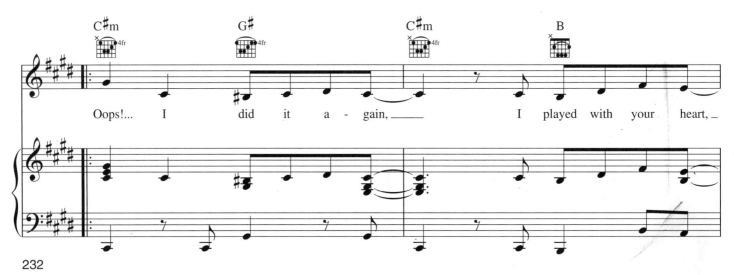

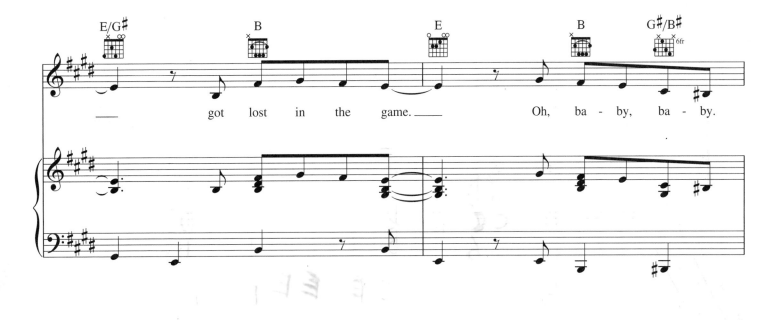

got lost in the game. _____ Oh, ba - by, ba - by.

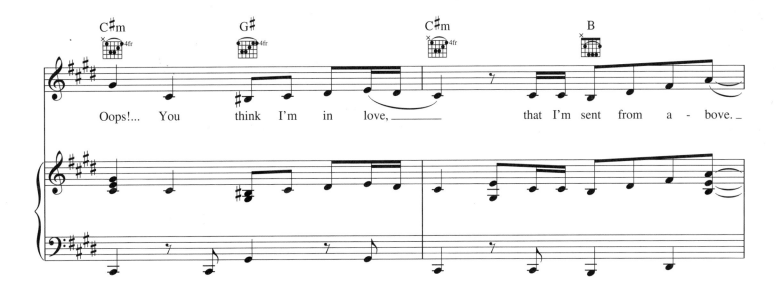

Oops!... You think I'm in love, _____ that I'm sent from a - bove. _

I'm not that in - no - cent. not that in - no - cent. _

Ordinary People

Words and Music by
John Stephens and Will Adams

May - be we'll crash and burn. _ May - be you'll stay; may - be you'll leave; may - be you'll _ re - turn. _

May - be an - oth - er fight; _ may - be we won't sur - vive.

D.S. al Coda II

But may - be we'll grow. We _ nev - er know, ba - by, you _____ and I. _

Coda II

slow. Take it slow, oh, ___ oh. _____

mp

239

240

Paper Planes

Words and Music by Joe Strummer,
Mick Jones, Paul Simonon,
Topper Headon, Thomas Pentz
and Mathangi Arulpragasam

fly like pa-per, get high like planes. If you catch me at the bor-der, I got vi-sas in my name. If you
Pi-rate skulls and bones. ___ Sticks ___ and ___ stones and ___ weed and ___ bombs.

come a-round here, I make them all day. I get one down in a sec-ond if you wait. I
Run-ning when we hit them. _____ Le-thal poi-son ___ through their sys - tem.

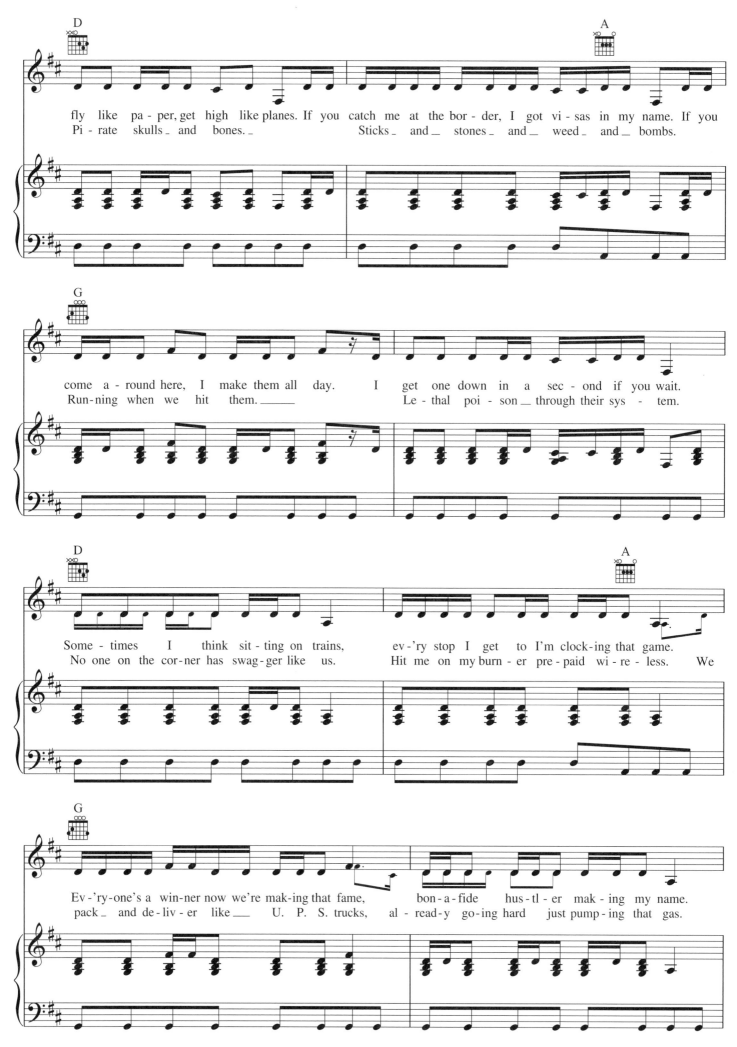

fly like pa - per, get high like planes. If you catch me at the bor - der, I got vi - sas in my name. If you
Pi - rate skulls and bones. Sticks and stones and weed and bombs.

come a - round here, I make them all day. I get one down in a sec - ond if you wait.
Run - ning when we hit them. Le - thal poi - son through their sys - tem.

Some - times I think sit - ting on trains, ev - 'ry stop I get to I'm clock - ing that game.
No one on the cor - ner has swag - ger like us. Hit me on my burn - er pre - paid wi - re - less. We

Ev - 'ry - one's a win - ner now we're mak - ing that fame, bon - a - fide hus - tl - er mak - ing my name.
pack and de - liv - er like U. P. S. trucks, al - read - y go - ing hard just pump - ing that gas.

Some - times I think sit - ting on trains, ev - 'ry stop I get to I'm clock - ing that game.
No one on the cor - ner has swag - ger like us. Hit me on my burn - er pre - paid wi - re - less. We

Ev - 'ry-one's a win - ner now we're mak - ing that fame, bon - a - fide hus - tl - er mak - ing my name.
pack_ and de - liv - er like ___ U. P. S. trucks, al - read - y go - ing hard just pump - ing that gas.

All I wan - na do is... and... and take your mon - ey.

All I wan - na do is... and... and take your mon - ey.

All I wan-na do is... and... and take your mon-ey.

All I wan-na do is... and... and take your mon-ey.

To Coda ⊕

(Spoken:) M.I.A., third world democracy, yeah, I've got

more records than the K.G.B, so, ah, no funny business.

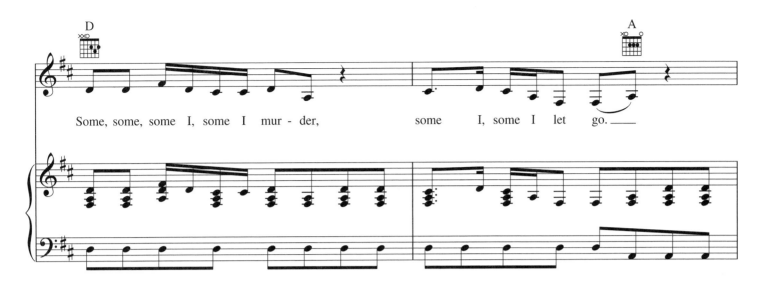

Some, some, some I, some I mur - der, some I, some I let go. _____

D.S. al Coda

Some, some, some I, some I mur - der, some I, some I let go. _____

CODA

N.C.

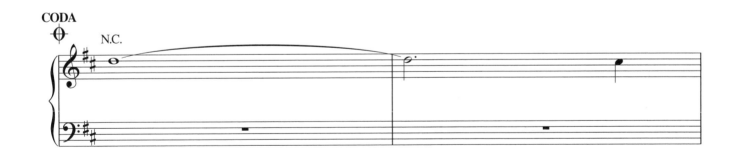

Photograph

Lyrics by Chad Kroeger
Music by Nickelback

*Guitarists: Tune down one half step.

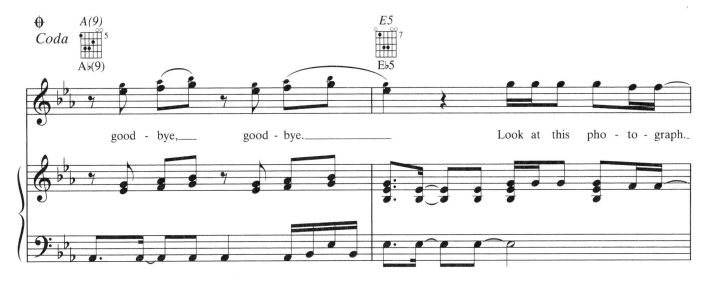

good - bye,___ good - bye._____ Look at this pho - to - graph.___

Ev-'ry time I do, it makes me laugh.___ Ev-'ry time I do, it makes me...

Realize

Words and Music by
Colbie Caillat, Jason Reeves
and Mikal Blue

*Recorded a half step higher.

Guitarists: Capo at 6th fret to play along with recording.

254

Take time ___ to re - al - ize ___ this all can pass you by. ___

D.S. al Coda

Did - n't I tell ___ you? ___

nev - er have to won - der if we missed out on each oth - er but... ___ It's not ___ the same, ___

we missed out on each oth - er now, _____ ow, _____ ow, ___ yeah. ___

Real - ize, _____ real - ize, _____ real - ize, _____ real-

ize. _____ Oo, oo. _____

The Reason

Words and Music by Daniel Estrin
and Douglas Robb

Moderately slow ♩ = 84

Verse:

1. I'm not a per- fect per- son,_____ there's man- y things_ I wish_ I____ did- n't do.___
2. I'm sor- ry that____ I hurt____ you,_____ it's some- thing I____ must live____ with_ ev- 'ry- day.___

you.

But I con - tin - ue learn -
And all the pain___ I put you
3. I'm not a per - fect___ per -

ing._____ I nev - er meant___ to do___ those things___ to you.___
through,_____ I wish that I___ could take___ it all___ a - way.
son._____ I nev - er meant___ to do___ those things___ to you.___

And so, I have___ to say___ be - fore___ I go,___
And be the one___ who catch - es all___ your tears.___
And so, I have___ to say___ be - fore___ I go,___

that I just want you to know___
That's why I need you to hear.___
that I just want you to know___

260

Chorus:

I've found_ a_ rea - son for me_ to change_ who_ I used to_ be._

A rea - son_ to start o - ver

To Coda

1.

new, and the rea - son is_

The Remedy (I Won't Worry)

Words and Music by Graham Edwards,
Scott Spock, Lauren Christy
and Jason Mraz

Moderately, with a beat

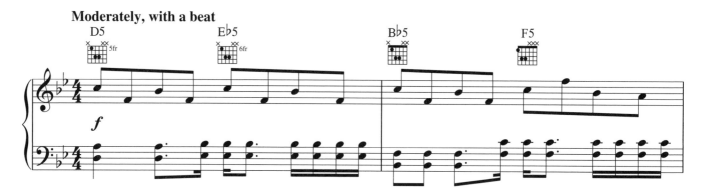

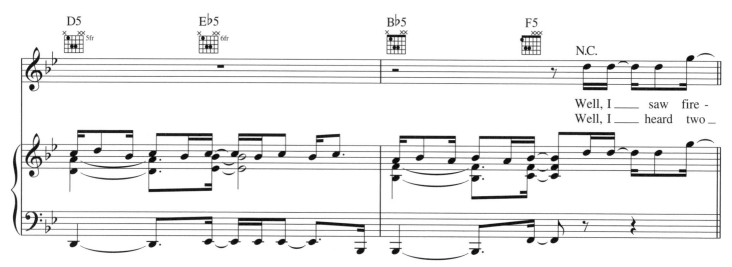

Well, I ____ saw fire -
Well, I ____ heard two ____

-thin' on the sur-face real-ly kind of makes me nerv-ous. Who says
___ af - ter this. The un - a - void - a - ble kiss where the

___ that you de-serve this and what kind of God would serve this? We will
mint - y fresh ___ bad ___ breath is sure to out - last ___ this ca-

cure this dirt - y old ___ dis - ease. ___ Well, if } you've gots the poi - son, I've _ gots the rem - e - dy. The
tas - tro-phe, dance _ with me. ___ 'Cause if }

rem - e - dy ___ is the ex - per - i - ence. This is a dan - ger - ous ___ li - ai - son. I ___ says, the

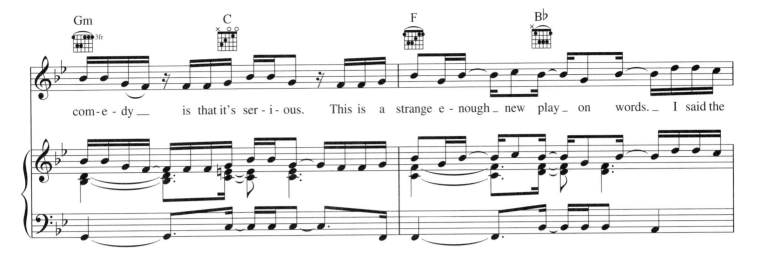

com-e-dy __ is that it's ser-i-ous. This is a strange e-nough __ new play __ on words. __ I said the

trag-e-dy is how you're gon-na __ spend __ the rest __ of your nights __ with the light __ on. So shine the

light on all __ of your friends __ when it all __ a-mounts __ to noth-ing in __ the end.

I, _____ I won't wor-ry my life __

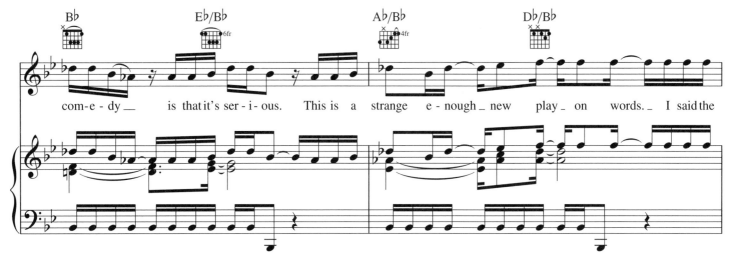

com-e-dy __ is that it's ser-i-ous. This is a strange e-nough __ new play __ on words. __ I said the

trag-e-dy is how you're gon-na __ spend __ the rest __ of your nights __ with the light __ on. So shine the

light on all __ of your friends __ when it all a-mounts __ to noth-ing in __ the end.

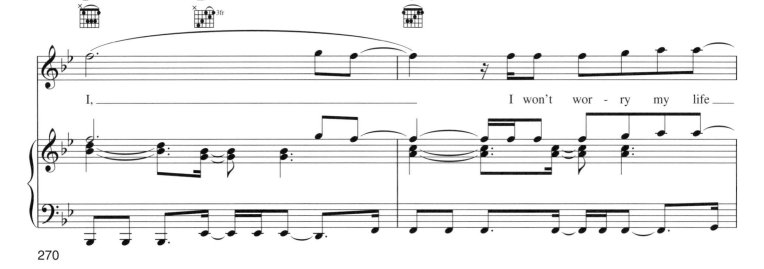

I, _____ I won't wor-ry my life __

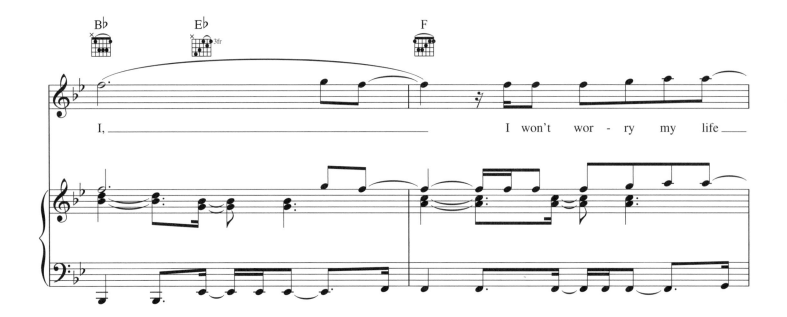

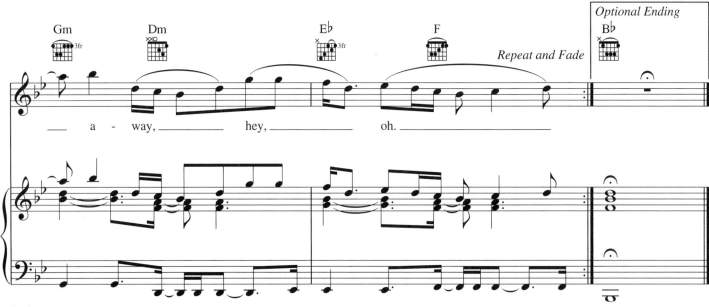

The Scientist

Words and Music by Guy Berryman, Jon Buckland,
Will Champion and Chris Martin

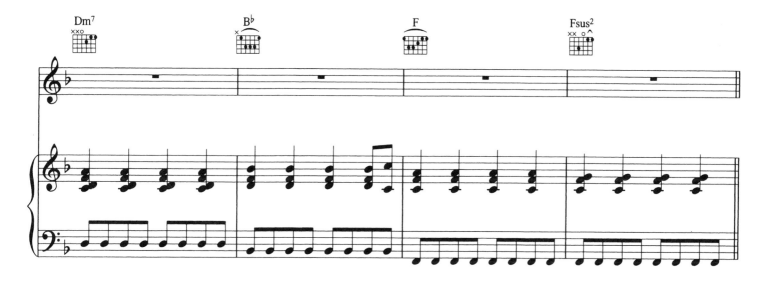

1. Come up to meet__ you, tell you I'm sor - ry, you don't know how love-
(Verse 2 see block lyric)

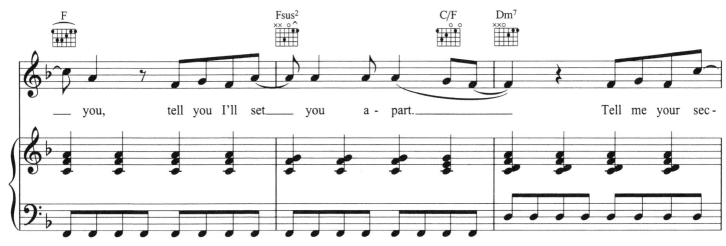

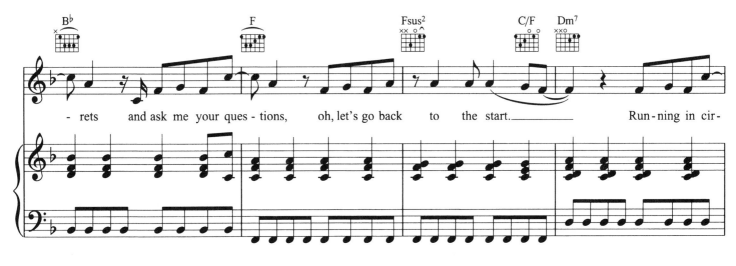

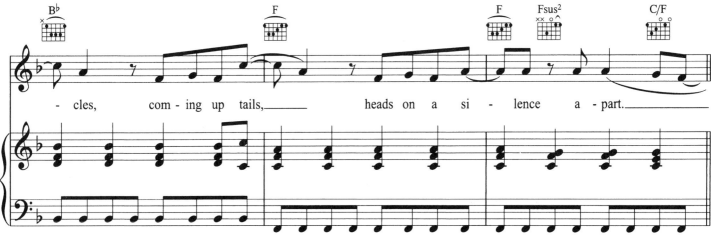

Verse 2:
I was just guessing at numbers and figures
Pulling your puzzles apart.
Questions of science, science and progress
That must speak as loud as my heart.
Tell me you love me, come back and haunt me
Oh, and I rush to the start
Running in circles, chasing our tails
Coming back as we are.

Nobody said it was easy *etc.*

Seven Nation Army

Words and Music by Jack White

Bluesy Rock

I'm gon - na fight them all,
Don't want to hear a - bout it,
I'm go - ing to Wich - i - ta,

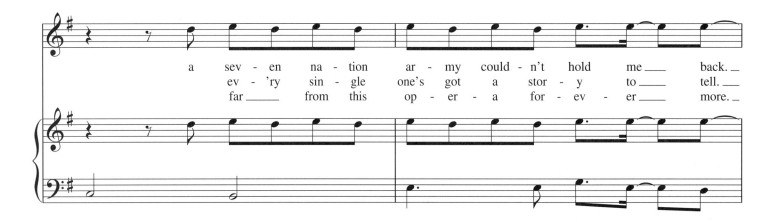

a sev - en na - tion ar - my could - n't hold me ___ back. ___
ev - 'ry sin - gle one's got a sto - ry to ___ tell. ___
far ___ from this op - er - a for - ev - er ___ more. ___

They're gon-na rip it off, ___ tak - ing their
Ev - 'ry-one knows a - bout it, from the Queen of
I'm gon-na work the straw, ___ make the sweat

time right be - hind my ___ back. ___ And I'm
Eng - land to the hounds of ___ hell. ___ And if I
drip out of ev - 'ry ___ pore. ___ And I'm

talk - ing to my - self at ___ night ___ be - cause I can't for - get. ___
catch it com - ing back my ___ way, ___ I'm gon - na serve it to you. ___
bleed - ing and I'm bleed - ing and I'm bleed - ing right be - fore the ___ lord. ___

Back and forth through my ___ mind, ___
And that ain't what you want to ___ hear, ___
All the words are gon - na bleed from ___ me, ___

279

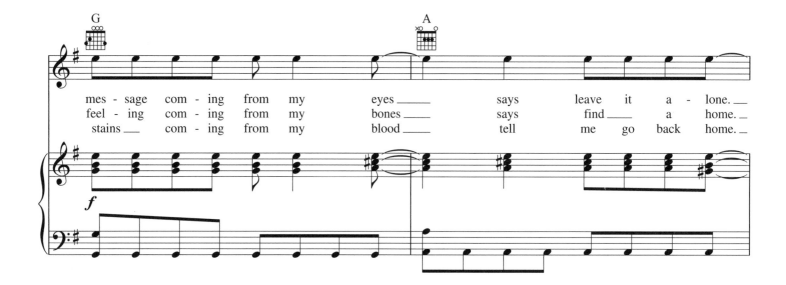

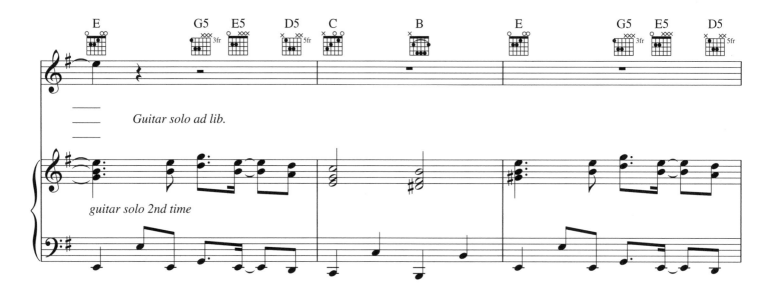

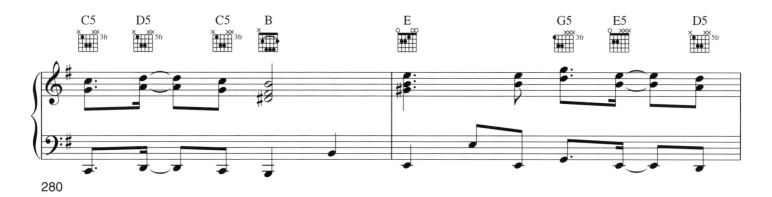

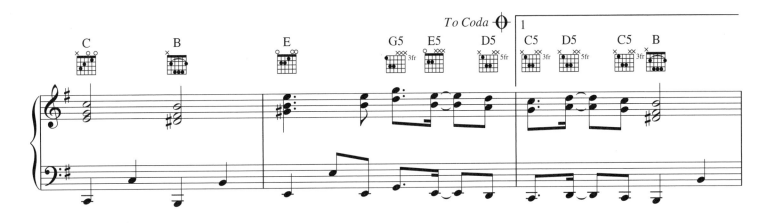

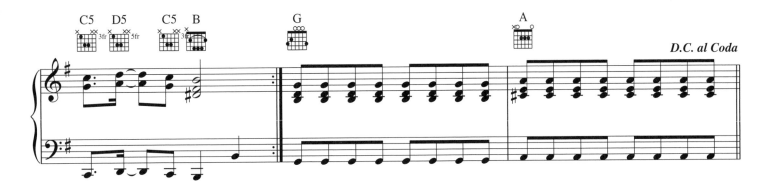

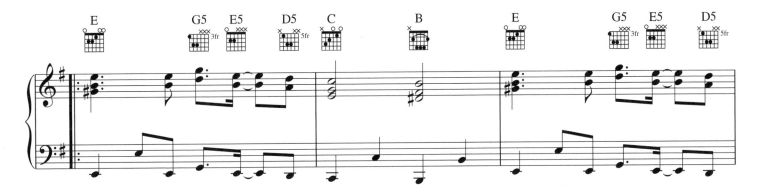

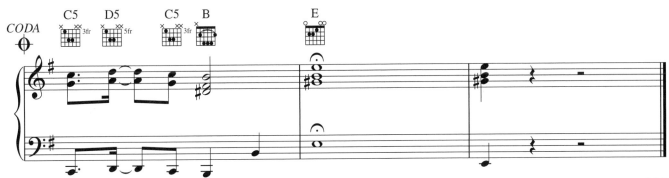

Smooth

Words by Rob Thomas
Music by Rob Thomas and Itaal Shur

words melt ev - 'ry - one. But you stay so ____ cool. ____
word I hear ____ your ____ name call - ing me ____ out. ____

My Mu - ñe - qui - ta, my Span - ish Har - lem Mo - na
Out from the bar - ri - o, you hear my rhy - thm on your

Li - sa. Well, you're my rea - son ____ for ____ rea - son, ____
ra - di - o. You feel the turn - ing of the world so soft and slow;

the ____ step in my groove. ____
turn - ing me round and round. ____

And if you said ____

this life ain't good e - nough, I would give my world to

lift you up. I could change my life to bet - ter suit ___ your ___ mood. ___

___ 'cause you're so ___ smooth. ___

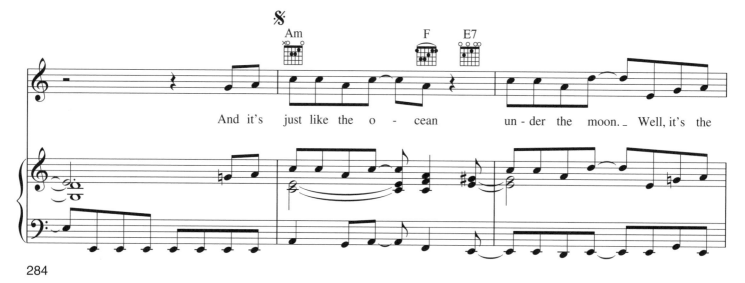

And it's just like the o - cean un - der the moon.___ Well, it's the

same as the e-mo-tion that I get from you.____ You got the kind of lov-in' that can

be so smooth,___ Give me your heart.__ Make it real or else for-get a-bout it.

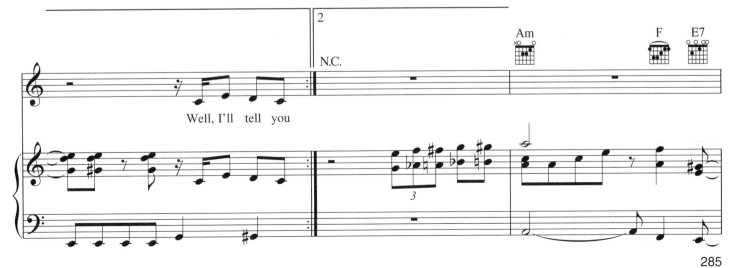

Well, I'll tell you

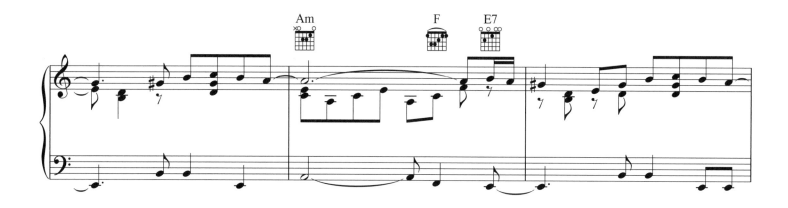

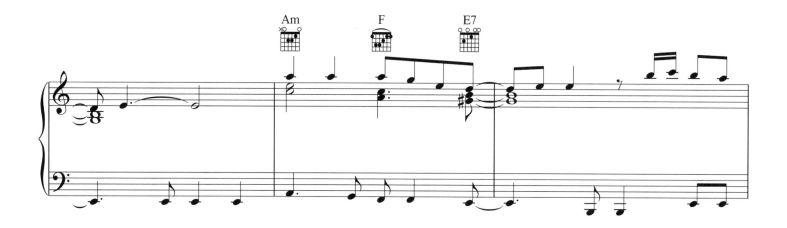

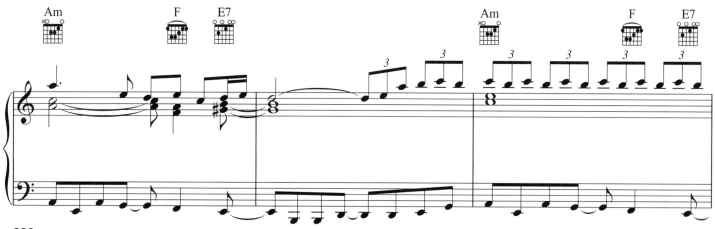

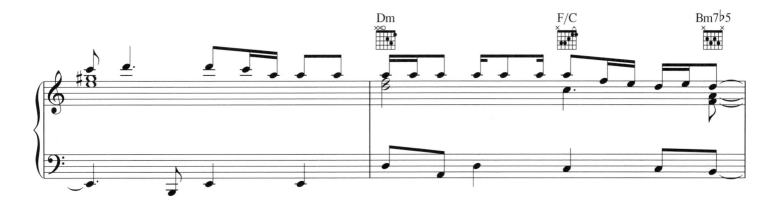

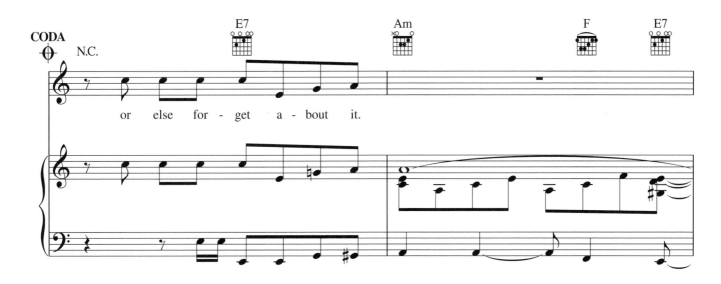

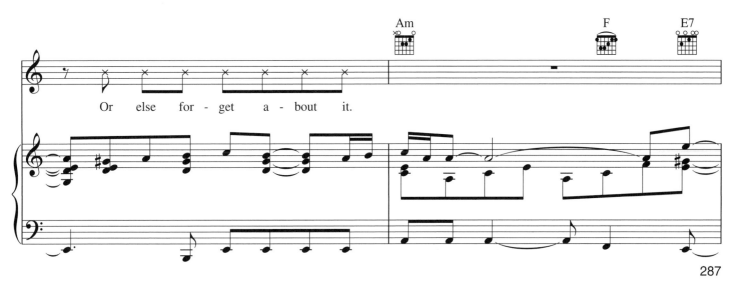

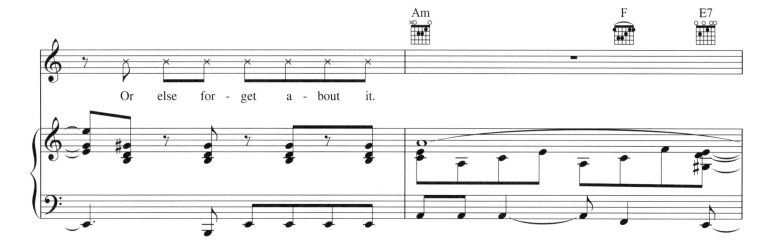

Or else for - get a - bout it.

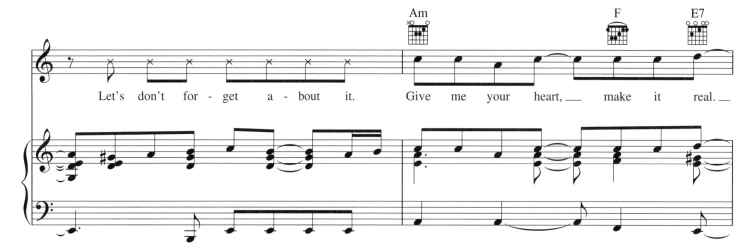

Let's don't for - get a - bout it. Give me your heart, ___ make it real. ___

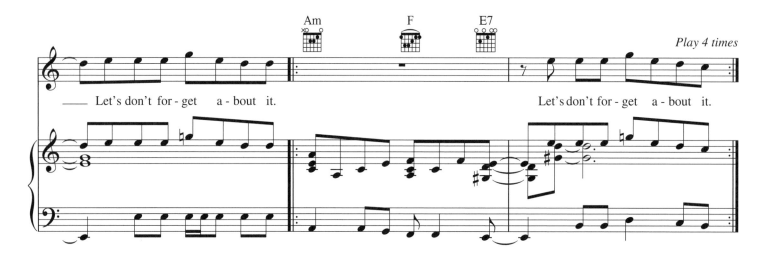

Play 4 times

___ Let's don't for - get a - bout it. Let's don't for - get a - bout it.

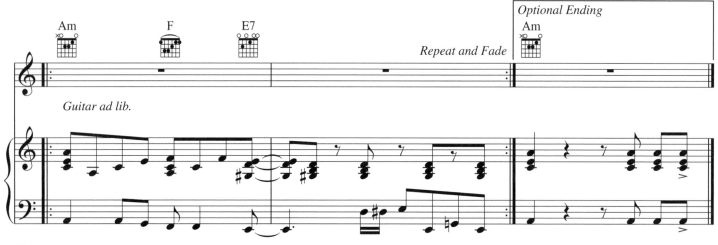

Repeat and Fade

Optional Ending
Am

Guitar ad lib.

Somebody

Words and Music by Bonnie McKee

I sit a - lone, a dark the - a - ter, watch - ing the peo -

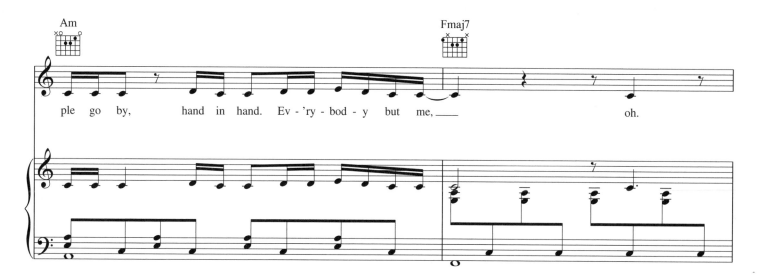

ple go by, hand in hand. Ev - 'ry - bod - y but me,___ oh.

290

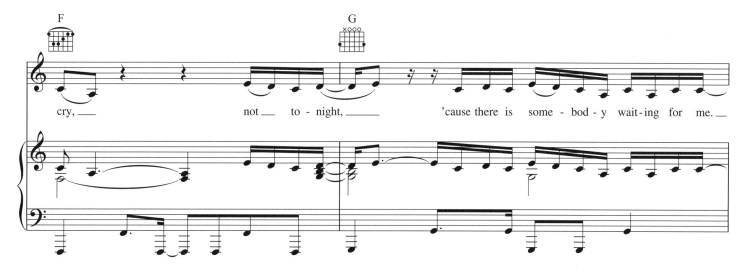

cry, ___ not ___ to - night, ___ 'cause there is some - bod - y wait-ing for me. ___

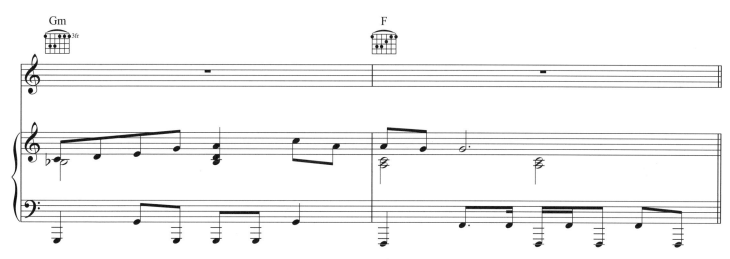

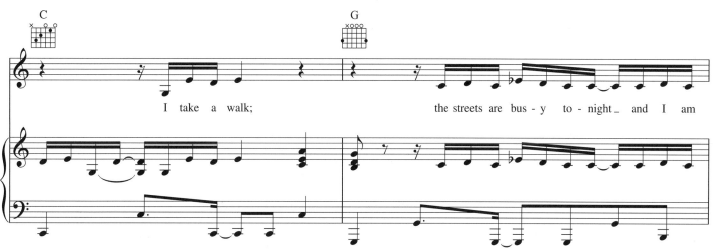

I take a walk; the streets are bus - y to - night ___ and I am

search - ing for you, wait - ing to brush _ your shoul - der. _

But I'm a - lone, _____ I watch the fac - es roll _ by,

roll, _____ roll, _____ roll _ right _ by me. _____

But I know _ I won't _ cry _____ 'cause there is some - bod - y, some - bod - y,

Los - in' track of the nights __ I spend __ heart - bro -

ken. _____

Oh, but to - night I __ know _____ I won't

cry no __ more. _____

I lie a - wake.

I left the porch __ light on;

I hope it helps you to find your way.

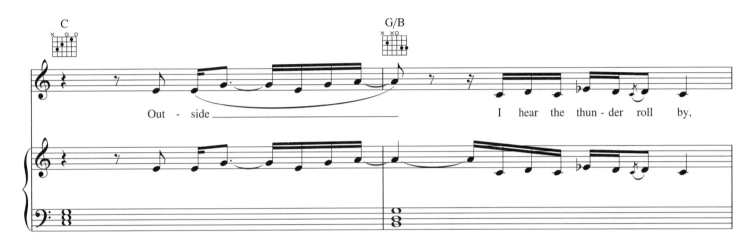

Out - side _____ I hear the thun - der roll by,

roll, _____ roll, _____ roll ___ right ___ by me. _____

cresc.

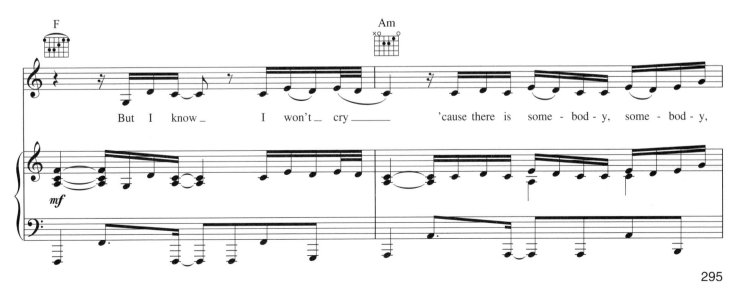

But I know ___ I won't ___ cry _____ 'cause there is some - bod - y, some - bod - y,

mf

The Space Between

Words and Music by David J. Matthews and Glen Ballard

The space be-tween _____ the tears we _____ cry _____

_____ is the laugh-ter keeps _____ us com-ing back _____ for more. _____

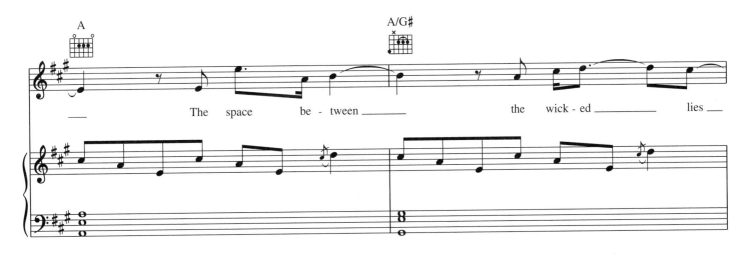

_____ The space be-tween _____ the wick-ed _____ lies _____

_____ we tell _____ and hope _____ to keep us safe from the pain. _____

But will I hold you a - gain?

These fick - le, fud - dled words con - fuse me,

like, will it rain to - day?

We waste the hours with talk - ing, talk - ing,

these twist - ed _____ games we're play - ing. _____

_____ We're _____ strange al - lies with war - ring hearts. _

_ What a wild - eyed _____ beast you _ be. _____

_ The space be - tween _____ the _____ wick - ed lies _____

we tell_____ and hope_____ to keep us safe from the pain._____

But will I hold you a-gain?_____

will I hold..._____

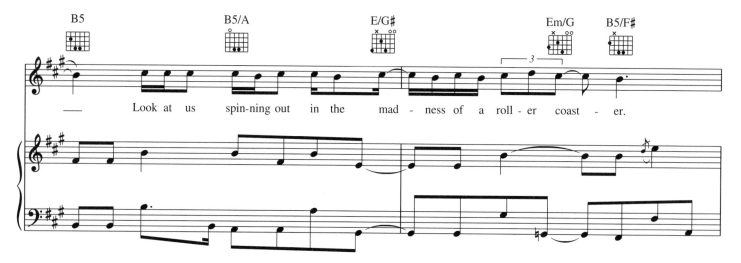

Look at us spin-ning out in the mad-ness of a roll-er coast-er.

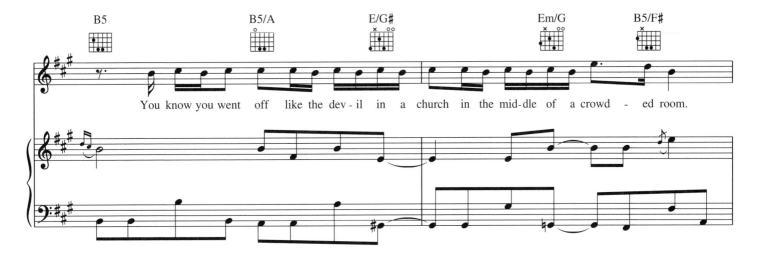

You know you went off like the dev-il in a church in the mid-dle of a crowd - ed room.

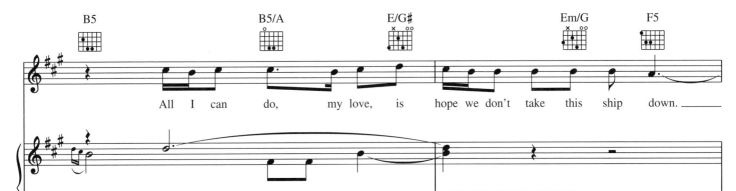

All I can do, my love, is hope we don't take this ship down.

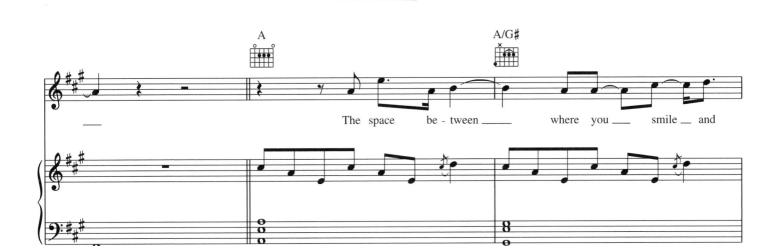

The space be - tween ___ where you ___ smile ___ and

hide ___ is where you'll find ___ me if I ___ get to go. ___

1. The space be-tween _____ the bul-lets in our fire-
2.-5. *See additional lyrics*

fight is where I'll be hid-ing, wait-ing for you.

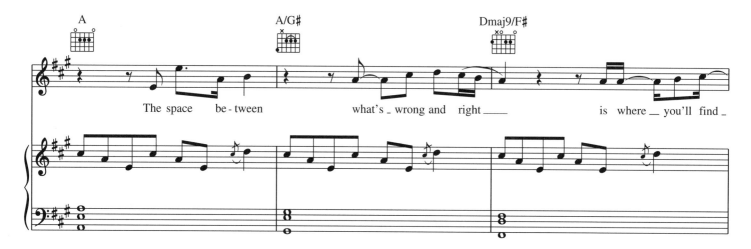

The space be-tween what's _ wrong and right _____ is where _ you'll find _

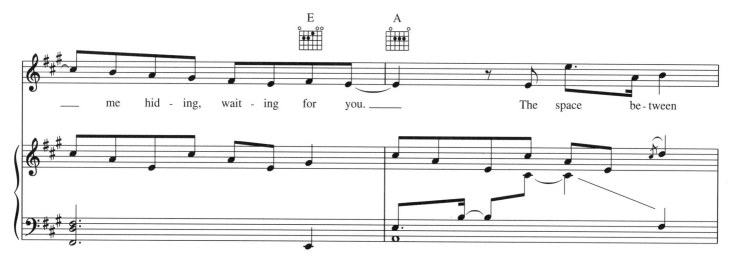

_____ me hid-ing, wait-ing for you. _____ The space be-tween

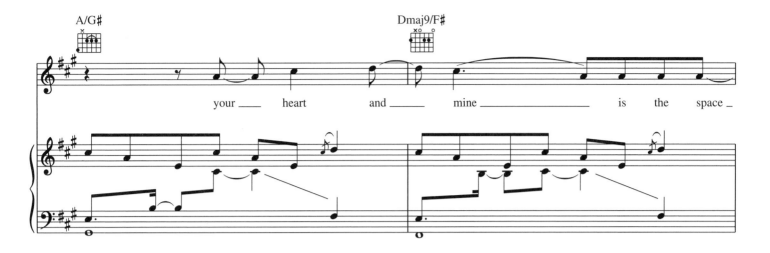

your ___ heart and ___ mine _____ is the space _

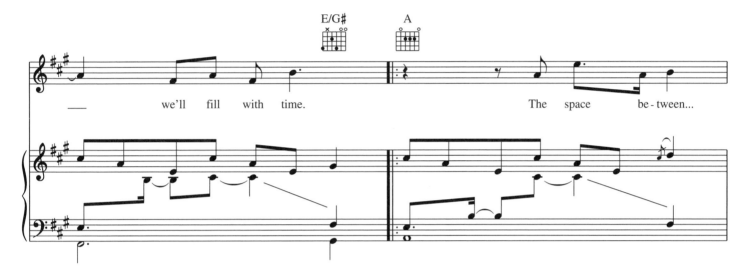

___ we'll fill with time. The space be‑tween...

Repeat and fade

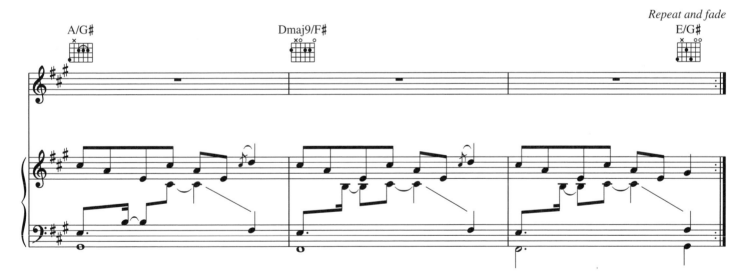

Additional Lyrics

2. The rain that falls splashed in your heart,
    Ran like sadness down the window into your room.

3. The space between our wicked lies is where
    We hope to keep safe from pain.

4. Take my hand 'cause
    We're walking out of here.

5. Oh, right out of here.
    Love is all we need, dear.

Stacy's Mom

Words and Music by
Chris Collingwood and Adam Schlesinger

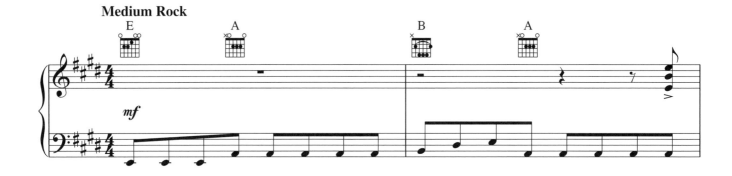

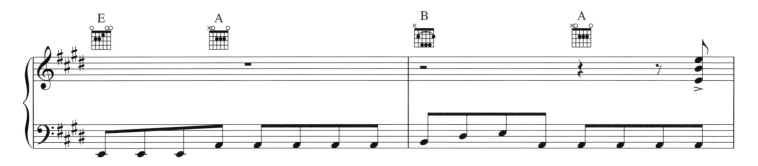

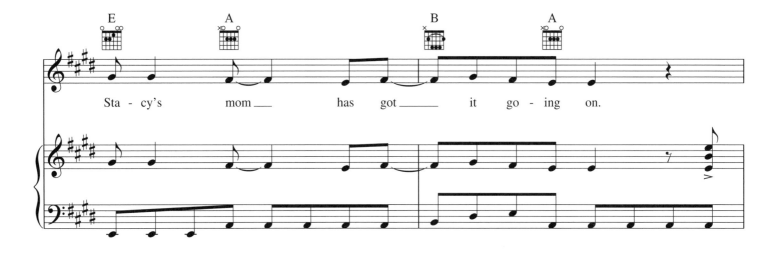

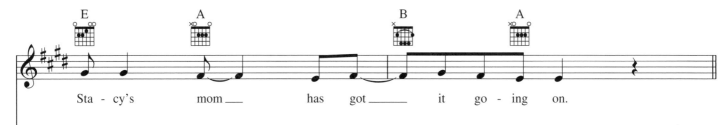

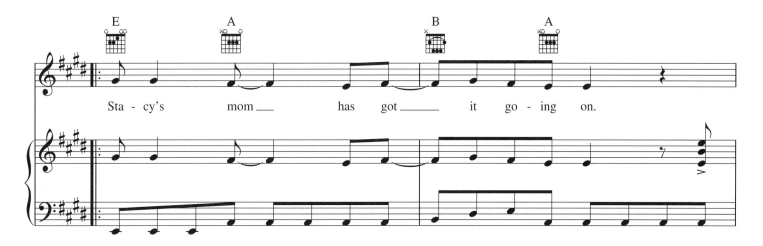

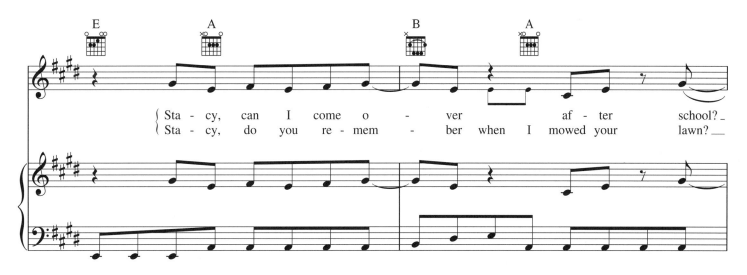

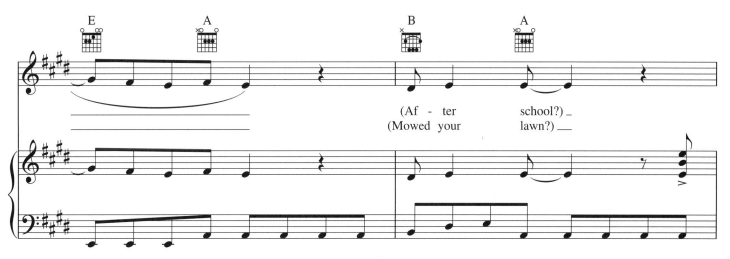

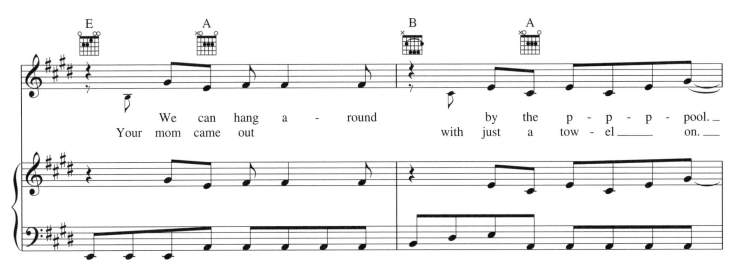

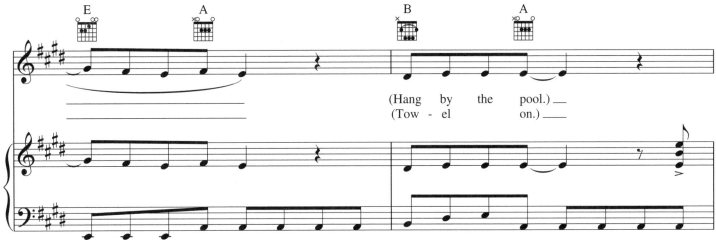

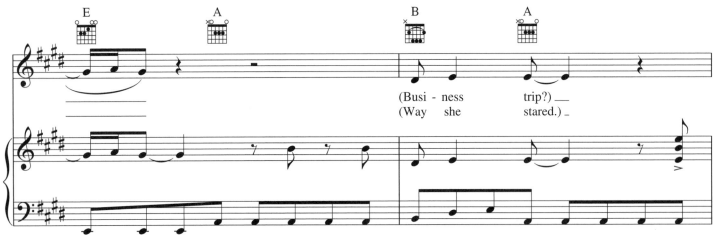

308

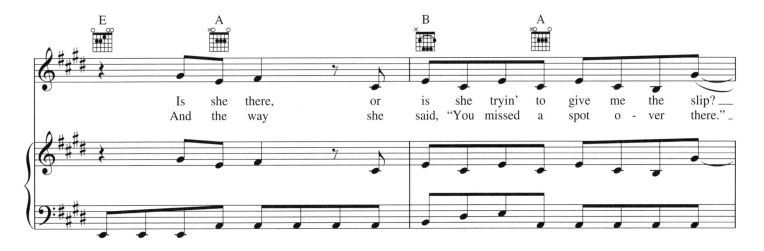

Is she there, or is she tryin' to give me the slip? __
And the way she said, "You missed a spot o - ver there." __

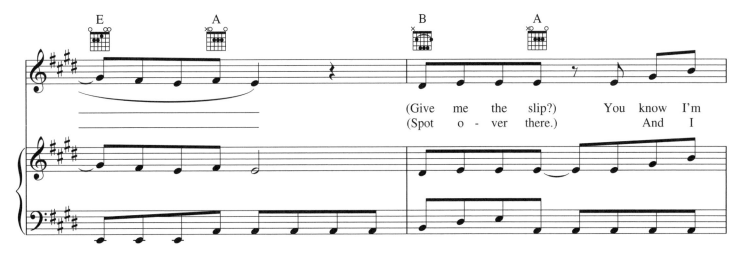

(Give me the slip?) You know I'm
(Spot o - ver there.) And I

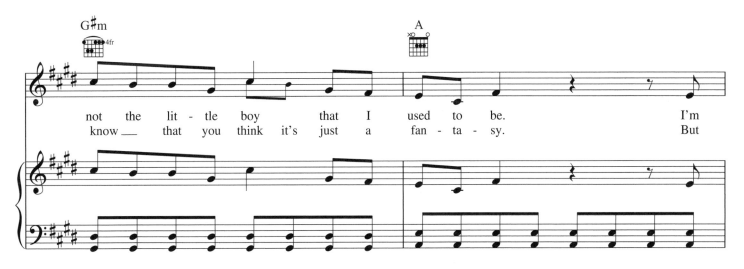

not the lit - tle boy that I used to be. I'm
know __ that you think it's just a fan - ta - sy. But

all __ grown __ up now, ba - by, can't you see?
since your dad walked out, your mom could use a guy like me.

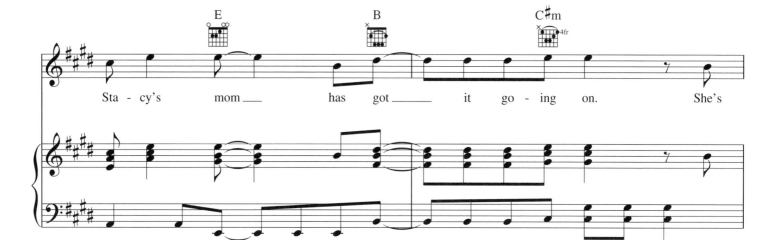

Sta - cy's mom ___ has got ___ it go - ing on. She's

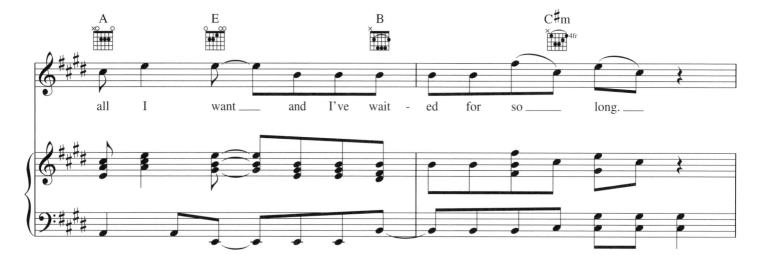

all I want ___ and I've wait - ed for so ___ long. ___

Sta - cy, can't you see you're just not the girl ___ for me? ___ I

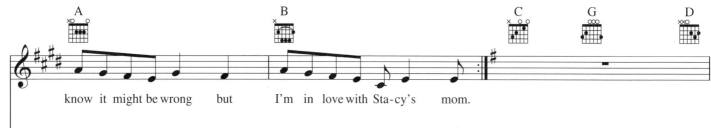

know it might be wrong but I'm in love with Sta - cy's mom.

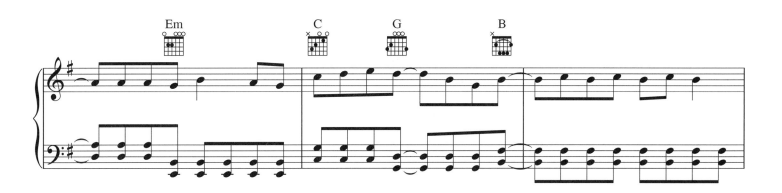

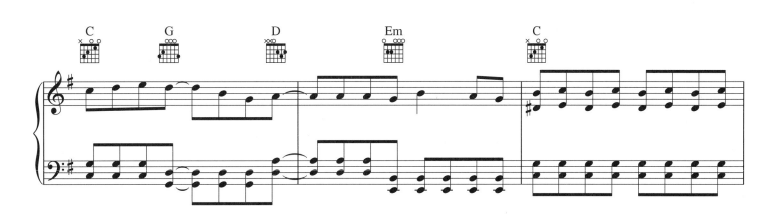

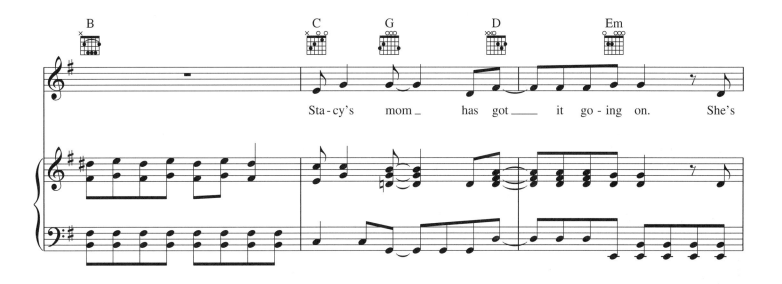

Sta-cy's mom ___ has got ___ it go - ing on. She's

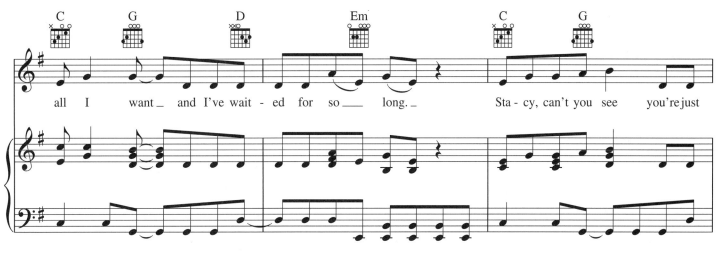

all I want ___ and I've wait - ed for so ___ long. ___ Sta - cy, can't you see you're just

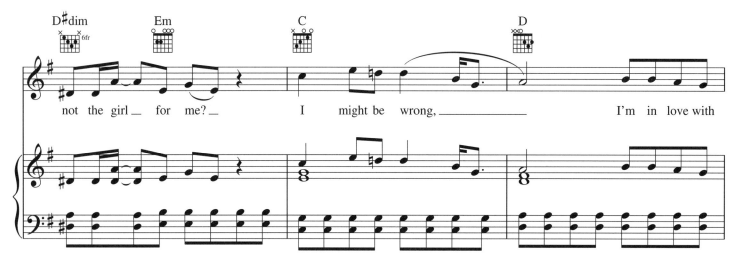

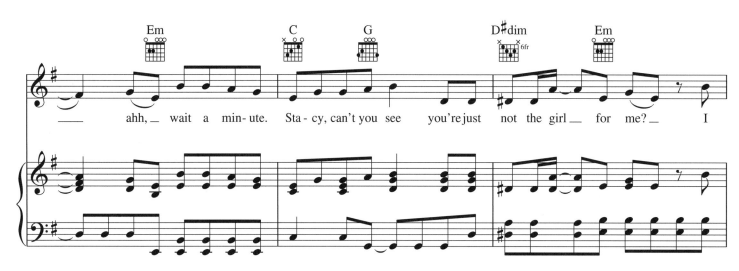

Suddenly I See

Words and Music by Katie Tunstall

Energetic Folk-Pop

Her face is a map of the world, __ is a map of the world. __
feel like walk in' the world, __ like walk in' the world. __

You can see she's a beau-ti-ful girl, __ she's a beau-ti-ful girl. __
You can hear she's a beau-ti-ful girl, __ she's a beau-ti-ful girl. __

And ev-'ry-thing a-round her is a sil-
She fills up ev-'ry cor-ner, like she's born

-ver pool of light.
in black and white.

Peo-ple who sur-round her feel the ben-
Makes you feel warm-er when you're try-

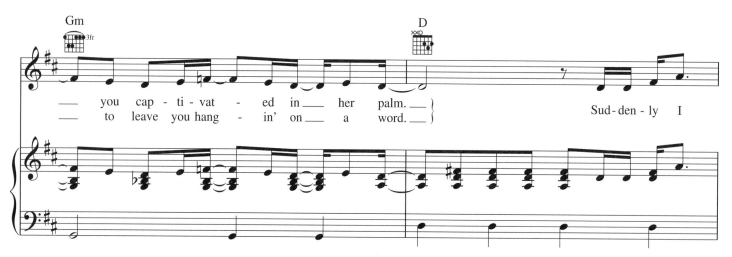

-e-fit of it, it makes you calm.
-in' to re-mem-ber what you heard.

She holds
She likes

you cap-ti-vat-ed in her palm.
to leave you hang-in' on a word.

Sud-den-ly I

314

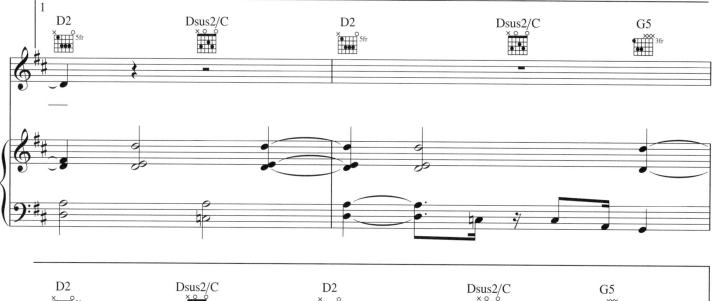

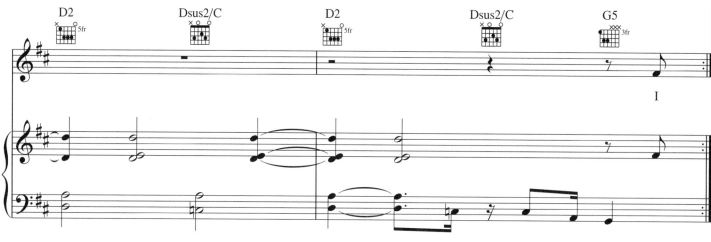

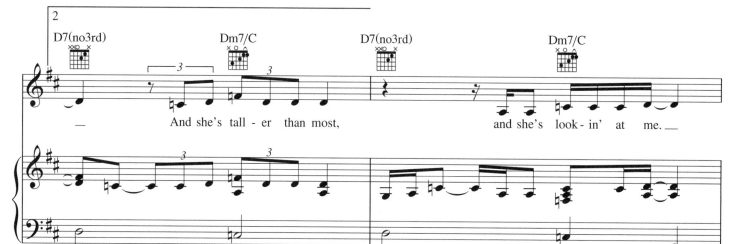

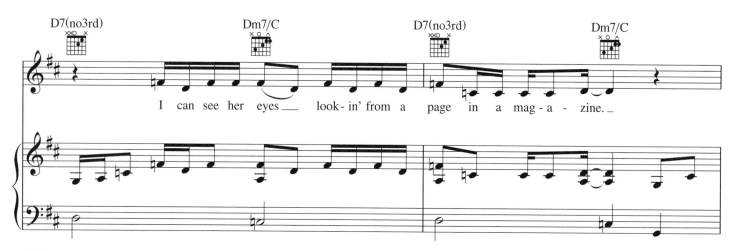

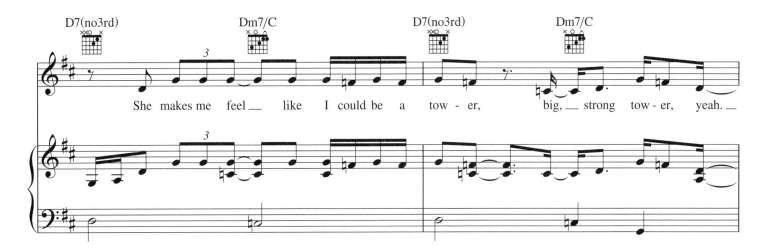

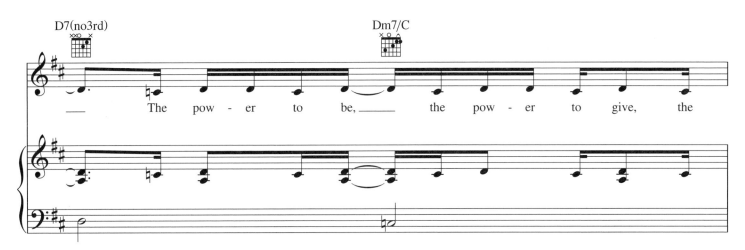

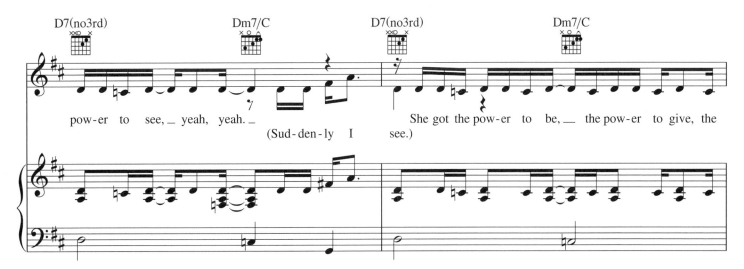

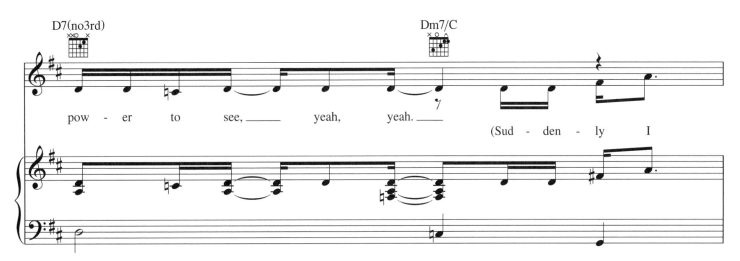

This Kiss

Words and Music by Annie Roboff,
Beth Nielsen Chapman and Robin Lerner

I don't want an-oth-er heart-break. I don't
Cin-der-el-la said to Snow White, "How does

need an-oth-er turn to cry, _____ no.
love get so off course?" _____ Oh.

I don't want to learn the hard way. Ba-by,
All I want-ed was a white knight with a

hel-lo, oh no, good-bye.
good heart, soft touch, fast horse.

But you got me like a rock-et shoot-ing
Ride me off in-to the sun-set, ba-by,

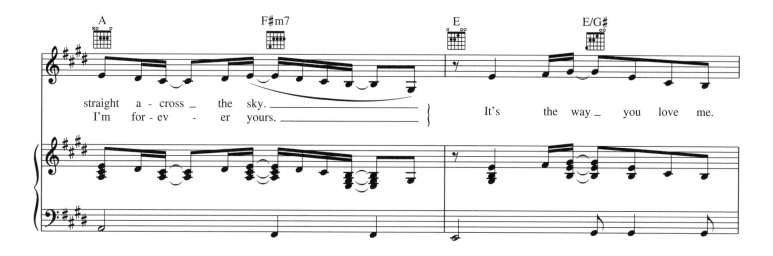

straight a - cross _ the sky. _____
I'm for - ev - er yours. _____

It's the way _ you love me.

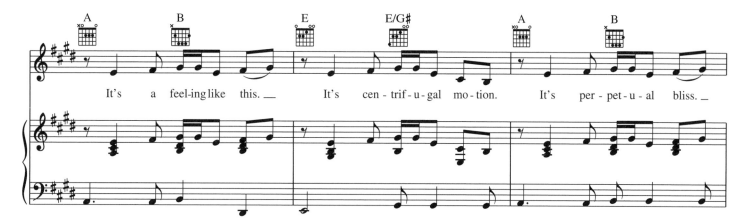

It's a feel-ing like this. __ It's cen - trif - u - gal mo - tion. It's per - pet - u - al bliss. __

It's that piv - ot - al mo - ment. It's ah, ____ { im - pos - si - ble. } { un - think - a - ble. } This kiss, __ this kiss, _

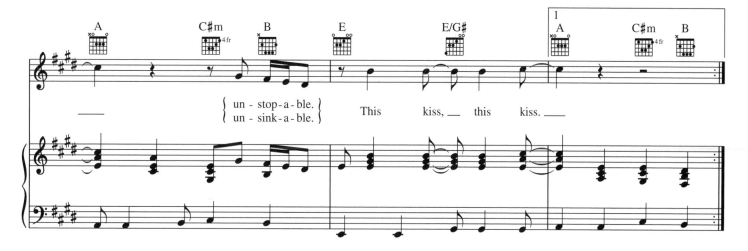

{ un - stop - a - ble. } { un - sink - a - ble. } This kiss, __ this kiss. __

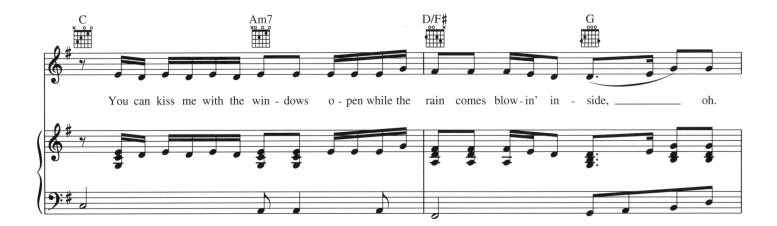

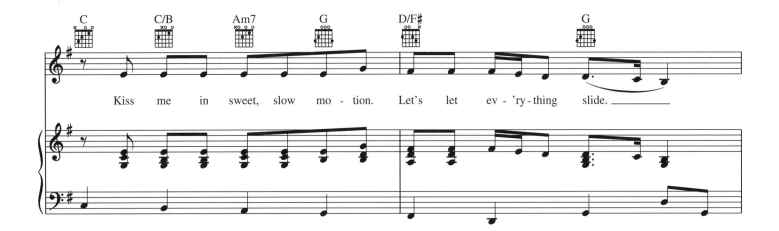

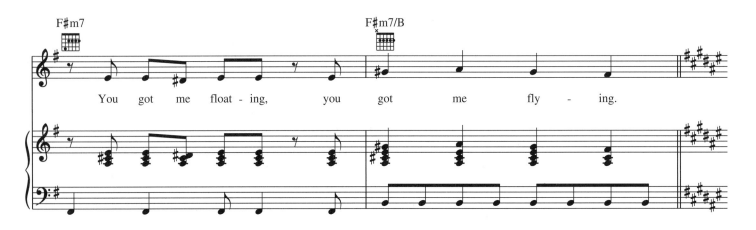

It's the way __ you love me. It's a feel-ing like this. __ It's cen-trif-u-gal mo-tion.

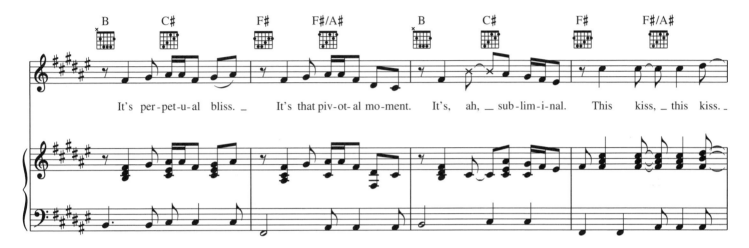

It's per-pet-u-al bliss. __ It's that piv-ot-al mo-ment. It's, ah, __ sub-lim-i-nal. This kiss, __ this kiss. __

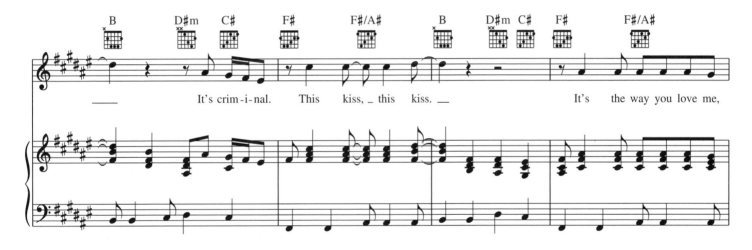

__ It's crim-i-nal. This kiss, __ this kiss. __ It's the way you love me,

Repeat and Fade | **Optional Ending**

ba - by. __ It's the way you love me, dar - ling. __

This Love

Words and Music by
Adam Levine and Jesse Carmichael

Moderately

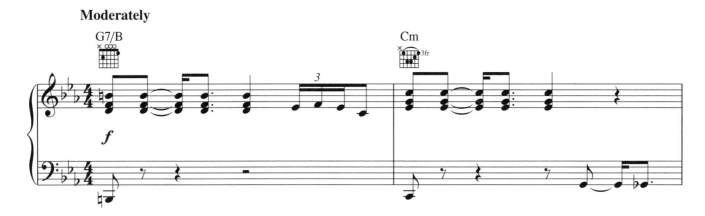

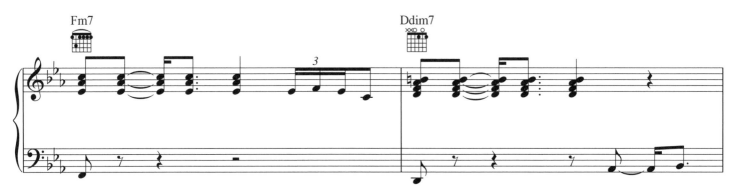

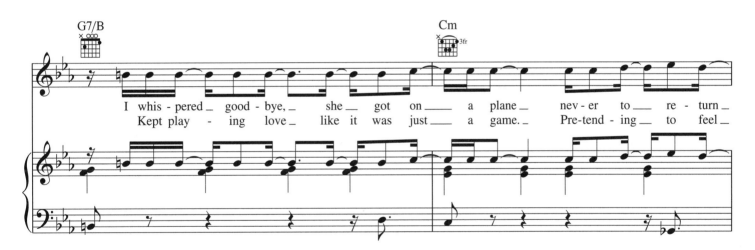

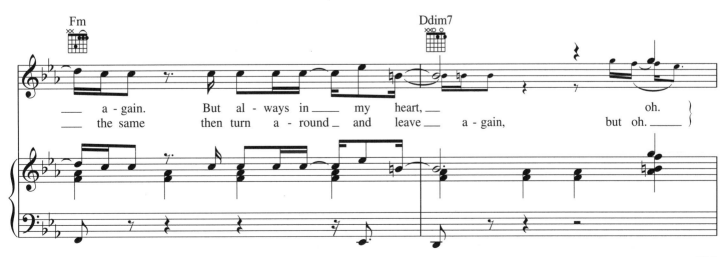

325

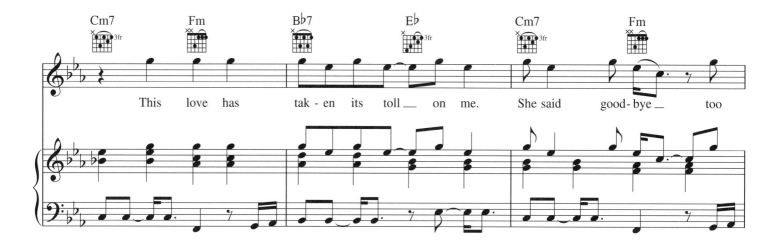

This love has tak-en its toll __ on me. She said good-bye __ too

man-y times be-fore. And her heart is break-ing in front __ of me. And

I have no choice __ 'cause I won't say good-bye an-y-more, __ whoa, __

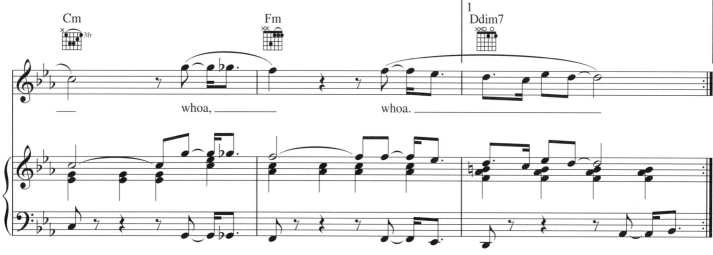

whoa, __ whoa. __

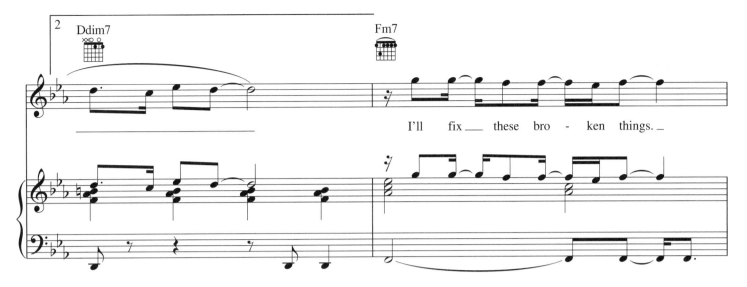

I'll fix __ these bro - ken things. __

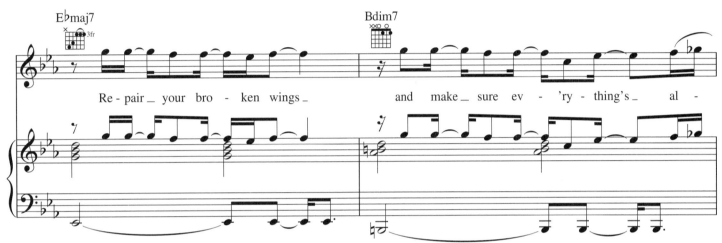

Re - pair __ your bro - ken wings __ and make __ sure ev - 'ry - thing's __ al -

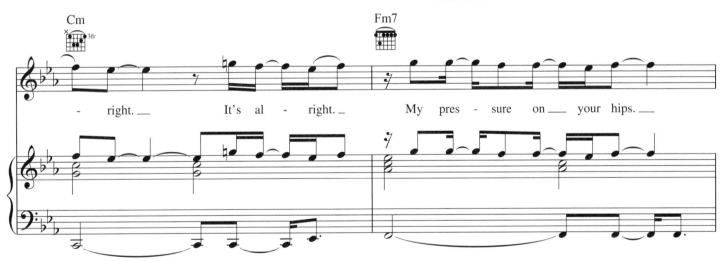

- right. __ It's al - right. __ My pres - sure on __ your hips. __

Sink - ing __ my fin - ger - tips to ev - 'ry inch __ of you __ be - cause I know __

that's what you want me to do. This love has

tak-en its toll on me. She said good-bye too

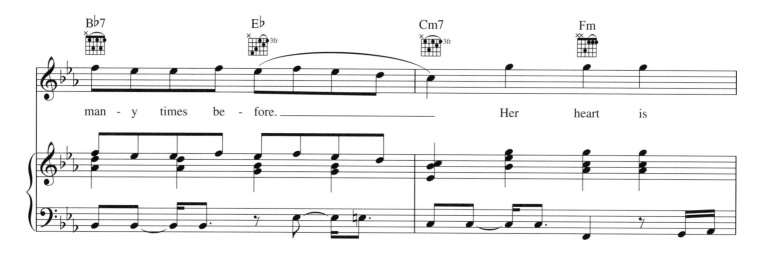

man-y times be-fore. Her heart is

break-ing in front of me. And I have no choice 'cause

328

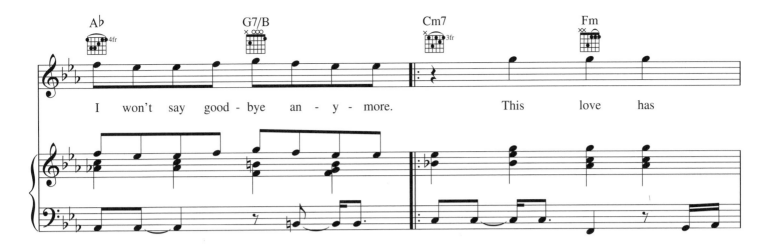

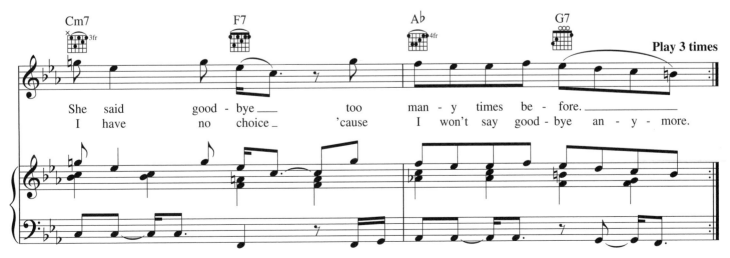

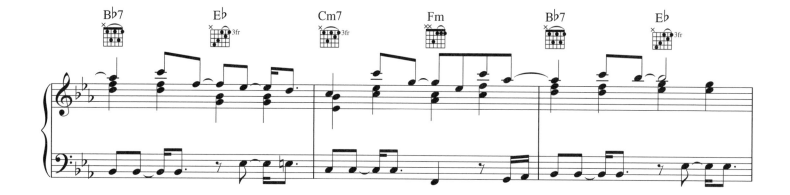

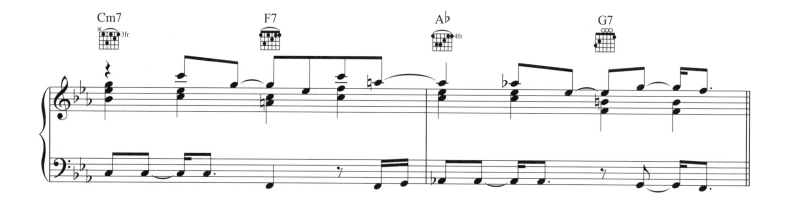

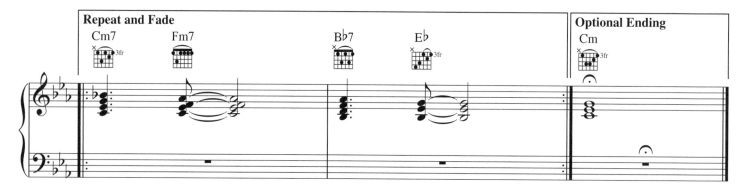

Times Like These

Words and Music by Foo Fighters

Driving Rock

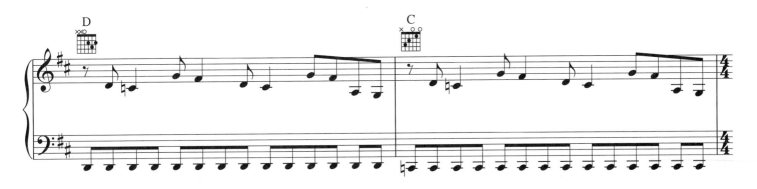

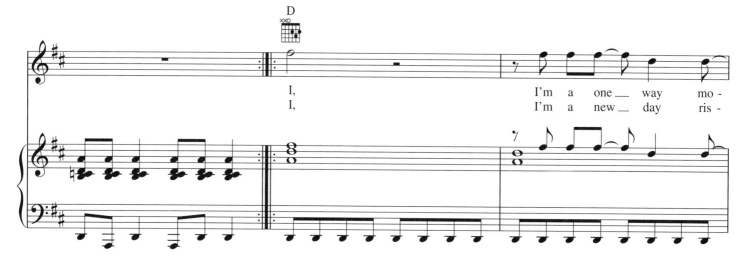

I,
I'm a one __ way mo -
I'm a new __ day ris -

- tor - way.
- ing.
I'm a road __ that drives __ a - way __ and fol -
I'm a brand __ new sky __ to hang __ the stars __

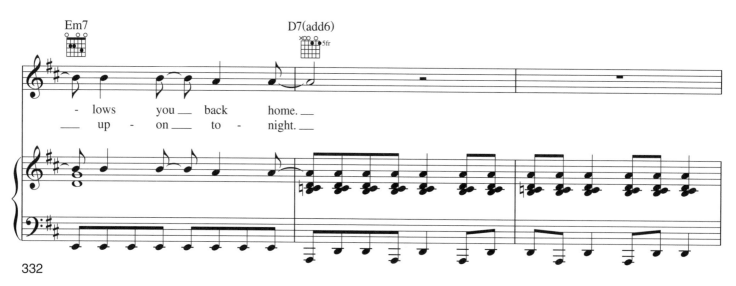

- lows you __ back home. __
__ up - on __ to - night. __

I, _____ I'm a street - light shin - ing.
I, _____ I'm a lit - tle di - vid - ed.

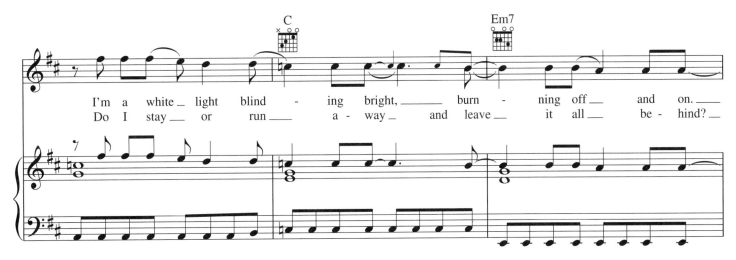

I'm a white _ light blind - ing bright, _____ burn - ning off _ and on. _____
Do I stay _ or run _ a - way _ and leave _ it all _ be - hind? _

Uh _ huh. _

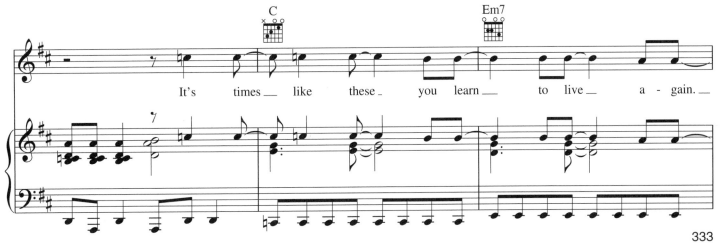

It's times _ like these _ you learn _ to live _ a - gain. _

It's times like these you give and give a - gain.

It's times like these you learn to love a - gain.

It's times like these time and time a - gain.

and time a - gain.

Umm,

woah,

Umm,

woah,

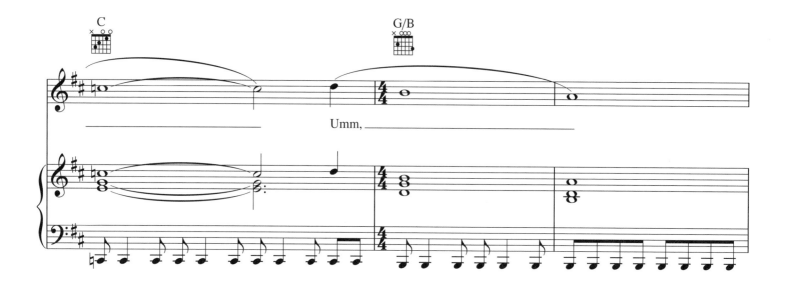

Umm, _____

Uh ___ huh, ___

Uh ___ huh

It's   times _

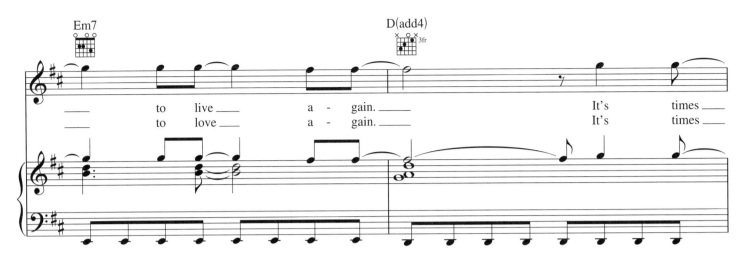

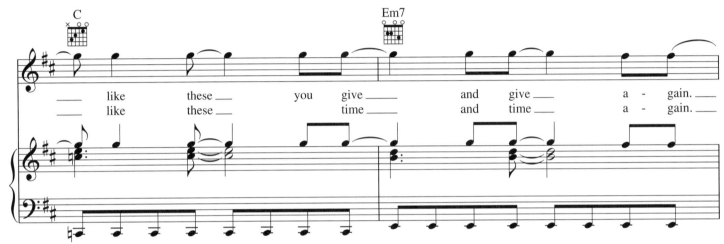

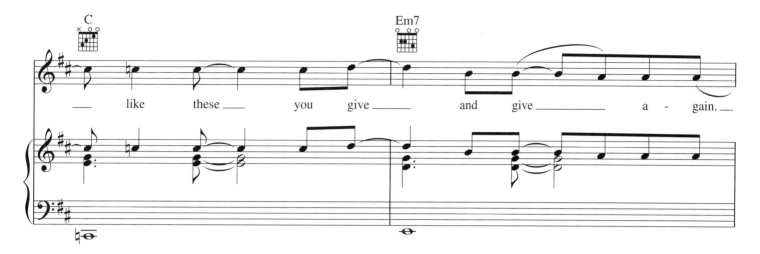

like these _____ you give _____ and give _____ a - gain. ____

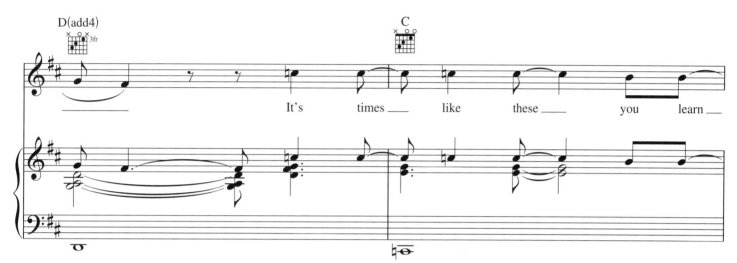

_____ It's times ____ like these _____ you learn ____

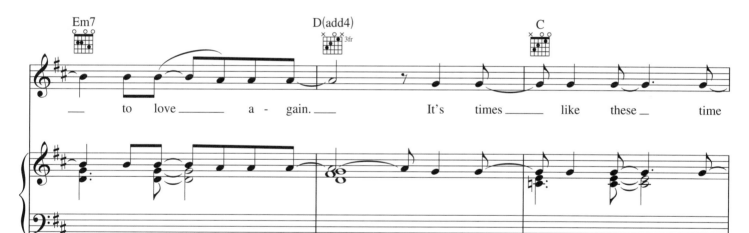

___ to love _____ a - gain. ____ It's times _____ like these ___ time

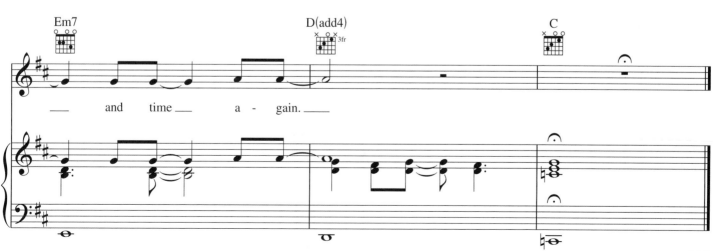

___ and time ____ a - gain. ____

Underneath Your Clothes

Words and Music by Shakira
Music co-written by Lester A. Mendez

Moderately slow

You're a song _ writ - ten by the hands of God. _
'Cause of you, _ I for - got the smart ways to lie. _

_ Don't get me wrong _ 'cause this might sound to you a bit odd. _ But you own the place _
_ Be-cause of you _ I'm run - ning out of rea-sons to cry. _ When the friends are gone, _

_ where all my thoughts go hid - ing. Right un - der your clothes _ is
when the par - ty's o - ver, we will still be - long _

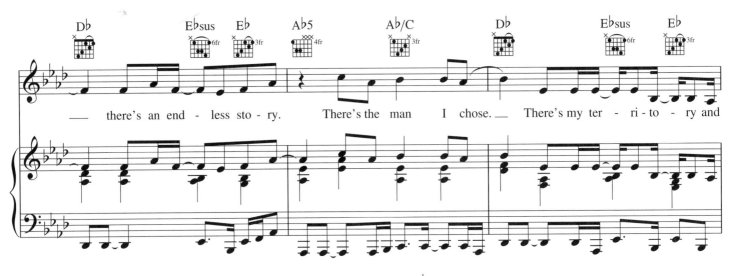

al - most don't be - lieve it.____ As ev - 'ry voice is hang - in' from the si - lence,____

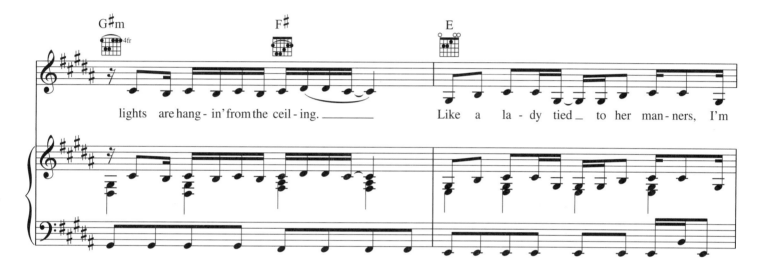

lights are hang - in' from the ceil - ing.____ Like a la - dy tied__ to her man - ners, I'm

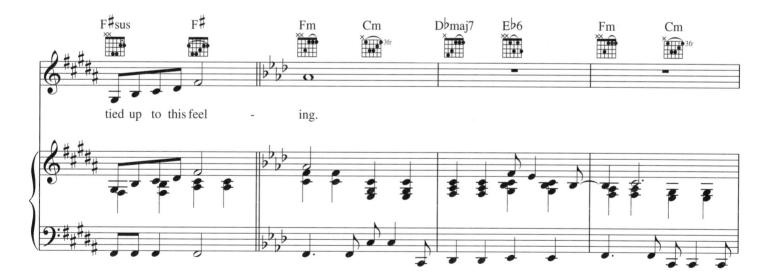

tied up to this feel - ing.

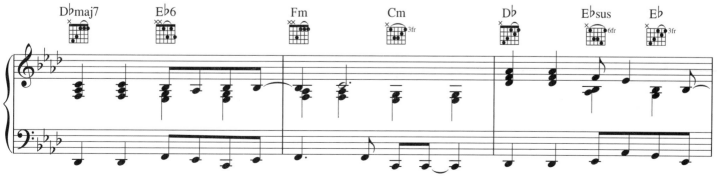

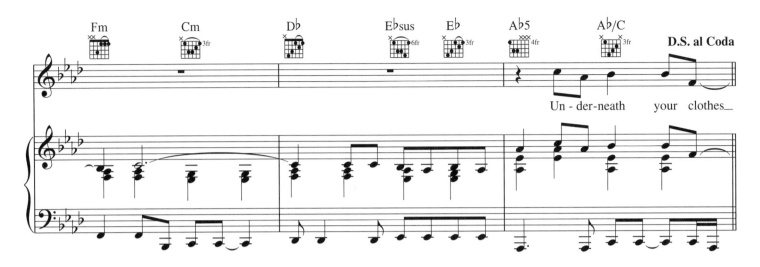

D.S. al Coda

Un - der - neath your clothes__

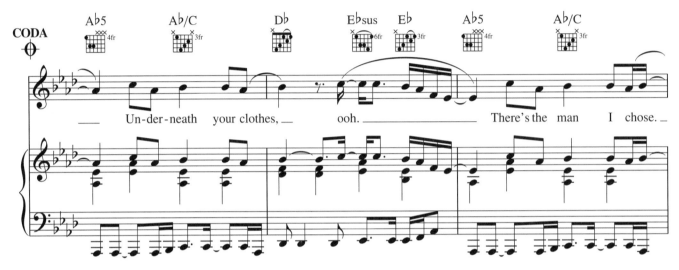

CODA

__ Un - der - neath your clothes, __ ooh. _____ There's the man I chose. __

There's my ter - ri - to - ry and all the things __ I de - serve _____ for

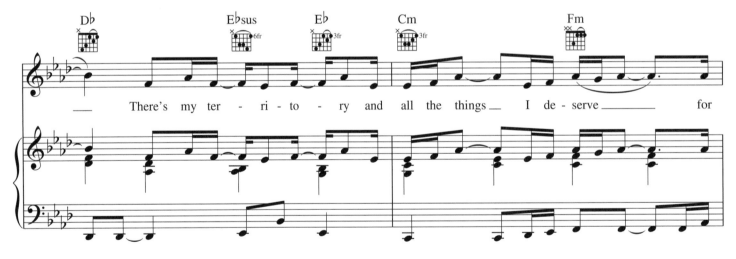

be - ing such a good __ girl, __ for be - ing such a good __ girl. _____

344

Used To Love U

Words and Music by
John Stephens and Kanye West

love — you.
I — don't love — you. Oh, I used — to love — you.
Oh,

I — loved you. — And you gon-na miss me now, —
I — don't love — you.)

— yeah. — Ba-by, when I used to love — you, — there's

noth-in' that I would-n't do. _____ I went through the fi - re for ___ you, but I'm

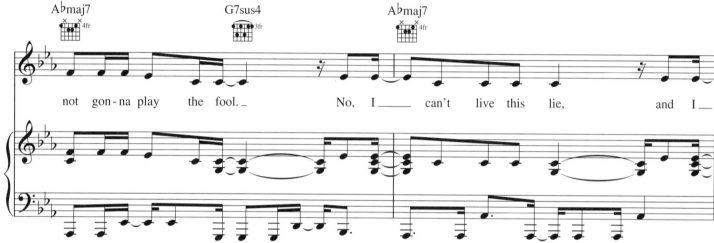

not gon-na play the fool. _ No, I _____ can't live this lie, and I _____

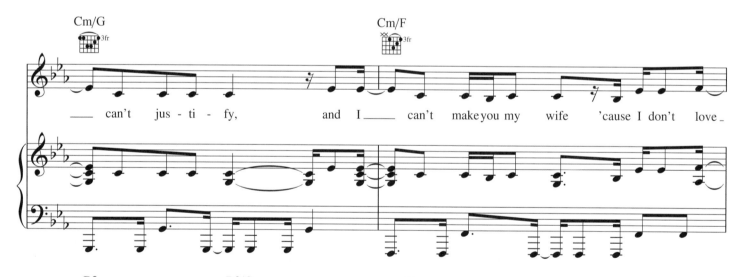

___ can't jus-ti-fy, and I _____ can't make you my wife 'cause I don't love _

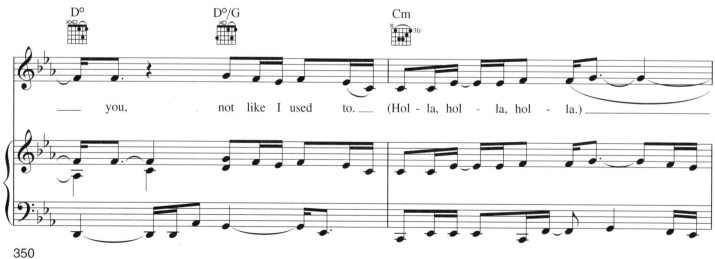

___ you, _ not like I used to. _ (Hol - la, hol - la, hol - la.) _____

Welcome To The Black Parade

Written by Gerard Way, Ray Toro,
Frank Iero, Bob Bryar and Mikey Way

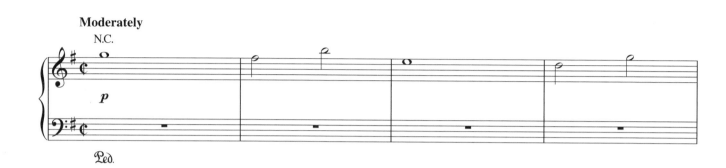

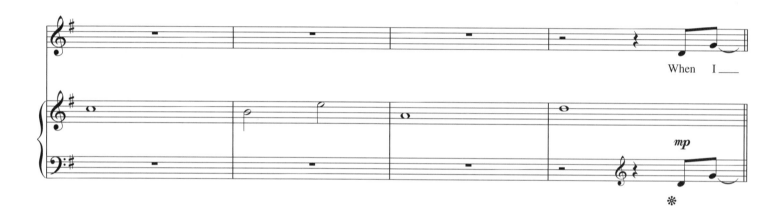

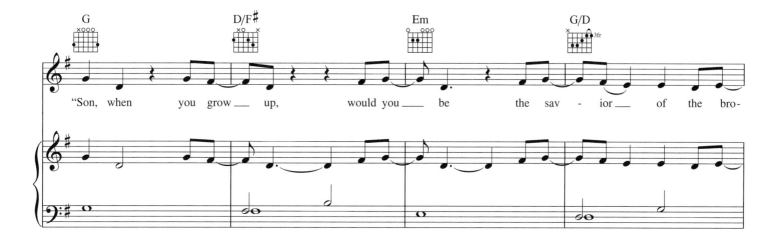

"Son, when you grow __ up, would you __ be the sav - ior __ of the bro-

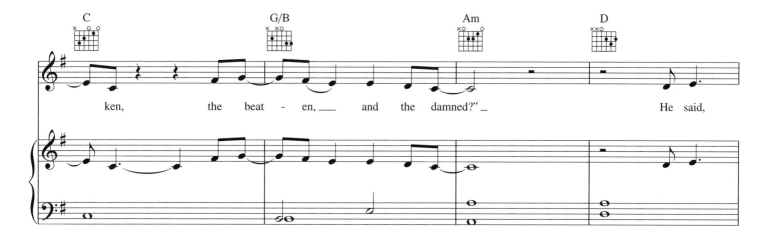

ken, the beat - en, __ and the damned?" _ He said,

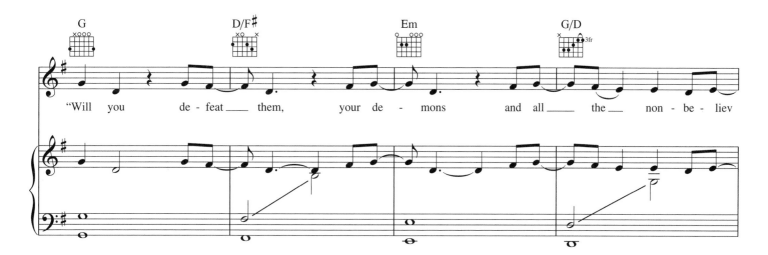

"Will you de - feat __ them, your de - mons and all __ the __ non - be - liev

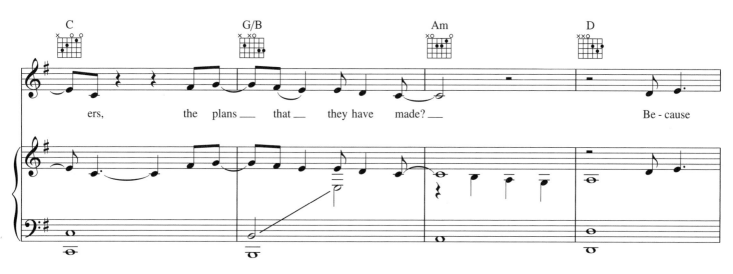

ers, the plans __ that __ they have made? __ Be - cause

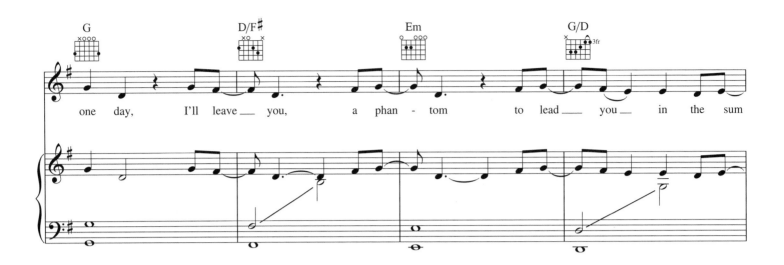

one day, I'll leave ___ you, a phan - tom to lead ___ you __ in the sum

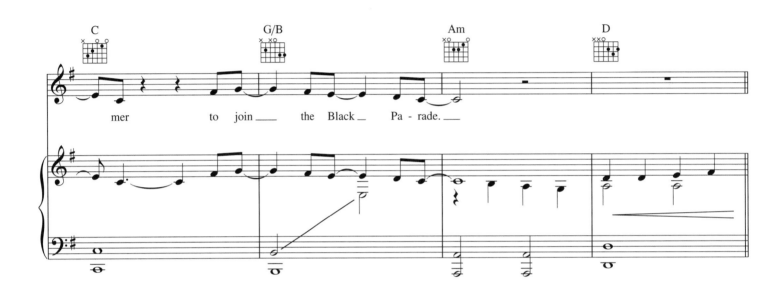

mer to join ___ the Black __ Pa - rade. ___

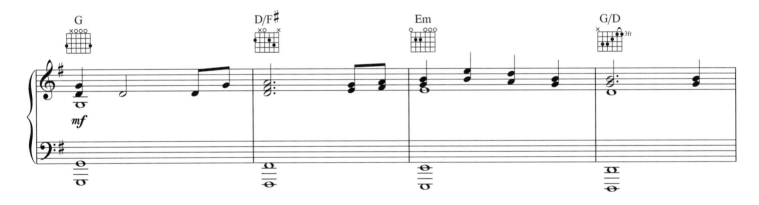

When I

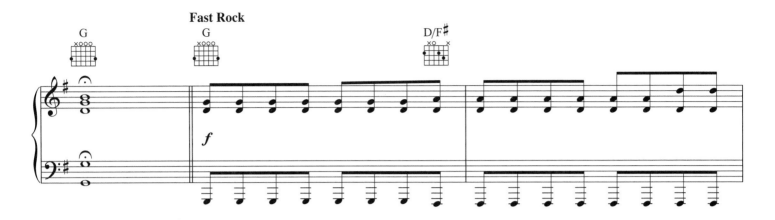

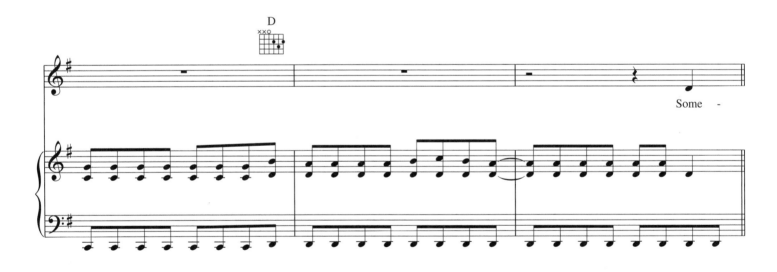

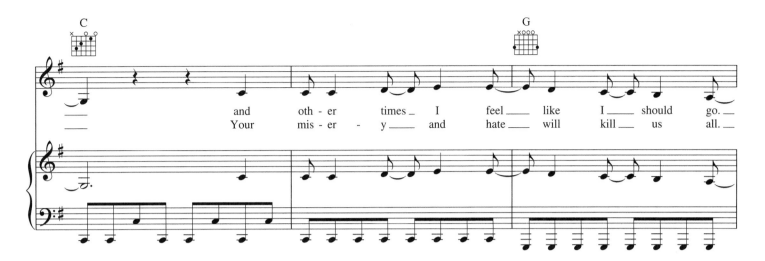

and oth - er times I feel like I should go.
Your mis - er - y and hate will kill us all.

And through it all, the rise
So paint it black and take

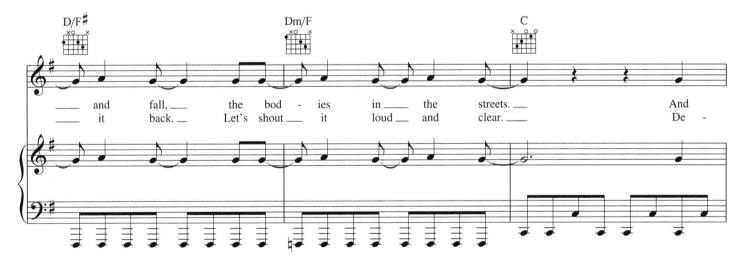

and fall, the bod - ies in the streets. And
it back. Let's shout it loud and clear. De -

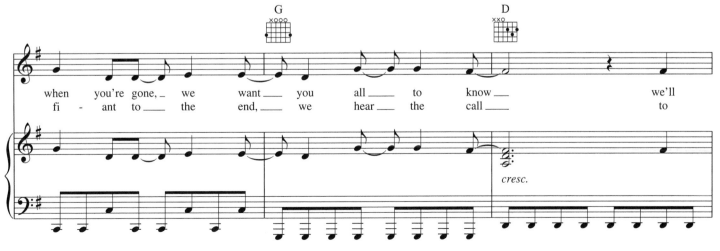

when you're gone, we want you all to know we'll
fi - ant to the end, we hear the call to

cresc.

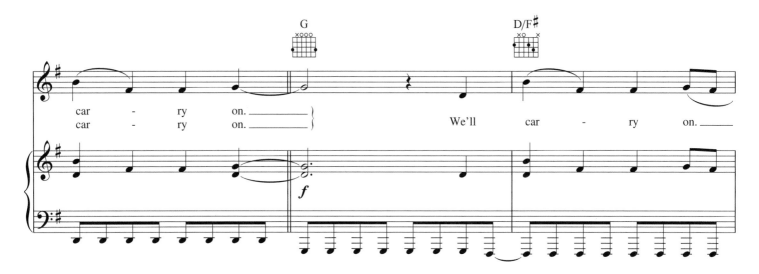

car - ry on. _____ }   We'll car - ry on. _____

_____ And though _____ you're dead and gone, __ be - lieve _

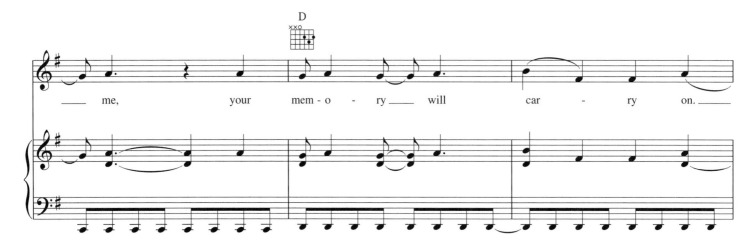

_____ me,   your mem - o - ry ____ will car - ry on. _____

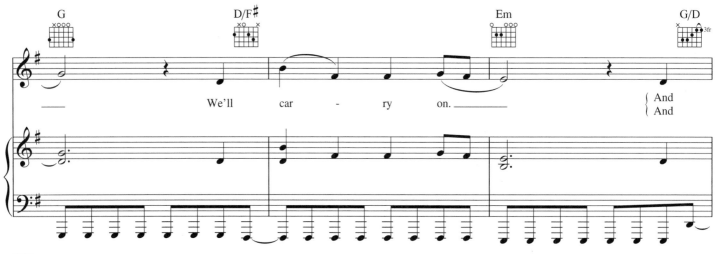

_____ We'll car - ry on. _____   { And
  { And

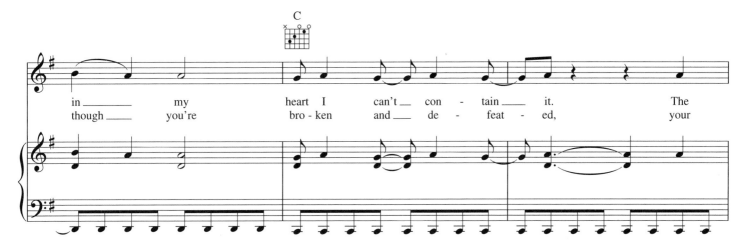

in _____ my heart I can't __ con - tain __ it. The
though ___ you're bro - ken and __ de - feat - ed, your

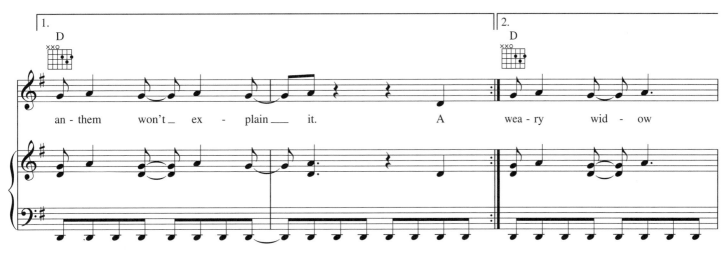

1.
an - them won't _ ex - plain __ it. A

2.
wea - ry wid - ow

march - es. On and on, ___ we car - ry through _ the fears. __

__ Oh. _____ Dis - ap - point - ed fac -

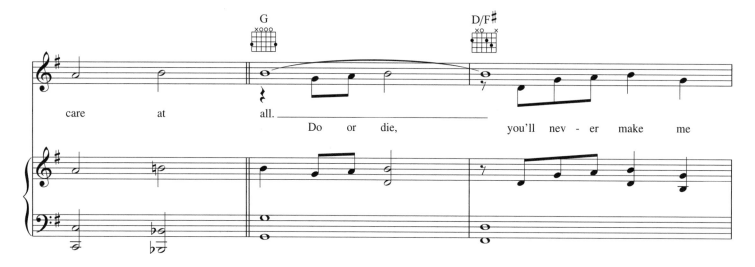

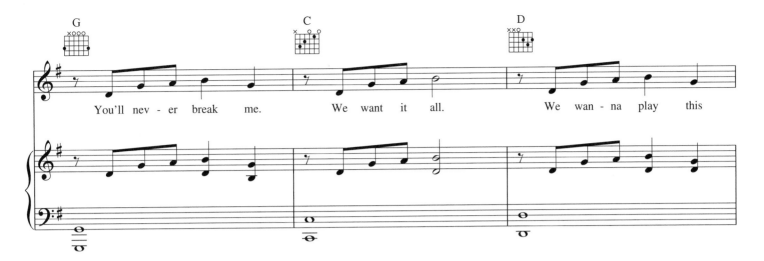

You'll nev-er break me. We want it all. We wan-na play this

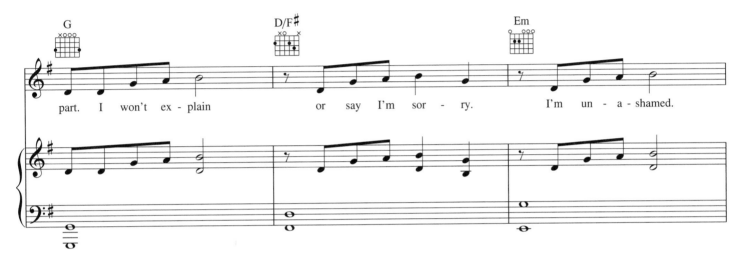

part. I won't ex-plain or say I'm sor-ry. I'm un-a-shamed.

I'm gon-na show my scar. Give a cheer for all the bro-ken.

Lis-ten here, be-cause it's who we are. I'm just a man,

dead and gone, be - lieve me, your mem - o - ry will

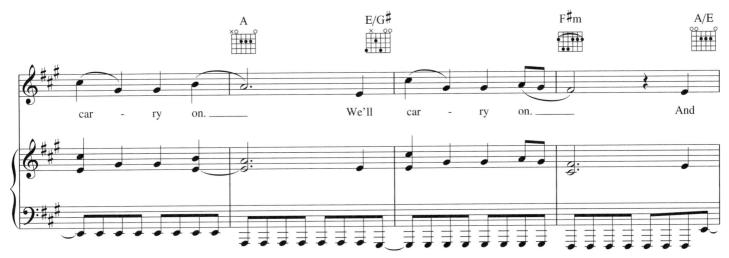

car - ry on. We'll car - ry on. And

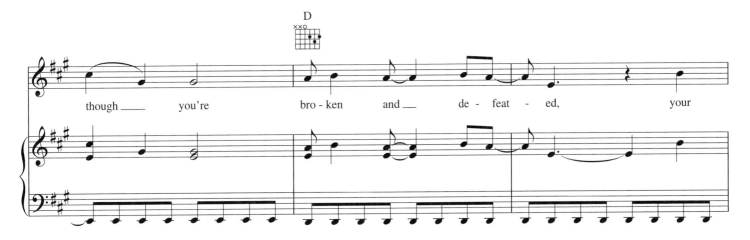

though you're bro - ken and de - feat - ed, your

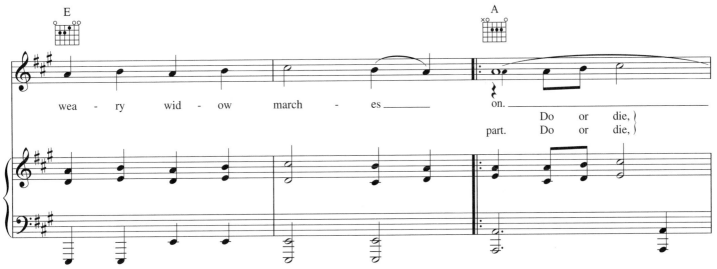

wea - ry wid - ow march - es on.
part. Do or die,
Do or die,

you'll nev - er make me   be - cause the world   will nev - er take my

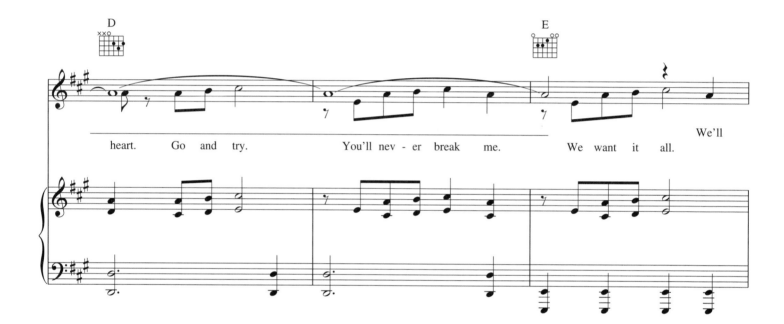

heart.   Go and try.   You'll nev - er break me.   We want it all.   We'll

car - ry _____   car - ry _____   on. _____
We wan - na play this   We wan - na play this   part.

Where Is The Love

Words and Music by Will Adams, Allan Pineda,
Jaime Gomez, Justin Timberlake, Michael Fratantuno,
George Pajon Jr., Printz Board and J. Curtis

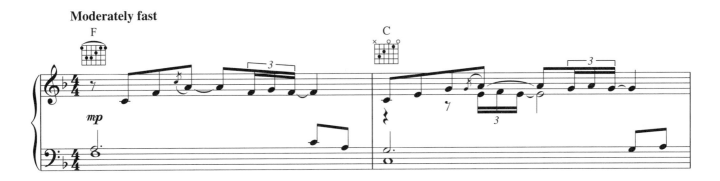

What's wrong with the world, ma-ma? Peo-ple liv-in' like they

ain't got no ma-ma. I think the whole world's ad-dict-ed to the dra-ma, on-ly at-tract-ed to

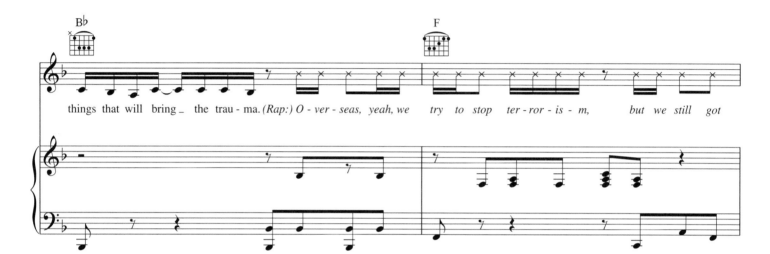

things that will bring _ the trau-ma. *(Rap:) O - ver - seas, yeah, we* try *to stop ter - ror - is - m,* *but we still got*

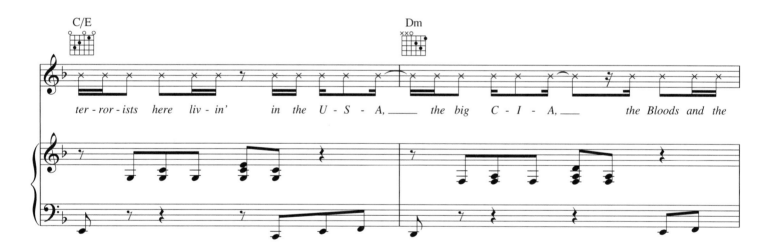

ter - ror - ists here liv - in' in the U - S - A, ___ the big C - I - A, ___ the Bloods and the

Crips and the K - K - K. ___ But if you on - ly have love for your own race, _ then you on - ly leave

space to dis-crim-i-nate, and to dis-crim-i-nate on-ly gen-er-ates hate. And when you hate, then you're

bound to get i-rate, yeah. The bad-ness is what you dem-on-strate. And that's ex-act-ly how

an-ger works and op-er-ates. Man, you got-ta have love just to set it straight. Take con-trol of your mind __

__ and med-i-tate. Let your soul grav-i-tate to the love, y'all. *(Sung:)* Peo-ple kill-in', peo-ple dy-

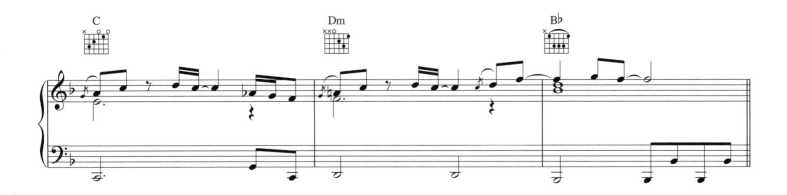

*loco

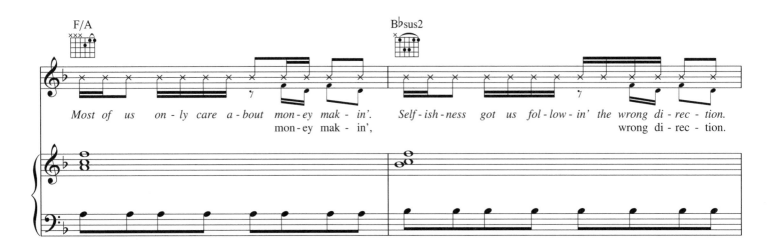

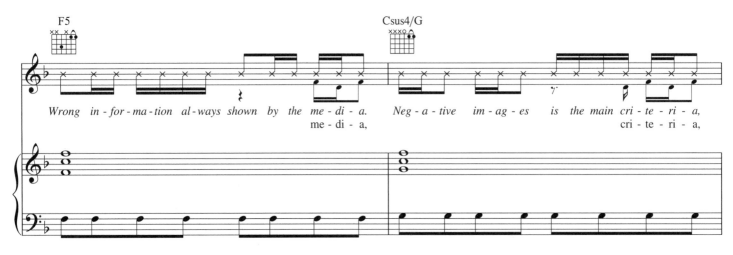

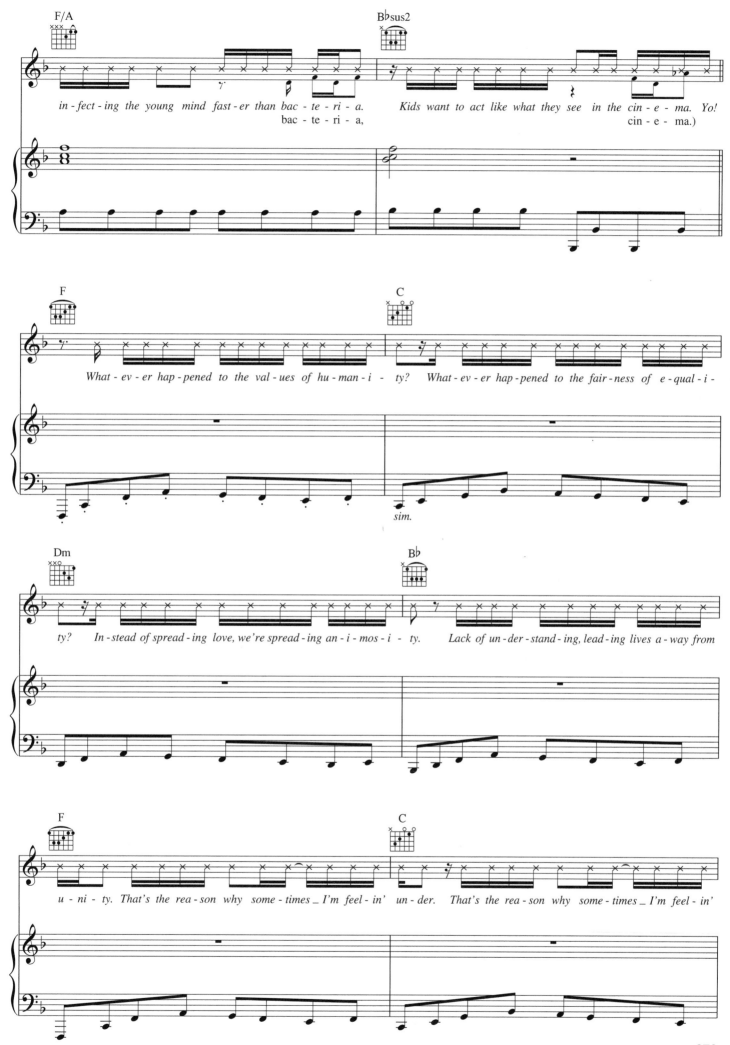

down. There's no won-der why some-times __ I'm feel-in' un-der. Got-ta keep my faith a - live __ till love is

found, and ask your-self.*(Where is the love? _____ Where is the love? __ Where is the love? __

*Sung an octave lower.

__ Where is the love? __ *Fa-ther, Fa-ther, Fa-ther help __ us; send some guid-ance from __ a - bove, __

*loco

__ 'cause peo-ple got __ me, got __ me ques - tion-ing: _____ Where is the love? __

White Flag

Words and Music by Rick Nowels,
Rollo Armstrong and Dido Armstrong

I know you think that I should-n't still love you, I'll
I know I left too much mess and de-struc-tion to come

tell you that. _
back a-gain. _

But if I did-n't say it, well,
And I caused noth-ing but trou-ble; I

I'd still have felt it. Where's the sense _ in that? _____
un-der-stand if you can't talk to me _ a-gain.

I prom-ise I'm
And if you live by the rules ___

___ your life hard - er; I'll re - turn ___ to where ___ we were. ___
___ that it's o - ver, then I'm sure ___ that that ___ makes sense. ___

But ⎱ I will go down with ___ this ___
And ⎰

___ ship; and I won't put ___ my hands up ___ and sur - ren - der. There will be ___

no white flag a-bove ___ my ___ door; I'm in love, _

___ and al-ways ___ will be. ___ ___ will be. And when we _

meet, which I'm sure we will, all that was _ there _ will be there _

___ still. I'll let it ___ pass, _ and hold my ___ tongue, and you will _

think ___ that I've moved ___ on. _____

___ { I will go down with ___ this _____ ship; and I won't put ___

___ my hands up ___ and sur - ren - der. There will be ___

no white flag a - bove ___ my _____ door; I'm in love, ___ and al - ways _____

You'll Think Of Me

Words and Music by
Ty Lacy, Dennis Matkosky
and Darrell Brown

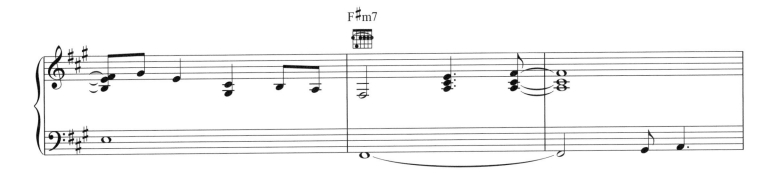

I woke up ear -
I went out driv -

keep - in' me ___ a - wake.
that seems ___ to still ex - ist.

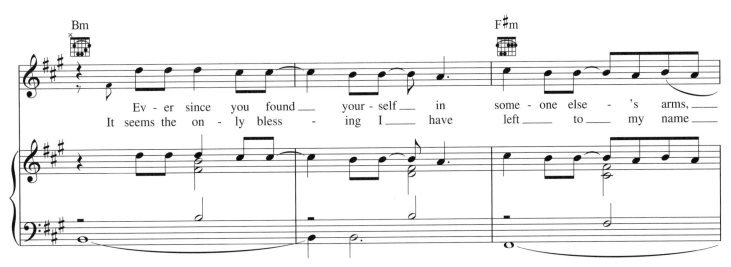

Ev - er since you found ___ your - self ___ in some - one else - 's arms, ___
It seems the on - ly bless - ing I ___ have left ___ to ___ my name ___

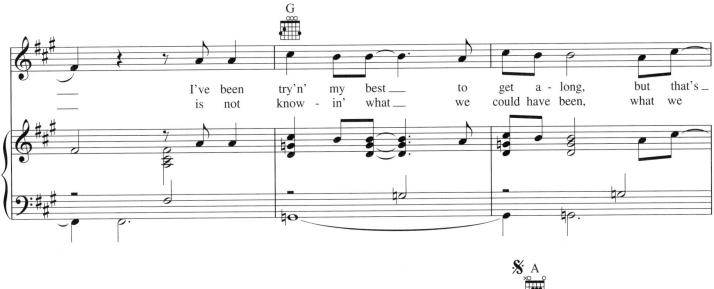

I've been try'n' my best ___ to get a - long, but that's ___
is not know - in' what ___ we could have been, what we

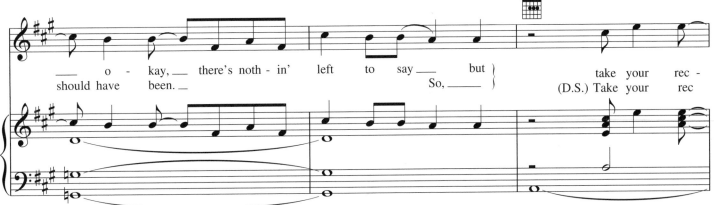

___ o - kay, there's noth - in' left to say ___ but
should have been. ___ So, ___ } take your rec -
(D.S.) Take your rec

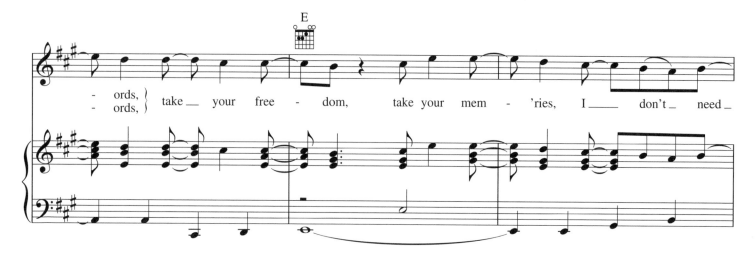

- ords, } take your free - dom, take your mem - 'ries, I don't need 'em.

'em. Take your space and take your rea - sons, but you'll

think of me. And take your cat and leave my

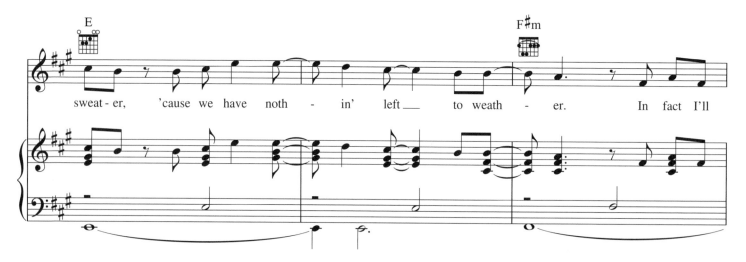

sweat - er, 'cause we have noth - in' left to weath - er. In fact I'll

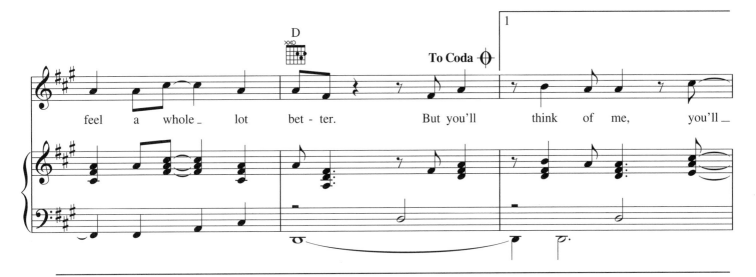

feel a whole ___ lot bet - ter. But you'll think of me, you'll ___

think ___ of me.

think of ___ me. ___

Some - day ___ I'm gon - na run a - cross ___ your mind, ___

but don't wor - ry, I'll ___ be fine. ___ I'm gon - na

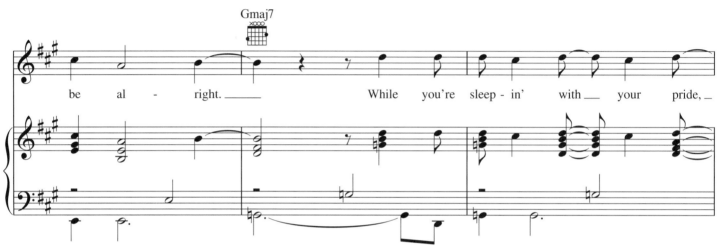

be al - right. ___ While you're sleep - in' with ___ your pride, ___

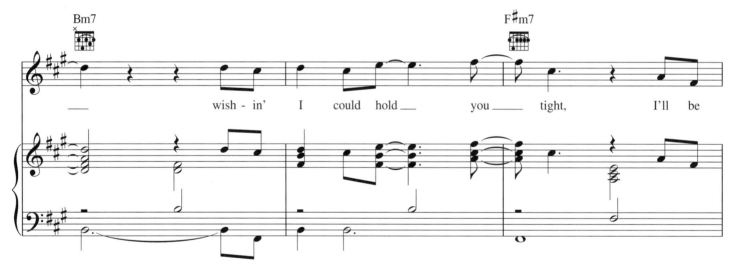

wish - in' I could hold ___ you ___ tight, I'll be

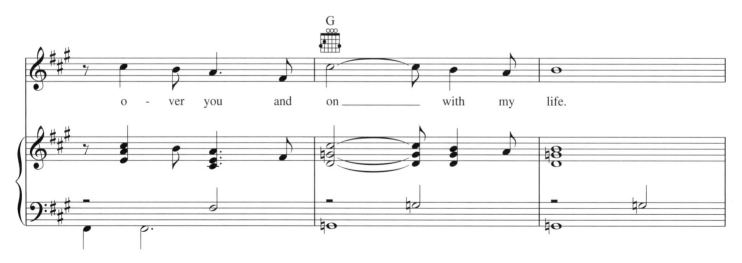

o - ver you and on ___ with my life.

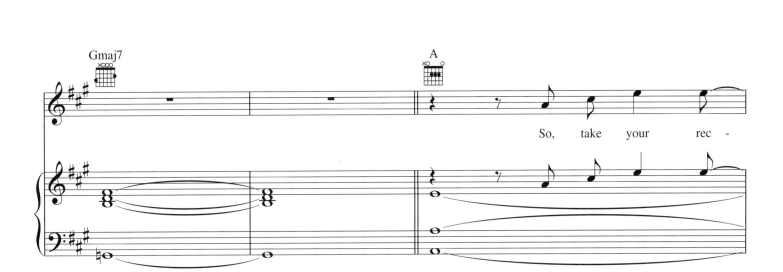

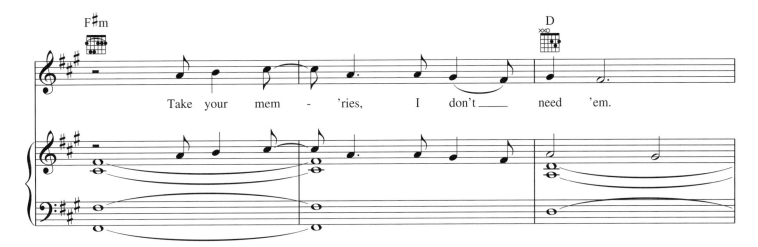

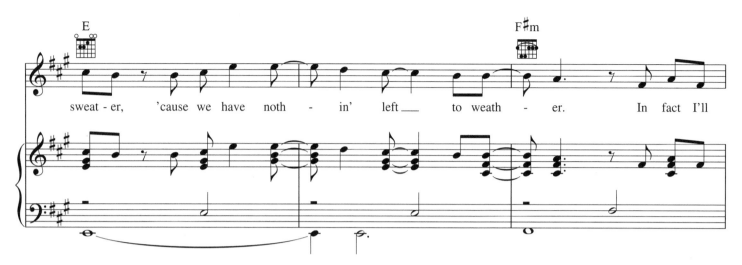

sweat- er, 'cause we have noth - in' left ___ to weath - er. In fact I'll

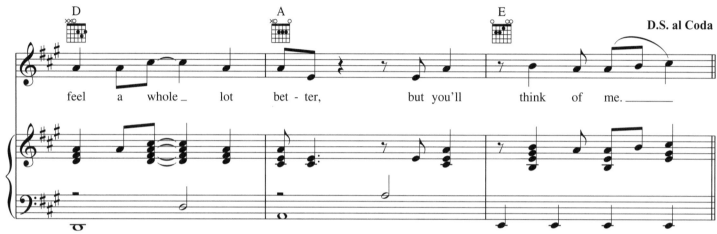

feel a whole ___ lot bet - ter, but you'll think of me. ___

D.S. al Coda

CODA

think of me, you'll _____ think ___ of me, _____

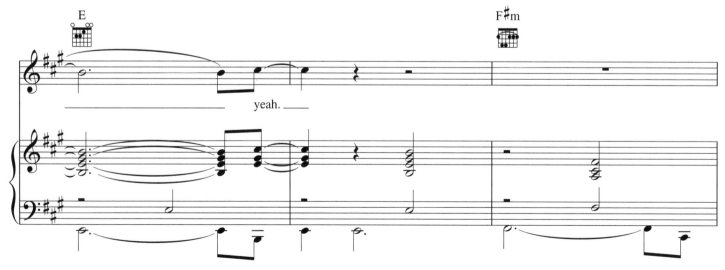

yeah. ___

And you're gon - na think__ of me.

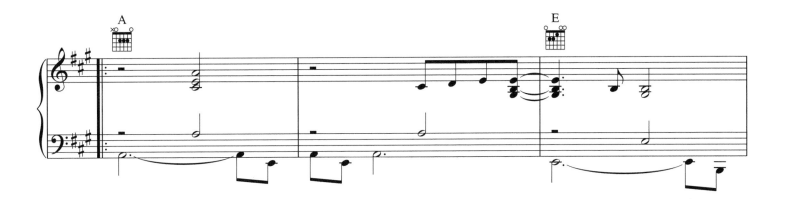

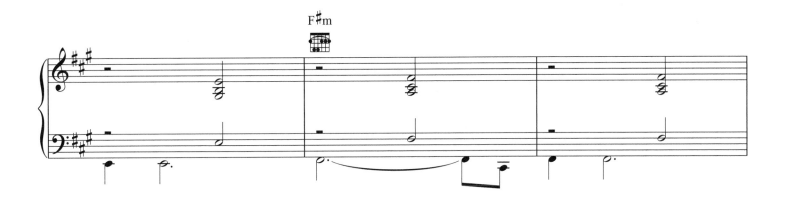

Your Body Is A Wonderland

Words and Music by John Mayer

Moderate Rock

We got ___ the af-ter-noon. ___ You got ___ this room ___
One mile ___ to ev- 'ry inch of your skin, ___ like por -

___ for two. ___ One thing ___ I've left to do: dis-
ce - lain. ___ One pair ___ of can - dy lips ___ and your

cov - er me ___ dis-cov - er - ing you. ___

Your bod-y is ___ a won-der. I'll ___ use ___ my ___ hands. ___

To Coda

___ Your bod-y is ___ a won-der-land. ___

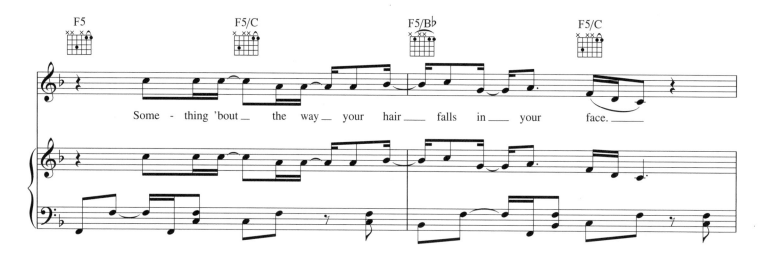

Some-thing 'bout ___ the way ___ your hair ___ falls in ___ your face. ___

I love ___ the shape ___ you take ___ when crawl-ing towards ___ the pil-low-case.

You tell ___ me where ___ to go, ___ and though I ___ might leave ___ to find ___ it, I'll

D.S. al Coda

nev - er let ___ your head ___ hit the bed _____ with - out ___ my hand ___ be - hind ___ it. You

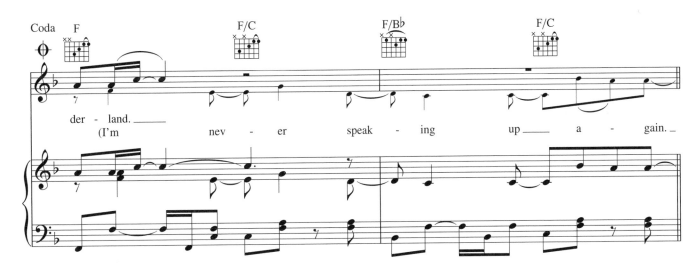

Coda

der - land. _____
(I'm nev - er speak - ing up ___ a - gain. ___

___ I'll ___ use ___ my ___ hands.) _____   Damn, ba - by. ___

393

You frus - trate __ me. __ I know you're mine, all _____ mine, all __

mine, _____ but you look __ so good, __ it hurts __ some - times.

Dm9

F5/D

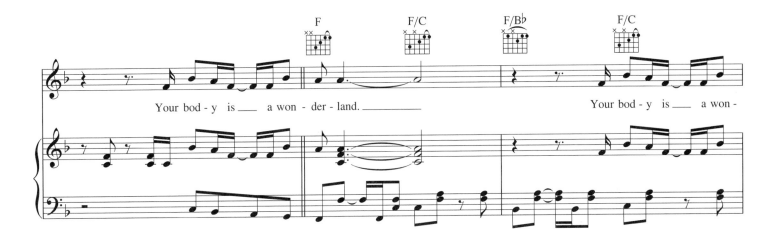

Your bod-y is ___ a won-der-land. ___ Your bod-y is ___ a won-

der. I'll ___ use ___ my ___ hands. ___ Your bod-y is ___ a won-

der - land. ___ Your bod-y is ___ a won-der-land. ___

Repeat and fade

Da da da, da da da da da, da da da, da da da ___ da.

You're Beautiful

Words and Music by James Blunt,
Sacha Skarbek and Amanda Ghost

Moderately slow

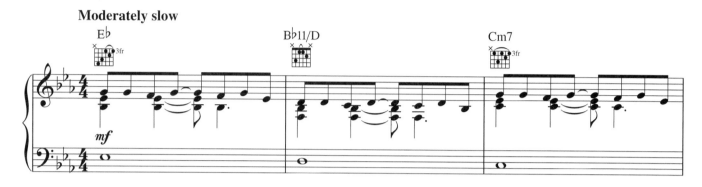

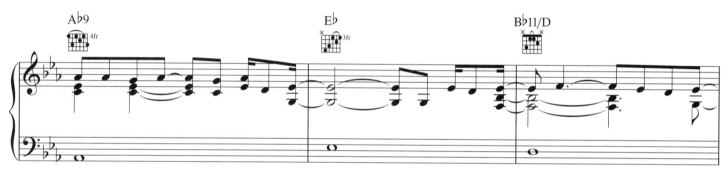

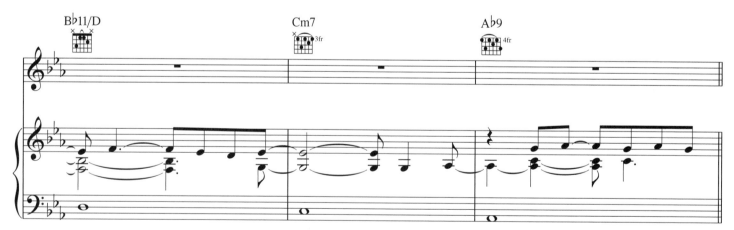

My life is bril - liant.

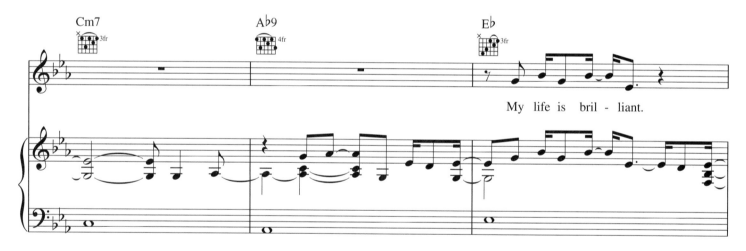

D.S. al Coda I